ANATOMY
OF A SPLITTING
BORDERLINE

ANATOMY OF A SPLITTING BORDERLINE

Description and Analysis of a Case History

René J. Muller

PRAEGER

Westport, Connecticut
London

The author gratefully acknowledges the publishers' permission given for the following:

Extract on pp. 175–177, reprinted from *Neurosis and Human Growth: The Struggle Toward Self-Realization,* by Karen Horney, M.D., by permission of W. W. Norton & Company, Inc. Copyright 1950 by W. W. Norton & Company, Inc. Copyright renewed 1978 by Renate Patterson, Brigitte Swarzenski, and Marianne von Eckhardt.

Table on p.188, reprinted from p. 58 of *Psychotherapy of the Borderline Adult: A Developmental Approach,* by James F. Masterson, by permission of Brunner/Mazel, Inc., and James F. Masterson. Copyright 1976 by Brunner/Mazel, Inc.

Library of Congress Cataloging-in-Publication Data

Muller, René J.
    Anatomy of a splitting borderline : description and analysis of a
case history / René Muller.
      p.   cm.
    Includes bibliographical references and index.
    ISBN 0–275–94975–3 (alk. paper)
    1. Borderline personality disorder—Case studies. 2. Splitting
(Psychology)—Case studies. I. Title.
RC569.5.B67M84 1994
616.85'85209—dc20   94–16995

British Library Cataloguing in Publication Data is available.

Library of Congress Catalog Card Number: 94–16995
ISBN: 0–275–94975–3

First published in 1994

Praeger Publishers, 88 Post Road West, Westport, CT 06881
An imprint of Greenwood Publishing Group, Inc.

Printed in United States of America

The paper used in this book complies with the
Permanent Paper Standard issued by the National
Information Standards Organization (Z39.48—1984).
10 9 8 7 6 5 4 3 2 1

To David Helbros,
who lives this illness

Contents

Part III
THREE GLOBAL ANALYTICAL VIEWS

Introduction

This is a story — whatever else it may be called, it is a story — about someone who is mentally ill. It is a description and analysis of that illness, of the person who lives it, and of the world he creates.

The illness described here fits the clinical picture of borderline personality disorder as characterized by James F. Masterson, Otto F. Kernberg, and others and by DSM-III-R. Most of what has been written on this pathology is presented either from a psychoanalytic perspective, in psychoanalytic language, or strictly from the perspective of behavior. I have tried to understand and write about this illness mainly from the existential-phenomenological point of view, a perspective that owes its start and ground to Husserl and its development and further existentialization to Heidegger, Sartre, Merleau-Ponty, Jaspers, Binswanger, Boss, and Laing, among others. The technique is description and reflection. A fundamental assumption is that if the surface of a phenomenon, in this case a mental illness, is described well enough, the structure — the *anatomy* — will show itself, and the phenomenon will reveal its meaning. This text has the feel of the surface, in contrast to the subterranean feel of so much psychoanalytic writing.

The book has three parts. Part I is a journal of the therapy sessions between David Helbros (not his real name) and myself that took place over a period of fifteen months; the journal is primarily descriptive. In Part II, the description is focused more sharply into analysis. In Part III, David's illness is interrogated from the existential-phenomenological perspective, as an instance of what Karen Horney in her descriptive-analytic classification of neurotic types called the "resigned person," and then in dialogue with Masterson's and Kernberg's psychoanalytic theories of borderline personality disorder.

Each journal entry in Part I is like a snapshot taken from a different distance or a different angle. As the reader moves through the text, the pictures accumulate into a gestalt of David and the world he lives in and through — its surfaces, contours, and textures. I like to think of the reader's consciousness assembling these pictures as a computer assembles pictures of numerous slices of the brain in a CAT scan.

A good deal of repetition occurs in the journal entries here, and some readers may find it cloying. But I believe these worded representations of the day-to-day, topsy-turvy, rollercoaster existence of a borderline patient struggling with his illness offer a glimpse of borderline phenomenology and borderline dynamics not seen before in the literature.

David Helbros is one of a subtype of patients meeting DSM-III-R criteria for borderline personality disorder who uses the splitting defense (many with this diagnosis do not). That splitting is the core of David's pathology becomes obvious from reading the journal and from the extensive exploration of the psychodynamics of this defense in the analysis that follows. That David is a *splitting* borderline patient has particular significance for me because I have proposed that borderline splitting has a neural substrate (see Appendix) — a notion that will, I believe, eventually lead to subtyping the highly heterogeneous *Diagnostic and Statistical Manual of Mental Disorders* borderline personality disorder diagnosis and significantly alter the way borderline patients are treated in therapy and with medication. David Helbros is a paradigmatic example of the splitting borderline patient. His story shows how splitting is ultimately lived out as "split" behavior and how this defense can devastate a life, as well as how difficult it is to challenge the borderline splitting defense in a psychotherapeutic encounter.

Prologue

David Helbros was born in Atlanta in 1949 into an upper-middle-class, socially prominent family. His father owned a successful wholesale grocery business started by David's grandfather, an immigrant from Greece. David lived in Atlanta, except for one year when he attended a prep school in Connecticut, until he finished most of the credits for an undergraduate degree at a university there. Literature and philosophy were his primary academic interests. He was alternately a good and an indifferent student.

During summer vacations, David worked in his father's business. By late adolescence, he was trading in the stock market and, with a stake from his father, made a considerable amount of money before he was twenty-one. At about this time, David's life-story begins to revolve around a serious mental illness. He was first hospitalized in Atlanta at twenty-one, in 1971, after a relationship with a girlfriend ended. Several years later, after the separation and eventual divorce from his wife, he was hospitalized again, for two years now, in this city. He was psychotic during part of that time and was treated with Thorazine. David was profoundly depressed during both hospitalizations.

David stayed in this city after his second hospitalization and began analysis with Dr. Alan Harris, an M.D.-psychoanalyst. He became seriously involved with a young woman, Sally, and worked for the Social Services Department. David finished his analysis with Harris in August 1976 and returned to Atlanta to work for his father in the wholesale grocery business. For about a year, David lived the good life there. He rented a fine house owned by his family, became reacquainted with old friends, took several courses at a local university, and became briefly involved with a number of women, continuing a pattern he established in early adolescence.

But a serious rift was developing between David and his father. David wanted a greater say in running the business and hoped to take it over after his father retired. Mr. Helbros felt David was not sufficiently committed to his work and refused to give him any more authority or an increase in salary. After working for his father for nearly two years, angry at how things had worked out, David moved back to this city in May 1978. He took courses in philosophy and literature and struggled with his options for the future: should he do something in business or with the stock market, or should he go to graduate school? He could not see returning to Atlanta, where old family conflicts had been renewed by his disagreement with his father. He saw Sally several times that summer, but it was obvious the relationship had been smashed beyond repair.

About halfway through the summer, David decided he would move to Chicago in the fall. He expected to find a job in a brokerage house and planned to look into graduate programs at the University of Chicago. He also hoped to take a course at one of the film schools there.

Once in Chicago, David enrolled in a film course, but he withdrew after several weeks because he felt it was not worth the effort or the money. One graduate program at the University of Chicago looked promising, but he did not apply for it. He sent résumés to several brokerage houses, but nothing came of that. He ended up working in a bookstore for several months.

In May 1979, after months of soul-searching, David's father decided to liquidate his business. David returned to Atlanta, hoping to change his father's mind. But, nearly sixty-five, Mr. Helbros had had enough. David tried to convince him to reorganize the business according to a plan he had worked out, but his father would not hear of it. Outraged at the rejection of his plan, David became seriously depressed. After he returned to Chicago, the depression deepened. He became emotionally paralyzed and was hospitalized there.

Not wanting to stay in Chicago and seeing no future in Atlanta, David moved back to this city again in the fall of 1979. He resumed therapy with Dr. Alan Harris, the psychoanalyst he had been seeing before he returned to Atlanta in 1976. David worked at several part-time jobs, saw Harris three times a week, and talked a good deal about his plans for the future. In April 1980, feeling he could no longer function on his own, he signed himself into the hospital where he had spent two years previously. He stayed for nearly six months. After leaving the hospital, David continued therapy with Harris, lived on his own in an apartment, and worked part time as a switchboard operator. His depression continued, as did his rage at his father who, David believed, had cheated him out of inheriting the family business, which David considered his birthright.

In March 1982, deeply depressed and unable to function on his own, David checked himself back into the hospital where he had been a patient twice before. He stayed three months and was released to a halfway house because it was felt he was not ready to function by himself. After four months, he moved to a hotel, and a month later into a house in a downtown section of the city that was being shared by a half-dozen people. David terminated his work with Dr. Harris just before leaving the hospital; and shortly afterward, he began seeing Dr. James Stacey, also an M.D.-psychoanalyst.

David improved somewhat during the next few months. He became part of the community life in the house where he lived and became close to one of his housemates, a young man who had just finished a Ph.D. in biophysics and was now writing electronic music. He took several graduate courses and made sporadic attempts to find work. His parents continued to support him, reluctantly, feeling he should be on his own by now. David's anger at his father for "cheating" him out of the family business continued, and David held him responsible for the illness that was paralyzing him, demanding reparations in the form of frequent checks.

In October 1983, feeling he had gone as far as he could after working with Dr. Stacey for nearly one year, David terminated with him. Three weeks later, David and I began our work.

... I regard mental illness as the "way out" that the free organism, in its total unity, invents in order to be able to live through an intolerable situation.

—J-P. Sartre

ε

... a single patient, no matter what his illness ... embodies the entire psychopathology.

—J. H. van den Berg

PART I

David Helbros: A Fifteen Months' Course of Therapy

Summaries of the therapy sessions were written after each hour. Not every session was written up. The dialogue in quotation marks was reconstructed from memory. No recording device was used.

Chapter 1

ം

Splitting Parents, the Lost Family Business, a Lost Girlfriend

October 26, 1983

David began our first session by describing an incident that occurred the day before. He was obviously upset, and his voice was shaky. After a poker game in a neighborhood bar, he was struck in the face and knocked down some stairs by a player who had lost about fifty dollars to him. He had a slight bruise on his face, but I would not have noticed it unless he pointed it out. He was concerned enough to have himself checked out at a hospital. The examination showed that no real damage was done.

David called the police and filed an assault charge, but he is not certain now he will press charges. His assailant was considerably larger and more powerful than he, and David is concerned about provoking him further. "He could break into the house and do something to me and my room-mates," he said. His concern for himself and his friends seems realistic and probably owes something to the fact that a man who lived in a house around the corner from his house was found murdered over the weekend. David feels that the person who hit him is both a sore loser and a loser in general. He doesn't want anything more to do with him.

"This reminds me of the situation I was in with Harris [a former therapist] and my father," David said when I asked how he feels about being beaten up. "I feel helpless." I was puzzled by his connecting this incident with Harris and his father. As far as I can tell, David did not provoke the person who hit him. He seems to have been a victim of the person's bad sports-manship and bad temper. On the other hand, he voluntarily stayed in therapy with Harris long after recognizing (or at least strongly suspecting) it was not helping him. Does David's connecting these three incidents mean he felt "helpless" when he was in therapy with Harris and working for his father? I asked him, and after considering the question for a moment, he said that he had. We stayed on this point for a while, and I let him carry the ball, which he was very willing to do. I did not want to jump to an interpretation because this would have taken the subtlety out of the moment and encouraged cognitive, rather than emotional closure. I am trying to help him stop thinking about his situation and *feel* it. This is the only way he can integrate those parts of his experience he has split off. I wanted him to live with the reverberations of my reflection on what he said about feeling helpless.

A teacher at a local college asked David to present a paper for a study group on Arthur Koestler's *Darkness at Noon*. He talked about some of the reading he has been doing recently. "Sometimes I interpret things to suit my own purpose and I lose the author's larger meaning," he said. I know what he means because I have seen him do this for some time. David uses books to justify his views about other people and about this culture. Most of the novels, films, and philosophical texts that interest him deal with violence and social revolution. Put another way, he uses ideas to rationalize and perpetuate his illness. I was surprised at how willingly he admitted doing this and that he did so without any prompting from me.

David had his thirty-fourth birthday last week.

October 29, 1983

David chose to use the first ten minutes of the session today to discuss some reading he has been doing. He read me a paragraph from *Anti-Oedipus,* a book by two French leftist thinkers, Gilles Deleuze and Félix Guattari, on the relationship between capitalism and schizophrenia.

I believe it is important for David to have someone with whom he can discuss his reading. He has criticized Harris for not understanding the ideas he brought into therapy. There is a potential problem here, as well, because David tends to intellectualize his situation and move away from it emotionally. He is aware of this and aware, also, of how doing it feeds his illness. He will continue to do it but, I suspect, less frequently as we get further along. If I am to meet him in his world and reach him where he is now, I feel I should respond to his request to talk about his books and ideas. For the last three years, David has not been able to concentrate and assimilate information while reading as well as before, and he feels bad about this. During the last three months, he told me today, his comprehension has been improving; and this clearly pleases him.

"How do you feel?" I asked when I sensed he was coming to the end of his talk about reading. My timing must have been right because he made the transition from books to feelings easily. "Most of the day I feel pretty good, but there is usually a period of an hour or two late in the afternoon when I'm in a different world. I really come off the wall. I lose touch with things. My mind wanders all over the place, and my thinking is in circles. It's a fantasy. I imagine this and that. It's not productive of anything good."

"My body becomes stiff when I feel this way," he said. "The stiffness is mostly in my left thigh." He indicated the place with his finger. Three years ago, when David came back from Chicago, his entire left side was rigid.

November 3, 1983

"How do you feel?" I asked as soon as we settled into the session. "Better," he said, with some reservation. "Better than what?" I asked. "Better than yesterday," he replied. "I feel better every day." David said he is taking a greater interest in the routine of the house where he lives and doing his share of the chores. "I've gotten interested in cooking again," he said. "And for the first time in three years, I've bought some new clothes."

I asked how the paper on Arthur Koestler is going. David is having problems with it. "I got to a point in the reading where I can't separate myself from one of the characters," he said. "I can't distance myself from his situation. This usually happens with a character who has to make a choice." David gets stuck at this point, and his concentration is broken. His thinking goes in circles and is not productive. Apparently, David's struggle to choose (his way out of his illness) fuses with the struggle of a fictional character trying to make a choice. I suggested this is similar to other situations — with his parents, therapists, women, and with work — when he makes a move forward, only to pull back because the forward move provokes an anxious response. He agreed.

"Doing this paper is like going up a 500-foot incline, and I can only go a few feet at a time," he said. I am not surprised he is having difficulty. I tried to prepare him for this kind of experience in our first session. I pointed out today that this is the first project of any importance he has undertaken in at least three years. A year ago, he would not even have considered doing it. I suggested that when he hits a snag in his reading by identifying with one of the characters, he take a break and do something else for a while. I am not satisfied this is the best way for him to handle the situation, but it was all I had to offer. The problem will come up again and again. We will have other chances to deal with it. I asked if he could recall a specific passage in his reading when this fusion with a fictional character occurred, but he could not. He said he would mark the passage the next time it happens, so we could look at this issue more closely.

November 6, 1983

"I feel isolated and cut off," David said today. "I miss certain friendships, and I miss not being close to a woman."

We talked about Sally — David had been involved with her for more than two years before he went back to Atlanta in 1976. He tried to minimize what she had meant to him. "She was too dependent on me and too much influenced by her mother," he insisted. "I told her she could come to Atlanta, but she played it safe and stayed here." He was saying, in essence, that the breakup of their relationship was Sally's fault and that she had not meant that much to him in the first place. As David said this, he did not seem behind his words. There was a forced smile on his face, and he sat rigidly in his chair. I did not point this out to him but let him continue. "Were you really disappointed that Sally didn't read the books you read?" I asked. "Was that so important to you?" "No," he said, his voice changing now.

The haughty, defensive tone disappeared, and the forced smile with it. He sat back in his chair and relaxed. He spoke more slowly. "That was probably the best relationship I ever had. Nothing since then has even been close. Sally was in touch with my needs; she was there for me. We essentially lived together for two years." David now took a good deal of the responsibility for their breakup. He admitted that the "demands" Sally made on him were not unreasonable but mostly what one who cares for another has the right to expect. He spoke now as if he regrets how things worked out. I asked if the outcome might have been different had he stayed in the city for another year or so. "It might have worked out very differently," he said as if he meant it.

We stayed with his feelings about losing Sally until the end of the session. I wanted him to settle into these feelings and touch them. David is very prone to flip back and forth between his positive and negative feelings, both about other people and about himself. His initial denial of what Sally meant (and, in a sense, continues to mean) to him is typical. Later, he was able to touch the ambiguity of his relationship with her and experience the pain of her loss. As long as he denies what the relationship meant to him, he can avoid the pain of its ending. I have seen David do this flip-flop about Sally before, and I suspect I will see it again.

"I compromised," David said about going back to Atlanta in 1976. "I should have known what going home would mean. I was just waiting for Harris to say, 'Why don't you stay? You have everything right here.' But he didn't say that. Instead, we had sessions that were supposed to get me ready for going back." I had the feeling David was behind his words as he told me this. I have often heard him say returning to Atlanta was a coura-geous move, motivated by his desire to help his father in the family business and repay him, in part, for the expense of his illness up to that time. David alternates between being the victim of his situation and the hero. Occasionally, as in some of our sessions, he is able to admit something closer to the truth. The therapeutic task is to encourage him to live this truth in the sessions so he can eventually live it outside therapy on his own.

November 7, 1983

We talked about work this evening, specifically David's feeling that he should find at least a part-time job to pay some of his expenses. It bothers him that he is dependent on his father for support, but he is also deeply conflicted about working. He likes to read and write, but he can't see his way to committing himself to pursuing a graduate degree that would be necessary for an academic job. He has some experience in business and brokerage, but he says he is not "cut out" for either. David is also having considerable trouble dealing with people. This started three or four years ago—the first time he experienced this kind of difficulty, he claims. "It used to be so easy," he said tonight. "I used to know everyone." David's feelings of being isolated and cut off are as detrimental to him in work as they are in relationships with women.

He spoke a good deal about his father and his bad experience with him in the family business when he went back to Atlanta in 1978. At first, he spoke as if it had all been his father's fault: his father had taken advantage of him by not paying him enough and by not giving him any real responsibility; he had not listened to David's plans for modernizing and "saving" the company; he was a tired and burned out man, who wrote "Don't despair" on his desk notepad; he wouldn't allow David to invest any of the company's excess capital; he didn't pass the business on to David, as he said he would, but liquidated it instead.

David continued in this way for about twenty minutes. He was the loyal son, done in by the powerful father. I then asked him to consider how the situation might have looked to his father, who was sixty years old at the time and had run the business for more than forty years. "Could it have been in the family's best interest that he liquidate the business when he did?" I asked. David considered this, and allowed it could have been so. "Could your father have sensed your ambivalence about the business and felt it would not be in your best interest to take over?" I continued. "My father did recognize my ambivalence," he replied. "You sound as if you feel your father owed it to you to hand over the business," I said. "No, he didn't owe it to me," David said thoughtfully, possibly realizing that this feeling is implicit in his anger at his father.

David is now willing to take a different attitude toward the situation—at least briefly. I suggested that after the liquidation of the business he no longer saw his father as an omnipotent figure and had trouble accepting his limitations. He denied this at first but then admitted it might be so. "Can you forgive your father for having limitations?" I asked. "Can you accept him if he is not perfect?" "Yes," he said with some difficulty, which I took to mean this would not be easy for him. David intimated this evening that after the business was sold, his family did not have quite the same status in the Atlanta community. I sensed he found this hard to accept.

David retold the story of his experience in the family business while we were discussing what kind of part-time work he would look for. "I'm not suited for business," he said. "Look at what happened in Atlanta." I said that sounds as though he feels any job in business would turn out the same way. He admitted that's how he feels. "It sounds as if you expect to fail in business because, as you see it, your father failed, ultimately, in his business," I added. David tried to deny this at first but then quickly reconsidered. "Yes, maybe that is how I feel," he said. While he was acknowledging this, I sensed that his basic conflict about business and trading stocks remained unresolved. "When I traded in the market, I felt bad about doing it," he said. "I hated going over the charts for the market. I didn't like having to keep up with it day after day."

David was considering another way of earning some money. "I could break the law," he said. From the way he spoke, I was convinced he was considering this possibility seriously. "Don't the big corporations steal?" he asked. "It's all in knowing how." He was not specific about what he had in mind, and I did not pursue the issue with him. (I should have. If it comes up again, I will.) He also said he regretted not "stealing his father blind" while he was working in the family business.

What David said this evening about work and his father took the same form as what he said yesterday evening about Sally and their relationship. First, it was his father's fault that David had soured on the business world, as it had been Sally's fault that their relationship ended. But when I challenged him on these points, he conceded that he probably contributed more to their breakup than Sally had, and that his father had every right to liquidate his business. He followed the same flip-flop pattern on both issues: initially, he denied his complicity in a painful situation involving another person, then later acknowledged it.

November 10, 1983

When we met this evening, David had just returned from a lecture on Martin Luther given at the house of a teacher at a local college who lives just a few blocks from David. The man had spoken for an hour and a half, and there were questions afterward. When we began the session, David had still not come down from the talk.

It seemed like a good time to point out to and explore with him something that occurred during our session on November 6 that I later wished I had brought up then: how his body had changed as he talked about Sally. He listened carefully as I described the change in his facial expression, voice, and posture while he talked about her. I pointed out that, at first, when he blamed Sally for the breakup of their relationship, he was speaking defensively (to defend himself from the truth?). His face had a forced smile, he spoke rapidly, and he sat tensely in his chair. I noticed David's interest deepen as I said this. He seemed surprised I had noticed. He was even more interested and surprised when I described the changes in his body when he admitted his part in the failure of their relationship: the defensive tone and forced smile disappeared, he spoke more slowly, and settled back comfortably into his chair. As I spoke, I could sense he was thinking something very much like, "Yes, that's the way it is."

I suggested that his initial tense body, in all its manifestations, was a lived body response to a coverup of his real feelings about Sally and the ending of their relationship. In essence, his body was going against the grain of his own truth — what he knew, but at that time did not want to admit and say. When he dropped the defense and his words matched his truth, his body, too, dropped its defenses. When I suggested that the body does not lie, I could sense he agreed.

I pointed out that he could get a pretty good idea whether his thoughts and words about a person or issue are matching his real feelings by paying attention to how his body responds as he thinks and speaks (Gendlin, 1978). If his body is as it was when he first talked about Sally, he should consider the possibility that he is out of sync with his real feelings. Conversely, if his body is as it was later, he could take this as a signal he is in touch with these feelings. I told him to look for a shift in his body as he goes from one attitude to another. I also suggested he try to get the feel of his body when things are going well for him, sink into this feeling, and savor it.

Just as I was about to point out how his body had shifted when he talked about his father during our last session, he brought this up. The shift had not seemed as pronounced, I told him. "I still feel I'm right about some things," he said as if he meant it. "My father was a slave to that business and had no life outside it. He kept his feelings to himself. When he came home in the evening, he deferred to my mother. He bought her expensive clothes and a new car every two or three years, and she went to her clubs with her socialite friends." I was surprised that these feelings about his mother were coming out now as he was talking about his father. Could liquidating the business mean to David, among other things, that his father has been defeated by his mother, who represents so much he finds objectionable (high social class and high living; emphasis on form and rules over feeling; the neglect of talent in favor of financial security)? David said some time ago his mother gave up a possible career as a pianist to marry his father.

Near the end of the session, when we both said all we wished to say, David sat relaxed in his chair. I sensed his gratitude for what happened during that hour.

November 11, 1983

David was clearly enthusiastic as he told me about his decision to take an accelerated course in German at a university here during the spring term. He wants to prepare for graduate study in contemporary literature. "It's time to go all out on this," he said several times as he talked about getting back to the work he was doing before he returned to Atlanta in 1976. "There's no point holding back now."

David showed me some articles in several recent literary journals he had brought with him. "I was always happiest reading and writing," he said. "Business and the market were a compromise. I did these things for other people, not me." As David spoke, he sat back comfortably in his chair but showed clear signs of tension. He flexed the fingers of both hands, opening and closing one hand, then the other. His eyes darted from side to side. His relaxed body told me he means what he says about wanting to study literature. The movements of his fingers and eyes told me he is anxious about doing it. He acknowledged this anxiety. "This would be just for you," I suggested. "Your parents won't be particularly pleased, and no one else will push you." He agreed. I also pointed out that this is the most ambitious plan he has had in at least four years. "I just can't compromise anymore," he said.

David spent Wednesday night with a woman he met several months ago. They had been at a party together earlier in the evening. "She kept me up all night," he said. "That's the best it's been in a long time. It's fun." He said this as if sex has not been fun for him lately. I have suspected as much from other remarks he makes from time to time. His sexual activity, vigorous and abundant until around 1978, has been sharply curtailed since then. During the last four years, David has become somewhat timid about becoming involved emotionally and sexually with women.

November 14, 1983

David spoke by phone to his father in Atlanta today. He has just been appointed director of a bank there. David appeared to be pleased by this and proud of his father, though he did not say so.

"There are many things we could do here if you would just get better," his father told him. David's face changed suddenly as he repeated his father's words, and there was some agitation in his voice. "This is starting to sound like a replay of 1976," he said. He repeated, once again, the familiar litany of disappointments that grew out of the period from 1976 to 1978 when he worked for his father in the family business.

It is clear David has no intention of returning to Atlanta to join his father in some business venture: "It would be the same old thing again. My father could never relate to me as I was. To his merchant mentality, I was just someone who could make money for him, in the business or in the market." What came through so clearly is that while David knows he can never win his father's acceptance, approval, and affirmation by going home again, he wishes he could. He has not given up the hope he might someday have the relationship with his father he has always wanted.

Using his words, I reflected back to him what he just said. Immediately, his face told me I had hit home. He offered no resistance. "You have said many times that your father is incapable of seeing you as a person in your own right," I continued. "I think this is exactly what you have never been able to accept. It is as if you tell yourself you will not take one step forward until your father gives you what you want but know he can never give you. You knew that was the situation, but you could not accept it."

Here, I believe, is one of David's major problems. He cannot let go of his disappointment that his father did not turn over the family business to him, but liquidated it instead. It was not the business he really wanted—he was highly ambivalent and conflicted about that—but his father's approval for doing something his father could understand and relate to. David claims that Mr. Helbros never really approved of his academic or artistic interests and accomplishments.

There are moments in the therapeutic encounter when no further words are necessary, when the space between therapist and patient opens up so as to allow the unique communication that comes when the truth of a difficult and painful situation is being touched and witnessed—at last. Our session ended this way tonight.

November 15, 1983

"My vision is better," were his first words when we met tonight. He smiled as he told me this, as if he knew something I did not. "I'm seeing things I haven't seen in years. I'm feeling better every minute." He did not appear at all hyper or manic. His words did not come in a rush, but at a normal pace, and he seemed behind what he was saying. "Do you think I'm going too fast?" he asked. I told him I do not and that I am not worried about where he is going with this. I told him I feel he is ready. (If anything, I feel this is long overdue, but I did not say so.)

David came to the session with a legal pad on which he had made notes. He had a pen and appeared to be checking off items as he talked.

It was immediately apparent that David had thought a good deal about what we said the last time we met. He spoke for some time about Harris and how they had worked together. "I must have played into Harris's Freudian expectations to please him," he said, "just as I played into my father's expectations in the business. I knew it was wrong, but I guess I wanted his approval.

"Harris couldn't separate out his own religious and ethnic feelings when he worked with me," David said. A week earlier, he read me parts of letters

Harris had written him after they terminated therapy (temporarily) in 1976. I was shocked by some of what I heard. I felt it was not appropriate for a therapist to be writing this way to a former patient. Now, David apparently thinks so too.

"He was obviously trying to apply Freudian constructs to my situation," David said. "He was trying to re-Oedipalize me and to become my father. He was an authority figure. He tried to keep me away from my parents." I could detect no bitterness, or even regret, as he told me he now feels his relationship with Harris had played into his illness. The real surprise of the evening came later, when David said that before he terminated therapy with Harris in 1976, Harris told him he was "healthier than ninety-nine percent of the people in this country." I did not comment.

That David seems more behind his words now is consistent with the fact that he is more willing to act on the meaning, as well as to take the consequences, of what he says. He knew Harris was not helping him as far back as two years ago but kept going to him anyway. Two months ago, when he realized that Stacey wasn't doing anything for him, he walked away.

David and I began therapy not quite a month ago. We have had just ten sessions. During this short time, I feel something significant has begun. He is, for the first time, starting to confront the issues that have caused him so much pain for so long. He is beginning to let go of some defenses and allow the disappointing experience with his father in the family business to have a new meaning for him, even if only for brief periods.

"Working with you I feel an anxiety I did not feel working with Harris and Stacey," he said tonight. I asked what he means by "anxiety," and he replied "tension." This is a word Albert Camus uses often in his books. To Camus, tension is living authentically in an absurd world. It is being in touch with a world that is ultimately unsatisfactory, because it will not give us all we want and need. Acknowledging and living in that tension is as good a way of moving beyond mental illness as I know.

November 17, 1983

"I was awake until 4 A.M.," were David's first words when we met this afternoon. He spoke without any sign of complaint or regret. "I tossed and turned." I asked if this happened because he couldn't turn his thoughts and feelings off, and he said it was. "I have these anxiety attacks," he told me. I asked what it is like for him when he is anxious. "I lose my footing and go around in circles. I back away from what I'm trying to get hold of." I asked how painful this is. "I can handle it," he said. I probed further, and was reassured he could.

David was obviously anxious this afternoon. His body must have been tight, because he kept opening and closing his hands and shifting in his chair. His eyes, too, moved nervously. "I'm still angry," he said, though he did not sound angry as he told me this.

He soon began to talk about Harris. "With him," he said, "as soon as I made a breakthrough, he would put on the brakes. He seemed afraid of what would happen. He played it safe. I got used to that." David told me today that in one of his letters he wrote, "I hope you are gritting your teeth, instead of clenching your fists." Harris suggested to David two years ago that he "control" his anger toward his parents because he was not ready to "deal" with it.

"How does it feel to be working with someone who is not asking you to put on the brakes?" I asked. "It feels good," he answered, without hesitation. "I don't want to hold back." I reassured him again that I feel he is ready for this. "There are no nets or parachutes now," he added. I took this to mean he hopes to jump out of his illness for good this time.

During our last few sessions, David has shown some faint glimmers of joy — intermittent and mixed with a good deal of anxiety. I asked if he senses the joy I see. He said he does. He seems to have some real hope now for more than just continuing to live his illness. "I'm on the ground again," he said, "and that's a good place to be."

I feel certain David is not building up a dependency on me, as he did with Harris and to a lesser extent with Stacey. He rarely even asks my advice. He has started each session spontaneously and introduces new issues throughout the hour. David sets the tone of the sessions and does at least ninety percent of the talking.

November 19, 1983

David is still having anxious nights. He was up until 4 A.M. again today, though he did sleep until about noon. Again, he did not complain. "I'll beat this," he said. "I don't care how many sleepless nights it takes."

David felt a good deal of anger last night, not only at his father and Harris but at himself for becoming involved in friendships and relationships with women that he now sees as destructive. He feels he often plays the other person's game and does what is expected of him, rather than what he wants and would be best for him.

David spoke today about how his parents had not encouraged his efforts to grow up and be independent. When he was thirteen, he went to Greece for a vacation. He visited the Greek islands and lost his virginity to a prostitute. He had grown from his experience on the trip, he said. But when he returned home, his father embraced him as if he were still a boy. David resented this, and pulled away from his father. Any time David acted on his own, he told me, his father would become sad. He feels his early success at athletics and in the stock market threatened his father, and that is why these successful efforts were not rewarded.

Nor did his mother encourage him, David claims. As his father was threatened by his success in the market and with women, his mother was threatened by his academic and artistic achievements. That, he said, she considered *her* domain. Before marrying David's father, his mother spoke four or five foreign languages and was an accomplished pianist. She had also studied literature seriously. After her marriage, she did not pursue these interests actively, and put her energy into running the house, bringing up the children, keeping up with Atlanta society, and raising money for the symphony. David recalls showing his mother a paper on Camus he wrote in 1976, just before returning to Atlanta. The paper was well received by his teacher, but his mother's only remark was, "How could you hand in something like that with so many typographical errors?"

David feels his parents did not expect success from him or reward it. What they rewarded was his failure. He also feels he played their game to please them, to not make them sad by acting independently and to fulfill their expectations. When he is down, David told me, as he has been after his breakdowns, they are sympathetic and offer help. But while he is well, as when he returned to Atlanta in 1976 to work in the family business, they put him down and hold him back. He feels that if he were to go back to Atlanta now and work at the bank where his father is a director, the same thing would happen all over again. "I'm not going to do it," he said.

David sees a lifetime pattern in the way his parents have, in effect, encouraged him to not grow up. From the way he spoke today, I sense he may be beginning to take responsibility for his role in coconstituting this situation, which he sees now as part of the structure of his illness.

At the end of the last session, David mentioned, almost as an afterthought, something that happened about three months ago. As he was walking to Stacey's office to keep an appointment, when he passed a Greek orthodox church, the church in which he was raised, he vomited. In the session today I asked how he felt at that moment. "Relieved," he said. David suspected for a long time that the analytic work with Harris and Stacey wasn't doing him any good. "I was sick of the sterility of my sessions with Stacey," he said. "I had enough. It wasn't helping. It was bad faith on my part. I knew I had to stop." I then asked how he feels about the Greek orthodox church. "I rejected that church years ago," he said. "I've had nothing to do with it." As he was walking past the church, his negative feelings about analytic therapy, what he calls the "psychoanalytic church," must have crystallized so he recognized that, for him, being involved with both "churches" was an act of bad faith. A Joycean epiphany?

November 21, 1983

David received a check for $100 from his father this morning. With it was a note that upset him very much. "He wants me to get myself together so I can conform and toe the line," David said. "Those were his words, exactly. I don't need this." David says his father equates being healthy with holding down a nine-to-five job. He tore the note up and immediately wrote a letter in response. He had it with him, sealed and stamped, but eagerly broke the seal to read it to me. The letter was handwritten, on legal-size paper. Essentially, David told his father he wants no part of his suggestions, his values, or his way of life.

"He's trying to manipulate me," David said angrily, "just as he always has. He's trying to hold it over my head that he's supporting me. He tried to use Harris and Stacey as intermediaries to deal with me. He could never deal with me directly. They were supposed to straighten me out for him. That's what he was paying them for.

"We should write to him and have him set up an account in my name, so I could pay you directly," David said. "This way I would have control. The last year I worked with Harris before going back to Atlanta [1975–1976], I paid for the therapy from my salary, and that made a difference." I realized then David was concerned that if his father paid me directly, I would take his side against David and be, in effect, his paid agent. I assured him this would not happen. He appeared to accept my assurance.

David continued to be angry and irritated as he talked about the note. "It's like pouring salt on an old wound," I suggested. "That's right," he said. I pointed out that his father's note is an invitation to David to live in a way he finds unacceptable and that he rejected the invitation firmly. "It's a sore point for you, isn't it?" I asked. He agreed it is. "That feeling will probably never go away completely," I said. "You don't *have* to do what your father wants. The trick is not to let your father's idea for what you should be paralyze you and to find something to do that satisfies you. There's no reason to feel bad that you don't want what your father wants for you." "Exactly," he said. I was more directive here than I would have liked to be. But I felt he needed this affirmation and support, and I was encouraged by the way he received it.

During an earlier session David told me he had murderous feelings toward his father. This point came up again today when he said he admired the way Violette, a young woman in a film of the same name, resolved her situation with the parents who had abused her: she killed them. She stood trial and was exonerated. I asked David if he is considering killing his father. Though I cannot recall his words exactly, I got the impression he strongly fantasizes about doing this but has no plan. I also asked him to consider the negative consequences to him of carrying out this fantasy. "They might catch you," I said. "Now they would," he replied, "because I'm not thinking very well. But it could be done."

David's strong ambivalence about money came to the surface again today. I reminded him that he will someday inherit enough money to make him financially independent, so he will not have to work. "I don't care about the money," he said. But earlier, as he was talking about how his father tries to influence and control him with his money, he said something very different: "My inheritance is the only reason I put up with this." His voice was low, and he held back some, as if he had trouble admitting it.

For the first time, David signaled the end of the session today. "Let's stop here," he said—my words, usually—after about an hour. He did not appear to be angry or frustrated. I sensed he wanted to stop because he accomplished all he hoped to today.

November 22, 1983

David was more relaxed today and sat comfortably in his chair. He appeared to be over the worst of his reaction to the note he received from his father yesterday.

He checked in with the state employment office several times last week but found nothing suitable. He is reluctant to take a job that would be distasteful because of what it would cost him emotionally. I asked if he feels such a job might interfere with his efforts to get well. He said it probably would.

David is considering asking either his father or his uncle for a loan of $5,000 to get him through the next six months. If he gets the loan, he says, he would not need to worry about finding a job and could concentrate his energy on therapy, taking courses, reading, and writing. He is thinking of drawing up a plan for how he would spend the money. He hopes this would increase his chance of getting the loan.

I was surprised he would consider asking his uncle for money. According to David, his uncle is everything his father is not that David wishes he were: He has a life outside his work; he knows how to relax; he trusts his son and asks his advice about running his business. He also experienced a serious two-year depression several years ago and came through it. David speaks of his uncle with affection and respect.

Money was very much on David's mind this afternoon. His family's money has caused him problems all his life, and he alternates between seeing it as a blessing and a curse. "I came out of the right womb," he told me. Yet, he also feels that money has limited and paralyzed his family. "My uncle knows how to use his money," he said. "For him and his family, it is liberating." He said he feels Joseph Kennedy had set things up so his sons would be free to use their inheritance. Today is the twentieth anniversary of JFK's assassination.

David saw a film last night, *Pauline at the Beach.* "It was nice to just sit back and enjoy the film, rather than analyze it as I usually do," he said.

November 23, 1983

David came to the session today with a legal pad and pen. He started by reading his notes. I was immediately struck by how similar his view of what we are doing is to my view. This gives me additional confidence that we are connecting in our meetings. When he finished reading from his notes, I pointed out several other issues we have been dealing with. As I talked, he wrote on his pad.

"I feel I've made more progress in the last month than I did in the last three years," he said as if he means it. Again tonight, I noticed the exhilaration David is feeling about getting on with our work. I told him I sensed this, and he acknowledged the feeling. "It's getting better every day," he said.

At our last session David told me he had spoken the day before to a young woman he was briefly involved with recently. He feels she is becoming too dependent on him, as other women have in the past. "I don't need this," he said. "I just walked away." Tonight he told me he spoke yesterday on the phone with Martin, a friend of several years. "He's depressed, and that gets me down," David said. "I don't want to get drawn into that again. I know what I was like when I was really depressed. I was very hard to be with. That's the way he is now." Two years ago, David felt comfortable with Martin and sought his company. As they talked radical politics, their illnesses fused. David saw him then as a minor hero of the counterculture. Now, David sees him as mentally ill, and though he still values their friendship, he seems no longer to need or want him to play into *his* illness. Raised a Catholic, Martin has become disenchanted with the church. Lately, he has been reading Freud very seriously. David feels he is trying to find a new religion and a new set of rules to live by in Freudian psychoanalysis. He also sees Martin doing this to avoid his own problems.

David called his father in Atlanta today and asked about borrowing $5,000. His father said he would think about it and that David should call him back. "My father closed the door on me," he said as if he didn't quite believe it. I was surprised that David said this. I told him it sounds like his father is leaving the door ajar. David got up from his chair, opened the door slightly, and held it there. "*That's* the way my father has kept the door open for me," he said emphatically but with no bitterness. "This is how," he added, slowly pushing the door shut.

David continues his reading. He said he was reading something by Lenin recently and found it boring though he feels Lenin is a great thinker. "I'm not using Marx anymore as an evasion," he told me. I was delighted to hear him say this because, for some time, David has used Marxist analysis of capitalistic society to justify his hatred of this country and all it stands for — what amounts to a pathological twisting of anything close to the truth of this world. I would like to believe he will not do this anymore, but I don't think he is ready yet to give up that crutch completely. If, at this point, he is just seriously considering letting this defense go, I would be pleased.

David is spending part of Thanksgiving, which is tomorrow, with friends who have invited him to dinner.

November 25, 1983

David was in a retrospective mood when we met this evening, musing over the last seven years, separating the good times from the bad. He has kept a journal for many years, and I suspect he spent some time yesterday and today going through it. He talked about how pleasant the first few months in Atlanta were, when he returned home in September 1976, then how things turned sour there, and how, later, there were good times and then bad times in Chicago in 1978 and 1979. After about ten minutes, he changed the subject to his father and the business and continued on this theme until the end of the session.

David has told me this story before. The essential details are the same each time, but quite often he brings in a new detail that adds yet another facet to this prismatic event in his life.

In May 1978, while he was in Atlanta working in his father's wholesale grocery business, a flood did severe damage to the warehouse. "I'm wiped out," his father told him. David did not feel the situation was that serious and offered his help. He worked with the stockroom employees, salvaging what could be saved in the warehouse. He also told his father about his plans for restructuring and revitalizing the business. But his father would not agree to try any of David's ideas. Angry and depressed, David left Atlanta for Chicago in the fall of 1978. "When I left, my father was shaking," he said. It was clear from the way he spoke that David was deeply upset by his father's loss of composure, which he took as a sign of his loss of nerve and, ultimately, I suspect, of his manhood. "I was dealing with a dead man," he said tonight, as he had several times before.

"My father dealt with me in bad faith," he continued. "He lied to me. He never had any intention of retiring and letting me run the business." I said it sounded as if his father may have been a confused and conflicted man at this point. David would not hear of this possibility, and insisted his father had deliberately taken advantage of him. He was angry as he spoke, though not as angry as when he has spoken about this at other times, when his face constricted and hardened.

Later, I suggested again that his father may have acted out of weakness and panic rather than malice. Suddenly, David's thinking, his mood, and his body changed together as he became willing to acknowledge that his father had been in a tight spot and may have had reasons other than malicious ones for not taking David's advice about the business. This was the same kind of body shift that had occurred in earlier sessions. Again, I pointed out this change to him, and he said he could sense it. "I'm focused on this," he said, as he sat back easily in his chair, with a smile on his face. "Now you are," I said, "but you will lose the focus and get angry again." He said he wouldn't, but I knew differently. I pointed out that there would probably be many more thought–mood–body shifts before he could accept and live the ambiguity of his situation with his father and no longer be paralyzed by living it as a victim of his father's supposed bad faith. When he can hold himself open to this ambiguity for longer periods, and not flee it back into the comforting (but destructive) negative polarization he so often makes, he will be on his way to getting over his illness. I told him so tonight, and he seemed to accept what I said.

I also pointed out no matter what he begins talking about in the sessions, he eventually comes back to telling me how his father deceived him by liquidating the business out from under him. "This must be the main issue for you now," I said, "because you keep coming back to it." He was not sure and suggested that other things that went on in his life at the time may be more important and that he may be covering up, using the experience with the business as an excuse. "If that's so," I said, "I think I would have picked up on it by this time." Later, I came to see how right about this he was.

"I saw the business and a whole lot of money slipping away," he said. "If the money was the most important thing," I suggested, "wouldn't you have kept making money in the stock market, to help offset the loss? Or find a job? But you didn't do that. You dropped out of the market, lost that income, became ill, and spent a good deal of money on therapy and hospitals." He seemed to accept what I said, but with a hesitancy grounded in knowledge I did not have at the time.

Earlier in the session, I said it sounds as though he has been devastated by what he sees as his father's betrayal and rejection. He hesitated at the word "rejection," but this resistance did not last long, and I sensed he saw, if only for a few moments, that he has taken up the liquidation of the business as an *abandonment* of him by his father. I have come to see this as the central issue in the phase of David's illness that began with his return to Atlanta in 1976.

November 26, 1983

"I just had a bad hour," was David's opening sentence when we met this afternoon. "There are a lot of things I want to do, but I can't get started. I begin reading one thing and then go on to something else. There's no continuity.

"I can't distance myself from what I read," he continued. Last night, he read parts of Michel Foucault's *Madness and Civilization*. He became angry at himself because he realized that for so many years what Foucault wrote about in this book has been *his* story. His main regret is that he allowed himself to become ill. I suggested it might be better to postpone reading books on psychopathology until he can get some distance on this subject. He agreed.

David is having the same problem reading other books. He can't distance himself from the characters and situations in the novels, plays, philosophical texts, and critical essays he reads. We have talked about this before. I suggested that, considering how much difficulty it causes him, perhaps he should not read at all for a while. I must have struck a nerve, because he flared up and said emphatically that he would not stop reading. Reading constitutes most of the work David is doing now, and it brings him satisfaction, as well as pain. Later in the session, I pointed out that he is not complaining about this pain and seems willing to pay the price for his reading, as he is willing to put up with the deep anxiety he feels at other times, particularly in the early morning before he goes to bed.

David's conversation turned to Harris. He admits he acted in bad faith in continuing therapy with him after returning from Chicago in 1979. "I knew what he would say. There was nothing new I had to learn from him. But I went anyway." He told me again that from January to September 1976, Harris had tried to prepare him for his return to Atlanta by rehearsing scenarios with him on how he should act in situations with his parents, uncles, and cousins. David sees this now as an exercise in bad faith. "It was pure persona," he said.

Two years ago, David felt conflicted about Harris, seeing him alternately as savior and demon. He was pathologically dependent on him (David admits this) and could not break away. Now, a year and a half after breaking off therapy with him, he is periodically angry at Harris but not bitter. He sees Harris's limitations as a therapist, as well as the outright mistakes that led to their therapeutic impasse. "It was a bad investment," he said.

Two years ago there were strong similarities between David's relationship with Harris and his relationship with his father. "If you can touch and live the truth of your situation with Harris, do you think you can do the same with your father?" I asked. "I'm starting to do that now," he said as if he means it.

David told me today that as he struggles with his reading, the only work, he says, he has ever really enjoyed, he is trying to get rid of the last traces of his involvement with business and the stock market. He says he cannot make the transition between the technical, numerical language of the market and the poetic language of literature and philosophy. He has tried to live in both worlds at the same time, but he could not. He is choosing now to let go of business and the market, which have caused him so much pain, and invest his time and future in the books and ideas that have given him more satisfaction than anything else. He is doing this without any specific career goal.

It has been in the back of my mind that effective treatment would resolve his conflict about working in the business world so he could use his obvious talent there, but during the last month I have recognized I was wrong to expect this. I must not try to "rehabilitate" David by trying to help him become someone his family and society would find more acceptable. I am hearing him more clearly on this point now and sense he realizes it. I believe he picked up on my expectation and resented it. I feel an obstacle to therapy has been partially cleared away. Some static has been removed from the therapeutic space.

November 27, 1983

Our next session was scheduled for Wednesday evening, but David called this afternoon to ask that we meet tonight. He had just spoken on the phone to his father, who turned down the $5,000 loan.

I was surprised to find him in good spirits. "I'll just have to figure a way to get through this on my own," he said. "Maybe it's better this way. I feel good about being free from my father financially."

David spoke mostly about his parents tonight. There were some new facts, though I had heard most of it before. What was new is the *way* he talked about his father and mother. What he said was not at all complimentary, but he spoke with equanimity and, most noticeably, with some empathy and appreciation. "My father was programmed to act just like his father," David said. "He never even thought about being anything else. He just fit into the mold. It is the old-world, immigrant style—work fourteen hours a day, and that's it. He would leave the house at six in the morning and come home exhausted at nine. He would be in bed by ten. It was that way since he was nineteen. He prided himself on saving the business after the Depression. He provided a livelihood for his brothers and their families. He didn't know how to enjoy the money he made. He never got around to asking what it was all for. It was total insanity." David compared his father to Tolstoy's Ivan Ilych, who lived his life from the outside in, with no thought of why he did what he did.

David had told me most of this before, sometimes with pride, sometimes with anger. Tonight he told it with acceptance. He laughed a good deal as he spoke, but it was not the mocking or sneering laugh I have heard at other times. It was a laugh that says, "That's the way it is."

"My mother was programmed, too," he continued. "She did just what her father wanted her to do, get married and have a family. She never complained that my father spent so much time with the business. She must have been totally frustrated, particularly when she was young. That's probably why she had breast cancer at forty-five and a recurrence several years ago. I never heard my parents fight, but my mother was always frustrated. She took it out on me. My father is still taking his frustrations out on me. Instead of facing up to his failure and sadness, he scapegoats me. He tells me I'm his only problem."

We talked more tonight about how David's parents may have encouraged

him to fail or, at least, not to succeed. We talked about how, without realizing it at the time, he may have cued into the feelings of anxiety and sadness
his autonomy seems to have evoked in his parents by becoming passive.

David spoke too of the city where he lives. "This city is provincial. All
the capital is tied up in conservative projects. I'm an outsider here, and I
don't know anyone who can do me any good. It's morally conservative, too.
You can't even talk to anyone here about young girls or incest." This last
observation surprised me. David seems always to have been interested in
women, but not particularly in young girls and, as far as I know, not at all in
incest. I did not pursue this with him.

November 30, 1983

David called his father several days ago to talk further about making a
financial arrangement that would allow him to survive for the next few
months. Mr. Helbros agreed to come here from Atlanta to talk with David,
and later with David and me together. He is due to arrive tomorrow and
will stay through the weekend.

David is deeply upset over what he feels his father owes him for the way
he exploited him during the two years he worked in the family business.
"He had me on a leash," David said, "paid me $145 dollars a week and made
a lot of promises he never had any intention of keeping." David is now trying to figure out how to collect the debt he feels his father owes him. He
has said several times he wishes he had "stolen his father blind," or made a
deal with one of his uncles to take over the business behind his father's
back. When he says he wants to be "financially independent," as he did in
the last session, he means he wants his father to set up an account, sufficient
to last, say, six months, so he can draw what he needs instead of receiving
it in $100 installments, each with some string attached. "I'm tired of him
trying to manipulate me with his checks," David said several times recently.
He also told me he has contacted two lawyers to see if he could get part of
his inheritance now.

David's anger at his father has him tied in a knot. "Should I punch him?"
he asked several days ago. "I have to assassinate him somehow," he told me
on the phone yesterday. I believe David is speaking symbolically here. He
wants to kill off the anger he feels toward his father because he knows this
anger is killing him.

David went to the state employment office this week and filled out
applications for three jobs, one as a medical research assistant. He plans to
take the civil service examination on December 7. But he remains deeply
conflicted about working. I suspect this will be one of the issues we discuss
over the weekend. I am looking forward to meeting Mr. Helbros and, even
more, to seeing him and David together. "I'm very doubtful anything good

will come from this," David said last night when he called. "I hate that man and want to get as far away as I can from him." I pointed out that, geographically, he is and has been far away from his father for several years, that he is not working for him now, and that his contact with him, even by phone, is minimal; it is David who makes the calls.

David's pessimism about the meeting with his father may owe something to a less than satisfactory day. He said tonight he spent several hours this afternoon with an old girlfriend who is having problems and that talking to her had dragged him down.

December 1, 1983

David and I talked about his father's visit, scheduled for tomorrow. "What's going to change?" he asked. "My father is the most conservative man I know. He doesn't understand me, never tried to, and never will. We have never been able to communicate." He said this with conviction and as if he regrets it is so. There was more than a touch of anger in his voice, though he said soon after he is not as angry now as he has been.

I challenged David on his negativity: "You say you have no hope, but you asked your father to come here and he accepted. Do you think you would have invited him if you really felt that way? And if he felt that way, do you think he would have agreed to come?" David did not respond, but it was clear from his demeanor he was hearing what I said. "You seem to be saying you are afraid of being disappointed if nothing good happens this weekend. Perhaps you don't want to risk being rejected by your father again. It's happened so many times. Now you are putting a lot on the line, and it's frightening you."

David sat back in his chair and did not move at all. He looked inward. In a sense, he left the room. The expression on his face became fixed. His eyelids closed partially. His eyes became glassy. He was somewhere else, somewhere I could not reach him and knew I should not try to. I could see it was hard to be there but good, too. Any word from me now would have shattered what he was feeling and touching. I kept silent but tried to be there with him in that silence. I could feel him connecting.

He sat this way for perhaps fifteen minutes. Then I asked, "How does that feel?" He said nothing for what seemed like another five minutes, looking inward in the same way. I, too, stayed silent and sat quietly. Finally, though the delay did not seem inappropriately long, he said, "It feels good, but I'm feeling more than I can say." I sensed his comment needed no response from me, and I made none. There was more silence. Then, he broke it: "This time, I'm going to get the whole pie." "Do you mean you are going to get all the way through this illness?" I asked. "Yes," he said. Not long after, he added: "I'm never going to let anyone play around with my

head again. I'm not going to compromise myself, as I did so many times."
In saying this, David is acknowledging implicitly that he has a *choice* about
how what happens to him will affect him.

"When we started, I decided I was going all the way on this," he said.
"You get your fifty dollars an hour and some ego gratification. . . ." He stopped
here, and I asked, "And you get well?" "Yes," he said. He sounded as if he
feels I deserve what I'm getting out of it.

"I just found out what this is," he continued. "Therapy is motion, flux.
I'm moving." I can't recall whether he or I added, "I'm [You're] breaking the
chains."

"You're letting go of the past?" I asked. "That's right," he answered.

"How long do you think this will take?" he asked, knowing I do not know,
because we have talked about this before. "We're moving, and we have a
direction," I said. "That should be good enough for now." "Let's keep it
open," he said, as if that is good enough.

December 2, 1983

David, Mr. Helbros, and I met from five to eight this evening. His father
started by taking from the breast pocket of his blazer a letter David had
written him just a year ago. He also had some notes on a piece of paper he
wanted me to read. David objected to his reading the letter aloud. "I wrote
that for you and only you to see," he said. His father handed him the letter,
and David read it to himself. After a short time, he read it aloud. The letter
was short and conciliatory and said, in essence, David was ready to put the
past behind him, find a job, and go on with his life. I presume Mr. Helbros
wanted me to read the letter to show that none of this has happened in the
last year.

David's father was presenting his side as one would in a debate. He was
firm but not unkind as he spoke about what he has done for his son and
what David has done with that. He handed me the paper with the notes
and asked me to read it. "These are some of my thoughts about David," he
said. David's sister had made a few notes of her own. Apparently, she was
visiting when Mr. Helbros was making up the list. Nothing I read surprised
me. Here was David's skeleton on a piece of paper: love–hate; unreliable;
unable to take responsibility; unappreciative; lying about having a job; a
con man. This hardly exhausts the list.

David interrupted frequently as his father spoke. He was angry, but his
father remained calm and became more rational and logical as the pressure
rose. Mr. Helbros talked about how he had tried to help his son: He had
bought him six cars; put him through private school and college; paid for
psychiatrists and three hospitalizations; sent him money, a good deal of
money over the years. He wanted to know why, after all this time, David is
not better and why he does not have a job. "A little self-respect, some disci-

pline, some autonomy"—this is what he wants for his son, he said. Instead, he gets promises and collect phone calls, recently five or six a week, asking for more money.

After about fifteen minutes, David said it was his turn. He retold his story about how his father had underpaid him and lied to him while he worked in the family business. All the familiar accusations and complaints were trotted out. His father tried to respond to some of them, but father and son kept missing, in large part because David's tone was combative. "I'm talking reparations," David said, lowering his voice enough so I was not sure his father heard him. Mr. Helbros insisted that he could not computerize the business, as David had suggested between 1976 and 1978. He had consulted an expert on computers who told him it would take $8 million a year in business to make that feasible. He was only doing $3 million. He also said he did not feel David was ready to take over the business. David did not question either point. Later, he said he feels the liquidation of the business is the best thing that could have happened for him.

"You asked me to come here so we could resolve something," his father said several times. "What is it you want to resolve?" David looked at a legal pad he had on his lap, and read from some notes. He said he was trying to get his body in shape. Mr. Helbros cut in and said he could do that in an hour or two after work and does not need the whole day. Then David said it would be hard to find a job that did not add to his frustration. He asked his father to lend him $10,000 to take him through the next year. Mr. Helbros balked at this, saying he had already given David a good deal of money. He and his wife consulted a psychiatrist in Atlanta about David who suggested that they cut him off.

I stayed out of the dialogue as much as possible, entering in only briefly now and then. I pointed out I was hearing frustration and hope from both sides in the stormy exchange. More than once, David said the whole situation is impossible, that he would get a job. But the dialogue about the $10,000 and other issues continued. Mr. Helbros then asked what I thought about giving David the money he is asking for. I started by saying I believe the letter David wrote him a year ago is more a reflection of his feelings and intentions now than then. He is making progress, I said. He is working very hard at this and experiencing a good deal of pain. If he doesn't have to worry about supporting himself for the next year, he could give more of his energy to the process of getting well.

"What I think I hear David asking is that you back the winner in him now, not the loser you may have backed before," I said. David nodded in assent. "It's a risk," I added. "No one can say for sure what will happen, but I think it is worth the chance." Mr. Helbros said he thinks so, too. A short time later, he agreed to give David the money, not the $10,000 David is asking, but $5,000. As he was saying he would do this, David turned his head as far away from his father as possible, as if what he was hearing was making him sick. "You seem to have problems accepting the money from your father," I said. David agreed. Soon after, David said his father has always dealt with him through intermediaries—Harris, Stacey, and now me—and that he could never understand what David was feeling. I pointed out to Mr. Helbros that David was saying he regrets not being closer to him. David sat back in his chair and his eyes filled with tears. He told his father how much he admired the way he took care of his family and how he built the business up after the Depression. David also said he was looking for his father's approval when he worked in the family business from 1976 to 1978 and became ill when his father turned down his plans for restructuring it.

Mr. Helbros said he realized how much pain David has suffered and he admitted some mistakes. "I never should have asked you to come back to Atlanta," he said. I pointed out that for the first time since we began talking, David and his father were communicating now. Each heard what the other was saying and responded. But this communication did not last long. David soon became accusatory and combative again, and the storm resumed.

About two hours after the meeting started, Mr. Helbros suggested that they go out to dinner. David immediately became defensive, saying he could get his own dinner. As before, when his father agreed to give him the money he asked for, David was turning against his father now. I pointed this out, and said it is characteristic of how David responds to success and intimacy: he backs away. As soon as a desired goal is in sight, he trashes it. Mr. Helbros thought so, too. "Two steps forward and one step back," he said. Twice this evening David showed that when his father offers him something, he feels compromised; if he takes the gift, he cannot be himself. This is a crucial element of David's problem with his father.

Mr. Helbros wondered out loud what he had done wrong with his son. I sensed his question was genuine and not an exercise in self-pity. He told us how he enjoyed the company of the young people in their twenties and thirties he works with and knows socially and how they seem to enjoy his. He mentioned that he and his wife had been to a formal dance recently. David got out of the chair, and stood in front of the door. "I'm leaving," he said, angrily. "You two can stay and talk if you like." He did not leave but became more negative and combative. "How can you spend time with those people?" he asked. David was talking about Atlanta society. He then said something about Marx, and then Castro, and quoted a line or two by Camus I did not recognize. He spouted some of the revolutionary jargon he uses frequently when he is defending himself against something unpleasant. I pointed out that David wants to choose the way he lives but is apparently not willing to let his parents have this same freedom. "Does it have to make you sick that we lead our lives the way we do?" his father asked calmly.

David was less combative for most of the last hour. He suggested that his father borrow $10,000 from a $30,000 life insurance policy his parents have on him. He also suggested that his father could cash in the policy, give him $10,000, and invest the remaining $20,000. Mr. Helbros suggested, in a kind way, that David "get with it," and pointed out that he could only recover the amount he had paid in, which is less than $9,000. "That policy is only good if I die," David insisted, as if this bothers him. His father then asked if he wants him to change the beneficiary. David said he does not. Then David suggested he take out the loan, and that his father co-sign the note. "That way I'd be more responsible," was his justification. He said nothing about how he plans to pay back the loan. How the $5,000 would be gotten for David was left unresolved.

David said he wants to pay all his expenses for the year with the money his father promised him—rent, clothes, food, utility bills, and me. I suggested he consider letting his father continue to pay me because I realized that my bill would probably take a good part of what he will be getting. Mr. Helbros seemed in favor of doing this. David seemed puzzled. It seems David's business sense and arithmetic were not very sharp tonight.

Just as we were finishing the meeting, Mr. Helbros asked if he could call me, or I him, about every six weeks, to see how things were going. David objected. He said *he* would call every month or so. I didn't press the issue because I know how sensitive it is for David. To him, if his father pays me and talks to me, he is buying me. Mr. Helbros told me he called and wrote to Stacey several times, but Stacey refused to discuss the case with him and said he would work with David alone. David told me last week that his father was angry at Stacey for not talking to him. I would like to open a channel between David and his father, but I must be careful to balance his father's interests and rights with David's.

Mr. Helbros suggested we meet again tomorrow. David was hesitant. His father asked my opinion. I felt it would be a good idea and suggested they sleep on it and call me by 10:00 A.M. to let me know. David asked what another meeting would accomplish. I pointed out that he and his father had communicated this evening, even if just for a short time, and according to David, this has not happened in some time. With the ice broken now, I hoped more communication would be possible.

David called, just after 11:00 P.M. "How do you think it went?" he wanted to know. "Well," I said. He agreed. But he still isn't sure if another session would accomplish anything more. He and his father are planning to drive to Washington tomorrow. David will call to let me know how that goes. "Your father is very nice," I said. "That's the trouble," he said.

December 4, 1983

Mr. Helbros flew back to Atlanta this morning. When David and I met this afternoon, his presence from the meeting two days ago was very much felt. David said his father cried as he was leaving. David immediately became defensive when I said I wished we could have had another session with his father. "With him, I'm dealing with an old-world, immigrant, Southern, Christian, upper-middle-class mentality," he said. "I have to stand on my own against this. I've closed the door on my family." I pointed out that while he is trying to stand straight on his own, this unresolved problem with his family is pulling him over. I told him I feel he will never get well until the conflict with his parents is untangled. As I tried to explain why, David became more defensive. "Have you read Sartre's 'Childhood of a Leader'?" he asked. "It's all there." I suggested his citing this essay amounted to an evasion of his present situation with his parents. He was running like crazy from my efforts to open up this issue. He was also getting fantasy gratification by identifying with Sartre's text. When I confronted him, he admitted it.

I repeated Mr. Helbros's question on this point at our meeting on Friday: "Does it have to make you sick that we lead our lives the way we do?"

DAVID: I know I can't change them. I hate them and all they stand for.

ME: But can't you try to accept them on the terms they choose for themselves?

David claimed his parents are trying to live through him. I pointed out that he seems to be trying to live through them.

ME: This is twisting you in a knot and keeping you ill. It's one thing that you refuse to come to terms with and accept your parents for what they have chosen to be. But it's even more destructive to you that you won't give them a chance to accept you as you want to be, as different as this may be from their present expectations.

DAVID: They'll never do that.

ME: I had hoped to talk about that while your father was here.

DAVID: It's no use (angrily).

ME: It's not over until it's over (quoting someone I could not remember).

DAVID: Is this what I pay you a dollar a minute for, to quote Yogi Berra? (Clearly, David missed the Heideggerian overtones here.)

ME: It sounds like you are afraid of the closeness to your parents that would come if they could accept you as you say you want to be. Could that be because you have been burned before by being close?

DAVID: I always get hurt then.

ME: Is that why you are running from the possibility your parents could someday accept you on your own terms?

I reminded David of his obvious anguish when his father agreed to give him the money he asked for. He admitted feeling this way. I also recalled how he had thrown his father's dinner invitation back at him. David told me that when he and his father were having dinner at an Italian restaurant on Saturday, his father gave him directions to the rest room. David became furious and accused his father of treating him like a child. I suggested if a friend had offered the directions under the same circumstances, David would most likely have been grateful. "It's better than stumbling around in the dark," he admitted. David assumed his father's giving him directions to the rest room meant he was patronizing him.

David sat back in his chair and said nothing. The silence lasted at least twenty minutes—the longest silence during any session yet. As before, he seemed to be looking inside himself. After about ten minutes, his eyes teared heavily. I did not know how to break the silence. I waited for him to say the first word. I tried to stay with him in the silence. Then, David cleared his throat. I waited for several seconds, and asked, "Where are you, David?" After a slight delay he said, "I'm relieved." He was breathing heavily now but was relaxed, too, as if he had let go of something that was making him tight. "I was considering other possibilities," he said. And then, a short time later, he added, "I'm going all the way on this."

I asked David to take note of what his body was telling him. "I can feel my stomach again," he said as if this surprised and pleased him.

December 5, 1983

"I'm feeling very well today," was the first thing David said when we met this afternoon. He had just had lunch with a woman he knows and she told him he is more interesting when he isn't "up in the air." I asked what this means. David said it means what he is like when he isn't running away from things and stays concrete.

We talked about his "running away" for a good part of the session. I pointed out the defenses he used during the meeting with his father on Friday and during our session yesterday. He sees, he said, what he is doing. I again repeated my hope that we could have met with his father a second time before he returned to Atlanta. Yesterday, David was still resisting this strongly. Today, his response startled me: "As long as you are on top of this, do you think we should ask him to come back? We could work hard for the next three or four weeks, and. . . ." He stopped there.

"How many fathers would have come that far to see a son who has given him so much trouble?" David asked. "Anyone else would have told me off a long time ago." He admitted he lost his temper many times on Friday, while his father behaved like a man during the entire meeting.

We talked about how David pulled away just when his father agreed to give him the money he asked for. "I just shut down after that," he admitted. I suggested this was because he feels uncomfortable being close to his father. When he should have felt grateful and happy, he was resentful and unhappy. "I have always had trouble letting people get close," he continued.

"My father, Harris, friends, girlfriends, teachers." "You told me your father could relate to you only when you were making money for him," I reminded him. "But on Friday, you could only relate to him as a lender of money and, even then, not very well." David said he recognizes this.

As we talked about his father, his problems with getting close to people, and his running away from the conflict with his parents, David became silent several times for periods of about five minutes. I believe that as he sat quietly, he was experiencing this conflict in a way different from the way he normally lives it. As he said after earlier silences, he told me today he is considering other possibilities for how it could be between him and his parents.

"How do we start?" he asked, meaning, I believe, how does he begin to face up to the pain the possibility of becoming closer to his parents causes him. "By doing more of what we have been doing in these sessions," I said. "When you start running away, I'll remind you of it." I pointed out again this afternoon that he can't integrate and live his good and bad feelings about his father because it is less painful to him to see his father at one moment as all good and then later as all bad. "As long as you see your father as all bad—in your terms, as long as you keep the door closed—you know what to expect from him. It's not what you would consider good, but it is predictable. It's very painful, but apparently not as painful to you as taking the risk that he could be someone other than the person you see him as. I sense you are struggling to take that risk now." David said he is.

What had been fifty-five minutes mostly of talk about the possibility of reconciliation with his parents turned suddenly into something very different. The change came when David talked about "all the shit my mother gave me," and I asked if he too hadn't given her a good deal of trouble, as he admitted before. "Does she expect me to be the number one socialite in Atlanta?" he asked angrily. And it went downhill from there. "They're not good people," he said, meaning his parents. "I get more out of talking with someone in the ghetto. It would have been better for me if my father had died in 1976." David was off and running again. There was about five minutes remaining in the session, and I had to be across town during the next hour, so I did not have time to challenge what he was saying. But he continued.

DAVID: If I had it to do all over again, I would have slowly done it to them.
ME: Done what?
DAVID: I would have poisoned them to death.
ME: And what about the consequences?
DAVID: I could have lived what that.
ME: Prison?
DAVID: I would have probably gotten away with it.

December 6, 1983
Afternoon

"Did you ever consider the possibility there was no confrontation with my father at all?" was the first thing David said when we met this afternoon. I was puzzled by this question and asked him to explain. "Maybe there was never anything to talk about," he continued. "We were in different worlds. He was dead, and I was youth. I was the best-read person in Atlanta. I was so far ahead of him it was ridiculous. He was scared of me. He told me that on Saturday, when he was here." Clearly, David was grandiose this afternoon. "Would Hitler's son have tried to talk to his father?" he wanted to know.

He said his parents have "led" him, and that he has been "conditioned" by them. I pointed out he is using terms that are part of a causal vocabulary, not the existential terms we have been talking in. That did not seem to bother him. I knew I was in for a rough session.

"I can do this without them," he continued. "I can dance around it. Why not?" I pointed out that he was going against much of what he has said during the last six weeks. "It's different now," he said. "I feel fine." He stretched his arms into the air, as if to show me how fine.

"You sound as if you feel there is no problem now," I said. "And if there is no problem, there is no reason why you have to deal with your parents. You're off the hook on that. You don't have to face up to it as we have been talking about doing."

"Maybe something else is more important here, and I'm using the situation with my father as a coverup." I asked what else this could be. He mentioned that while he was in Atlanta between 1976 and 1978, his best friend left his wife and became involved with a younger woman he later married. "He leaned on me during that time," David said. Was he really trying to say that his problems then, and those that followed, were due to the trouble his best friend had with his wife? (Only later did I recognize the significance of this remark and how much David was revealing through it.)

Once again, he trotted out the familiar accusations against his parents. "Have you read Donald Barthelme's *The Dead Father*?" he asked. "That's the way it is with my father. The dead should bury the dead. The only reason he wants a reconciliation is because he's going to die soon and can't face his mortality. His death is imminent. He wants me to be his immortality." I asked David if *he* can accept his father's mortality and the fact that he could die at any moment (Mr. Helbros is about seventy). He did not want to talk about this.

Then David said that many of the healthiest people he knows broke with their families and haven't had anything to do with them for ten or fifteen years. I pointed out he now equates being mentally healthy with complete separation from family. He said he thinks that is often the best way. "Stacey was right when he refused to talk with my father," he said. (And by implication, I suppose, I am wrong to suggest the opposite.) David attacked me this afternoon, directly and indirectly.

ME: So, what's the next step?

DAVID: I have to take small, concrete steps.

ME: What will you do?

DAVID: I'm going to call some people.

ME: Anything else?

DAVID: I'm going to two movies tonight. That's always creative for me.

I confronted David throughout the session but stopped short of telling him what I am very sure is going on: that he is in full flight now, running like crazy from dealing with what is keeping him ill. Toward the end of the session, I sensed David was feeling he had won a victory over me this afternoon. I asked if he still wanted to meet tomorrow evening, as scheduled. He wanted to cancel it and would call me later in the week.

About a half-hour later, my phone rang.

DAVID: Bad session today.

ME: Rough session. We can talk about it next time.

DAVID: I know where I was coming from on that.

ME: Are we on for tomorrow night?

DAVID: Yes, but I'd like to settle this now.

ME: How about tonight at 9:00?

DAVID: OK. You have to watch out for me.

ME: I know.

DAVID: We're the only ones for this.

A short time later, it occurred to me I might have added, "That's all it takes."

December 6, 1983
Evening

Where David was "coming from" this afternoon was a long conversation the night before with a woman he has known for some time. It was she, apparently, who put him onto this new way of looking at his situation with his father—as a nonsituation. David is suspicious of her motives. "She wants a piece of me," he said.

I was totally surprised by what happened this evening. When he called after our session this afternoon, David had flipped back in touch with his feelings about his father, after having been out of touch with these feelings for the entire hour we worked together. Now, at 9:00 P.M., he had flipped back again. He was not finished yet with his new escape.

I have never seen David quite this way before. Some of what he said didn't make sense and sounded bizarre. His logic seemed to be slipping. He couldn't, he said, see the difference between my getting a degree in psychology and a holdup man robbing a bank: I took knowledge from a university, the holdup man took money from a bank. "How are the two different?" he wanted to know. (Later, I suspected David's bizarreness during this period may have been due to a brief micropsychotic experience of the kind often seen with borderline patients.) And he was paranoid. He had heard from a third person that his best friend from Atlanta said he "hated women." He was angry at other friends, too, for things they said, angrier, it seemed, than what they said warranted. While we were talking about the situation with his father, he said, "The trouble wasn't with my father, it was in the streets." (This remark puzzled me. Later, I realized that, to David, "the streets" is a code term for his illegal activity, such as stealing and dealing in stolen goods and drugs, as well as his sexual activity. David left a powerful clue here that I did not recognize at the time.)

Suddenly, about halfway through the hour, David flipped back in touch. He admitted he uses socio-political-economic issues to mask and avoid his issues, as when he said, a few minutes earlier, that his problem with his father is really a displacement of problems "in the streets." This was the other David, the one who wants to get over his illness and asks me to work with him.

There are two Davids. I have seen them both many times during the last six weeks. Tonight I saw them both within a period of an hour. There is the "in flight" David, whom I spoke with for the first half-hour this evening, and there is the "in touch" David I spoke with for the last half-hour. (These terms are analogous to the commonly used terms "acting out" and "working through." I prefer them because they seem more descriptive.)

It's this way with David, back and forth, back and forth:

"In flight" David   ↔   "In touch" David

"In flight" David is angry, tense, self-deceiving, fantastical, grandiose, passive, feral. He runs from ambiguity by splitting everyone and everything in his world into all-good and all-bad constitutions that do not correspond to reality. "In touch" David is calmer, more relaxed, less self-deceiving, more behind his words, more realistic, more rational, more responsible, more "civilized." When "in touch," David can make some accommodation to ambiguous, unsplit reality, but not for long.

David admits now that he can't accept his father as he is and that he sometimes has trouble accepting me as I am — a "patrician," to use his word. "I'm coming from the same place with both of you on that," he said. "It's limiting for me, isn't it?" I told him I feel it is. Later, it occurred to me that David can't relate successfully to people who are different from him — which, ultimately, means everybody — because these differences threaten his efforts to fuse with every person he meets. Never having been sufficiently separate and individuated, he attaches himself to others to survive. But he finds this hard to do as soon as others present themselves to him, as eventually they always do, as "different."

"In touch" David and I finished the session tonight this way:

DAVID: I have to do this.

ME: You're strong enough now.

DAVID: How far can I go?

ME: I'm optimistic.

DAVID: How long will it take?

ME: I don't know.

DAVID: Harris missed this, didn't he?

ME: Yes.

December 8, 1983

David called this afternoon to ask that we meet this evening. I asked how things are going. "I'm open to the possibilities," he said enthusiastically. "Let's get down to work."

So, I was surprised when his first words to me tonight were, "Do you think therapy is surveillance?" I said I hope it is not. "I've been thinking about your background," he said. "That university you went to is a CIA factory. You liked the Kennedys, and they were imperialists." I told him I realize my university turned out some graduates who work for the government, both in science and politics, but that most do not, and that I never have. Several weeks ago, David told me he feels Bobby Kennedy was the last hope of this country.

"You like things as they are," he continued. "You never fought the system. In the late sixties I was at the marches and got tear-gassed." David hates the system. Our sociopolitical differences are a problem for him. In his words, he is a "revolutionary," I a "patrician." I once wore an Izod cardigan during a session. "Don't think I'm not noticing that," he said as if he just discovered something sinister about me.

"Have you seen *State of Siege?*" he asked. I had not. "The left kills the leader of the revolution because they find out he's a British agent and was trying to set them up." I got the impression David was suggesting I was somehow an agent of the system trying to undermine him in therapy. Was he thinking of killing me, as the revolutionaries killed their leader? He was talking as if I were part of a conspiracy against him. Clearly, his thinking was paranoid.

He went on about Vietnam and Central America, making connections between his situation with his family and the efforts of an imperialistic America to control and dominate Third World countries. At several points I had trouble following him and had to ask for clarification. Some of what he was saying didn't make sense to me. I thought back to our last session, when he said he couldn't see any difference between me taking a degree from a university and a holdup man taking money from a bank. At some point during the first half-hour of the session, I became concerned, frightened may be a better word, about what he was saying.

David read me several excerpts from an article on Nietzsche in an academic journal he had brought with him. First, there was a quotation from *Beyond Good and Evil*, where Nietzsche, in his dazzling language, says that Christian morality was invented by Christians and has no legitimacy beyond that. It was obvious that David was responding to the joy, lightness, and poetry of Nietzsche's writing, experiencing it emotionally as well as intellectually. He told me I was missing the poetry in him.

He read another excerpt, a joyous exploration of the possibilities of freedom and breakthrough that reminded me of Sartre. "That's the way I feel," he said. "Like I'm on the threshold of a breakthrough. I swam for an hour and ten minutes this evening. I didn't have the energy for that before. It felt good." I asked how the day had gone for him. "About noon, I started to loosen up," he said. "I could feel the anger go away." I asked if he feels letting go of the anger made it possible for him to swim that long. He said he thought so.

"Where are you in all this, David?" I asked, hoping his answer would clarify some of what he was saying. There was an abrupt change in his tone now. "I've been trying something out," he said. "I said those things about you to see if I would be angry when I said them. I wasn't." This took me completely by surprise. Perhaps he noticed it. It is the first time, as far as I know, he has put on a deliberate act in one of our sessions. If he can talk about our differences now without being angry, he may be starting to come to terms with them.

Now and then, David rereads the papers he wrote while taking courses in literature and philosophy between 1974 and 1978. This evening, he read me some of the comments his teachers made on papers he wrote during the summer of 1978, just before he left for Chicago. The remarks were complimentary and encouraging, and in at least one case, the teacher suggested developing his ideas further. "With comments like these, why do I need my parents?" he asked. "It's finished between us. I'll dance on their graves. They tried to hold me back. They were jealous of my freedom. My father was jealous of all the women I had. When I worked in the business, I would bring one girl after another to his office. He would sit there, depressed. 'I've had this one, Dad,' I would tell him later, 'you can have her now.' It was no big deal for me." David said that when Sally visited Atlanta, she and his father liked each other. "He could have had her," he said. "I wouldn't have minded."

David's father did not take up the offer of any of his women. According to David, his father is monogamous and frustrated. He would tell his son how this friend kept a woman here, that friend a woman there. "He just couldn't do it," David reported, as if this is a shortcoming. "If I had a wife with cancer and all my father's money, I'd get a woman."

Last week David said his mother was sexually frustrated, particularly during the early years of her marriage, because her husband spent most of his time and energy on the business. David is upset over what he sees his parents as having missed in life, sexually as well as in other ways. This is probably because he is fusing with them, so that in essence their frustration becomes his frustration. David is having his own sexual problems these days. He is anxious and cautious about making even casual sexual contacts with women, the kind that used to be so easy for him. He doesn't seem to be able to separate his parents' lives from his own, their presumed short-comings and disappointments from his.

"What a joke it all was," he said, laughing. He was talking about his family, how they—and he—had lived, and the business. He seemed behind his laughter, which is to say he seemed to see the genuine comic side of his family situation. I pointed out he was focusing on the comedy now, but that there is a serious, even tragic, side as well. He acknowledged this.

"You are going to have to stay on your toes," was one of David's last remarks this evening. He meant, of course, he knows he is still running and that if he is going to get better, I will have to keep chasing him down.

December 13, 1983

DAVID: I'm thinking of cutting this off for two weeks until after the holidays. I've been counting the number of sessions this month, and it seems like this has been taking up a lot of time. I've just been talking here, and I've always been better off when I'm doing things. There's nothing here I haven't experienced before. This is becoming a crutch.

ME: Has it been just talk? We've talked about how its been more than that. You've said it has, many times.

DAVID: (He nodded in agreement.)

ME: You say you have experienced nothing new here in the last six or seven weeks. But that's not what you said before.

DAVID: I know.

ME: Am I really a crutch to you?

DAVID: No.

That's how it began tonight. David is trying to convince himself he should stop our sessions for two weeks so he can get more done. His efforts to discredit me didn't work. Now, he's trying to talk himself into getting rid of me, just for a while. As I challenged him on each of his reasons for wanting to stop therapy temporarily, the reason evaporated between us.

Then, as he told me about his day, his tone changed suddenly. "When I got up this morning, I had a lot of energy. I swam at the gym at 7:30. It felt good starting the day that way. I wished I had a schedule for the whole day. I wished I had a class to go to." I said it sounded like he had an intimation of a day like the days he had here in 1976, before he went back to Atlanta. He said he felt that way. I pointed out this was probably the first time in at least four years that it was possible for him to look toward the future with such hope. He agreed. "Why not?" he asked emphatically, as if convinced it could be so again. "I lived every minute fully and concretely in those days." "Why not?" He repeated the question twice again before the session ended.

I resisted the temptation to suggest that the work we are doing together may have something to do with his glimpsing, today, a life fuller than the one he has now.

Tonight, after David finished suggesting we break off therapy for a while, we got back to working much as we had worked before his father's visit. I asked if he wanted to keep the appointment made earlier for Friday or if he wanted to think about it. He wanted to keep it.

December 14, 1983

David was in touch all through the session this afternoon. There was no running, no hedging, no hostility toward me. He was behind his words, undefended and vulnerable, as he was during many of the sessions before his father's visit nearly two weeks ago. Once again, he has a sense of urgency about what we are doing.

He had a rough night, he said. He was awake until 4 A.M. but slept for seven hours. He was angry last night, mostly at himself, as far as I could tell, and anxious. When anxious, David can't complete his thoughts. His thinking goes in circles or, as he described it today, in half circles along a certain path then back again. I asked if, as he experiences more anxiety, he is less depressed. He said this is so. I told him that is what I would expect.

Earlier this week, while we discussed the course in French David is planning to take during the spring term, he spoke easily of doing this and of how it would help him with his studies in philosophy and literature. But today, when I asked when he would register for the course, he became tense and his eyes darted from side to side. Clearly, he is anxious about taking this next step. He pictures himself going to the admissions office to get information about the course, and this terrifies him. "In 1976," he said, "this would have been no problem. But I don't know what I can do now." I pointed out that his anxiety is what would be expected for someone letting go of one kind of life and opening up to the possibility of a different one where he does not know what to expect. I hear David asking implicitly, "Can I do it? Am I up to it?" Anxiety and the inertia of the past hold him back. His desire for a better life keeps him pressing ahead. This is the essence of his struggle.

"What do I have to lose?" he asks over and over. But he does have something to lose—who he is now. As long as nothing much changes, he knows more or less what to expect from each day: anxiety, anger, pain, his sessions with me. But if he lets go of his past (and present) situation, what then? He often talks about "taking the risk." That is precisely what he balks at doing because to risk an uncertain future is to let go of a certain, though painful, past. David is caught now between who he is and has been and the person he would like to become, at least some of the time.

David was pleased with our session today. I pointed out that he did no running this afternoon. It was obvious he knew what I meant. "When I run from issues and give seminars in our sessions, you should stop me," he said as if I had let him down by not doing so. "I have to meet you where you are," I said. "I can take a stand against what you say as you run and point this out, but I can't tell you to stop running. If you bring something up, it has a meaning, and we have to deal with that. If it didn't mean anything, you wouldn't have brought it up." I told him his running in our sessions is his struggle being lived out between us. He accepted this.

December 15, 1983

Martin, a friend of David's for about six years, committed suicide Sunday evening by cutting his arms with a knife while sitting in a car in the parking lot of a local community college. He had been to David's house the preceding Wednesday, but David had not been there. Several days earlier, David mentioned that Martin had called and said he had not slept for four days.

David told me about Martin's death at the start of the session this evening. He had just called his friend's apartment a few minutes earlier and heard the news from Martin's brother. David had known Martin well.

A college graduate, Martin spent nearly a year making a film about the city. But he did not edit it, and the project was not completed. He then took a job as a heart-lung machine technician at a local hospital. He worked there full time for about a year, and then cut back his hours so as to have more time for other things. About six months ago, he quit his job. "They're killing people at that hospital," he told David, who, antiestablishment and paranoid though he is, doubted it. He took up the piano and sometimes practiced eight hours a day, David told me. About two years ago, a young woman he was living with ended their relationship and asked him to move out. "She didn't like his act," David said at the time, meaning, I believe, that she felt he was too dependent on her and was not interested in doing any real work. The breakup devastated Martin, and he became depressed. He withdrew gradually from people and from the world and became more depressed. David wrote him a letter several weeks ago, essentially telling him to pull himself together. As far as anyone knows, Martin never sought any professional help.

David has recognized for some time that he and Martin are alike in significant ways. He was one of the "dependent" people David has recently tried to distance himself from. Not long ago, he referred to him as a "wimp."

Martin came from an Irish-Catholic family and was raised in an industrial section of the city. He and David met while taking a course at a university here. They were both interested in film, but there was a deeper bond: they both hated this country and everything about it. Like David, Martin had a "revolutionary" spirit. Also, like David, he never committed himself to doing anything about what he hated. He would cite Camus on the meaninglessness of life, David said, but stopped there. He had no sense of Camus's response to the absurd — a revolt that led to taking a stand against it and in favor of life. Two years ago, David and Martin spent hours together trashing the country and speaking vaguely of revolution. During the last few months, David spent less time with him.

I'm not sure how much impact Martin's suicide will have on David. He must see how Martin took his — David's — basic attitude toward the world to one extreme and died for it. The issue was too sensitive to deal with today, but it will certainly come up later.

December 17, 1983

"I had two and a half hours of openness yesterday," David told me as we began the session this afternoon. Clearly, he was delighted. I asked if this is the longest good period he has had during the last few years. He said it is. He spent part of this good time talking on the phone with an old friend from Atlanta, who teaches at a university in Houston. The rest was spent swimming.

The hour went more slowly today than any other I can remember. For the first time, we had several brief awkward silences unlike the silences in earlier sessions that came out of the depth of encounter. Perhaps David was feeling more secure today and did not need to talk as much. He was both "in touch" and "in flight." He did some running around socio-political-economic issues and tried to put me on the defensive about the class system set up by capitalism, as he has done so many times. Dealing with these issues, over and over, has been the most difficult and unpleasant part of working with him. It is the point around which he does so much of his running and one of his main justifications for remaining ill: he is sick because society is sick. There are times when he recognizes and admits what he is doing. At other times, he covers it up.

I asked David how he feels about Martin's suicide. "I have no pity," he said, evenly and solidly. "I was not that close to him. He was a friend who listened to me when I was coming off the wall." I got the impression David is trying to put as much distance between himself and Martin as possible. I asked if he feels they were similar. He said he does not. His categorical answer surprised me somewhat because he previously acknowledged that they had a good deal in common. Perhaps Martin's suicide makes him appear ultimately different now, minimizing to David the similarities there were. I sense strongly David's resolve that he will not end this way. It would not surprise me if Martin's death helps catalyze David's recovery. "I'm going to get through this," he said at the end of the session with a smile that seemed a part of his brightening mood.

December 18, 1983

"I've had a very good day," were David's first words when we met this afternoon. He played tennis earlier and was clearly pleased by how it went. "I set the pace of the game," he said. "I made some good shots." He used the words "rhythm," "flow," and "continuity" several times to describe how he played. He has said many times that during the summer of 1976, before he left for Atlanta, he was "on top of his tennis game," but since returning here four years ago, his game has been off. He feels it is coming back now. Paralysis is relenting; rhythm, flow, and continuity are returning. It was cold today, in the forties, but David seemed exhilarated by playing in it. Last night, he said, he was asleep by midnight, and got seven hours of restful sleep.

David spoke again today about moving to New York. I asked what he would do there. "I would make contacts with intellectuals and people involved in what is going on off-Broadway and on the streets," he said. He would also try to find a job, he added. David visited friends in New York several years ago. "We were having dinner in a restaurant," he told me, "and the people at the next table sent over four bottles of wine." David speaks as if he expects all New York to treat him this kindly: the Big Apple as Big Breast. Obviously, this is a reunion fantasy, a pathological substitution for parental acceptance and love. He talks about New York as having the "energy" he feels is necessary to stimulate and sustain him. But he has no concrete plans for what he would do there, or for how he would support himself.

December 20, 1983

Again, David said he felt well today. He spent the afternoon at the main branch of the city library, watching a film about Angela Davis made in the late sixties or early seventies. He admires Davis as a militant and an intellectual. "The film was not a glorification," he said. "They showed her in her struggle."

David then talked about the present state of the economy. "Why do you think people are buying so much this Christmas?" he wanted to know. I said I think it is because they have more money to spend this year than last. "Why do you think the prices are so low?" he asked. "It's fixed," he said. From the way David spoke, it is clear he sees something ominous and conspiratorial here. But when I pointed this out, he seemed surprised. I said I think most people would see the heavy buying this Christmas as a normal response to supply and demand, as capitalism, greedy as it is, doing its thing. Where others see free enterprise taking its course, David sees conspiracy. And he takes it another step: he is a victim of the conspiracy, of the "they"—Republicans, capitalists, and his father.

David showed me a Christmas card he just received from an old friend, the one who teaches in Houston. There was a picture on the card of him and his wife. They were married about a year and a half ago, while David was still in the hospital.

"He could be a prep," David said as if this disappointed him. His friend's hair was well cut, and he wore a white, long-sleeved shirt with a button-down collar. His wife wore a white blouse, trimmed with lace, closed at the neck. They were both blond and looked, as some couples seem to, very much alike. Their blond hair, white clothes and the bright sun joined them together against a background of green foliage that was out of focus. David noticed how much alike they looked. "That's narcissism," he said. "Actually, the whole card is pretty middle class."

David and his friend from Atlanta had been against the Vietnam war and played out their rebelliousness together during the late sixties and early seventies. So here is his best friend now, a part of the system, married to a young, attractive all-American girl from the Midwest, saying "Merry Christmas" on a card with a picture that makes them look like recent graduates of the University of Virginia. And David is still fighting the Vietnam war, along with the more recent wars in Central America, the economic wars of capitalism, and the war with his parents. Embattled David is having problems with his friend's Christmas card. Today, he seemed more wistful than angry or resentful.

December 27, 1983

David spent Christmas alone and did not seem to mind. His housemates were away on the twenty-fifth, but some returned a day or two later. His closest friend in the house, the biophysicist-musician, is still away. David planned to spend Christmas with a friend, a painter, in a nearby city; but his friend became ill, and the visit was postponed until the end of this week.

David told me he invested $500 in an options move in the market. "Everything about doing it was painful," he said. I asked why. "It's all fixed," he told me. "It's controlled. It's a sure thing. I can't lose." The Dow-Jones, he said, went up fifteen points today. Essentially, David is saying he is having trouble with this transaction because it is *too easy*. The self-deception is clear; he is trying to avoid the pain in the ambiguity of the situation by denying there is any ambiguity. He is telling himself he cannot lose. He is splitting the positive and negative consequences of engaging in the trans-action, and is now living the positive side as if it were the whole thing. As long as he can hold on to this all-positive constitution, he can derive fantasy gratification from the *illusion* of success.

By investing $500 in the market, David is engaging in a concrete situation. And he is having concrete problems doing it. He brings these problems into the session, we discuss them, and I try to show him how he is deceiving himself on a particular issue. In a way, my words are his "unconscious" reflected back to him thematically. I pick apart the intertwined threads of his self-deception and hold them out to him for scrutiny. "It used to be so easy," he said. "I could buy and sell without any problem. If I lost on one stock, I'd sell, take the loss, learn something from it, and go on to another trade. Why can't I do that now?"

David was relaxed tonight, even mellow. He seems enthusiastic about what we are doing, and eager to go where he is going. He sees more clearly all the time the meaning of his illness. I pointed out that it is not enough for him to feel good and become engaged in projects again. He has done this in the past and still been ill. The illness was underneath the good times and the projects and surfaced when things went sour, as when his father liquidated the family business. "I'm not fooling around anymore with this," he said. "I want this to be for life."

December 28, 1983

David spent most of the afternoon in the library again today, doing re-search and checking out several books. He said he felt well and that the day had gone well. But then his mood suddenly changed as he started talking about his father and how his father treated him when he worked in the family business. As David spoke, I felt as if a switch had been turned on to activate a recording I have heard many times before. He was angry and combative now, but not so much as when he had covered this familiar ground in other sessions.

I took a stand against what he was saying, challenging him gently but firmly, point by point, over the old terrain, as I have done so many times. The "recording" went on for about a half-hour. At the end, I pointed out that he had been "in flight" during this time, running like hell. He quickly admitted this. His anger had evaporated. "Why do I do this?" he asked as if he was really puzzled by the flight. Then he answered his own question: "I guess I'm not facing up to my situation." I pointed out he seems to be defending less recently, but that we could expect him to continue (splitting, projecting, projecting and identifying, overidealizing, devaluing, etc.) until he can face the issues that are tying him in knots. He was "in touch" now, relaxed and mellow, as he had been during the entire session last night.

"During the last two or three weeks, I've had a lot more energy," he said near the end of the hour. Then, almost matter-of-factly, he added, "We have to be careful." When I asked why, he said, as if continuing his remark on being careful, "We don't, really. You're not like Harris about that." Clearly, David was referring to Harris's therapeutic hesitancy and contrasting this to my attitude of going all out against his illness.

ME: What do we have to be careful about?

DAVID: I'm not suicidal now. I'm not going to hurt myself.

ME: Do you think it could be the momentum you have now and what it could lead to that you feel you have to be careful about?

David's look told me he believes so. Immediately, he began recalling a number of situations and projects, starting with adolescence, when after gathering momentum, he suddenly pulled back, and, to use his word, "sabotaged" himself. He had described most of these events before. In each case, it was as if at some point a switch was thrown that cut off his power.

David talked again about how his parents seem to have been threatened by his independence and discouraged certain moves he made to be his own person. "This is a present my father brought me when he came up here," he said, holding out a small black and white photograph that had obviously been folded to fit into a wallet. The picture was of David and his father at the beach, when David was two or three. He was standing in the sand, his father bending toward him solicitously.

January 6, 1984

David returned from his vacation on Wednesday. We have met each day since. Today, Friday, is the first day I have been able to write anything because I have not had the time. On December 30, the building in which I had my office was totally destroyed by fire and the water used to fight the fire. Somehow, this manuscript survived in a burned-out room with a foot of charcoal on the floor from the incineration of the ceiling, the attic floor, and the roof.

Wednesday

David spent five days in Philadelphia with his friend, a painter, and his friend's girlfriend. He enjoyed himself and came back high on the city. It is the first time he left this city for more than a day since he returned from Chicago four years ago.

David talked about the "energy" he found in Philadelphia. He met about a dozen people who were friends and associates of his friend, mostly writers and other painters. "There's nothing going on in this city," he told me. "It's time I got out of here. There's nothing for me to do." David spent a good deal of time "in flight" this evening, fantasizing about what his life would be like if he moved. But when I asked how he would fit into this group of people he considers "creative" and "high powered," he said he does not know. He called later that evening to say he realizes he was being rather "abstract" for most of the hour.

Thursday

Tonight David said he hopes to move to Philadelphia by the third week in January, so as to be there in time for the beginning of the spring term at the University of Pennsylvania. He was grandiose for much of the hour, blaming this city for his malaise. "I've got nothing to lose," he said about the prospect of moving. When I pointed out moving would mean not being able to continue our work together, he said he has written to a phenomenological therapist in Philadelphia about the possibility of working with him. I asked again, and still David has no idea of what he would do once he got to Philadelphia.

Friday

David seemed a totally different person this evening. He was "in touch" for the entire hour and exhilarated by the progress he appears to be making. He did not seem angry at his parents, though he insisted he does not want anything more to do with them. He is sick of his illness, he said, and wants out. "I have to let it all go," he insisted, later adding, "This is going to be hard work." He admitted tonight he is not ready now to move to Philadelphia. "I have to get healthier first," he said.

Though he still oscillates between being "in touch" and "in flight," David seems to be getting stronger every day now. Clearly, he is excited by what he senses ahead. "I see no reason why I can't be in good shape in a year," he said tonight.

January 25, 1984

David returned today from Houston, where he has been since Saturday, visiting an old friend from Atlanta who teaches there, and his wife. This is the couple who sent him that very "middle-class" Christmas card with their photograph. His friend and his wife have rented a house, both are working at jobs they like, and appear to be happy. David seemed pleased by this, if not totally convinced. He doesn't think much of middle-class happiness.

David was "in touch" this afternoon, all the way. He liked Houston and the people he met there. His friends talked to him about moving, and David is considering it, but not in the frenzied ("in flight") way he talked about moving to Philadelphia three weeks ago. "I was actually glad to get back here," he said today.

"I feel good," he acknowledged several times during the session. And it seemed so. He was more relaxed and at ease than I have seen him since we began therapy. In Houston he had played tennis, run, and worked out in the weight room at Rice University. This evening he has his first class in one of the courses he chose. He has some doubts about the teacher who, he feels, is "off the wall," but is looking forward to reading the assigned books.

January 26, 1984

It was a warm, spring-like day, and David was responding to the fine weather when we met this afternoon. He had walked from his house, which is several miles away.

He talked more about his visit to Houston. He said he feels pressured by his friend to move there and resents it. He did not say so explicitly, but I sense he feels he would be in his friend's shadow, a buddy returning to remind him of the old days. "He compromised," David said at first, but then he hesitated as if reconsidering. "Maybe he didn't," he added. David and his friend were rebels together during the late sixties and early seventies. His friend found a place in the system. David has not and at times has said his friend sold out. He seems to have mellowed somewhat on this point.

David's face appeared more creased this afternoon. I think he is feeling the weight of his situation more now, what he has lost because of this illness and what he has to look forward to as he lets it go. "It's working," David said about the therapy after our last session before he went to Houston. "I've been thinking of thanking you," he said this afternoon. "I do." Later, he told me I am the only real Sartrean he knows. I said I consider that a compliment.

We talked more about the two courses he is taking. I pointed out that he is living a good deal of his life through books and ideas now. He immediately agreed, and I sensed he recognizes what this means: that he still has a long way to go.

Again, he talked about his parents and how his father had misled him about the family business. He spoke more loudly as he went over the familiar territory. He is still very angry. "There's no reason for reconciliation," he said. "If you don't see that, I'll find a really radical therapist." I took this more as an indication of how deeply he feels about the way his father treated him than of his intention to ditch me for someone more "radical."

David called this evening, more to check in, I believe, than for any other reason. "I hope to be out of this city by May," he said. "That's four months. We'll have to push hard." I didn't tell him I doubt he can get through this in four months but said I feel we should keep going as we have been. "Every day is getting better," he said today.

January 28, 1984

David appeared fairly calm when we began the session early this evening but became less so after about ten minutes. "I got up this morning and wanted to accomplish several things," he said. "But I had too much energy and didn't get anything done." I asked if he means he couldn't pace himself. That's what he meant. I also asked if this felt like the periods of anxiety he experiences now and then. It didn't.

He called home this afternoon, and spoke to his mother. "She resents me," he said. "She could never relate to me on a feeling level. The only things she cares about are money and her socialite friends. That's why I have problems about making money. I hate that woman. I really am the bastard child." "Bastard child" is a term used by the French writer Regis Debray, who was a friend of Sartre's. It signifies a child who is free of his or her parents.

ME: But are you really a bastard child? If you were, would you have called home?
DAVID: I guess that's right.

David was agitated and angry as he talked about his mother. "I'm going back to full revolutionary consciousness," he said. I asked if this is a way of intellectualizing his problem with his mother, a way around dealing with it. He said he feels it is.

DAVID: My mother has given up on me.
ME: You have said that before. Did she say it again today?
DAVID: Yes.
ME: Did you tell her about the courses you are taking?
DAVID: Yes.
ME: Did she seem pleased with that?
DAVID: Yes.
ME: When did she start to get resentful?
DAVID: When I told her she ought to look at her own life.
ME: So, she may have been threatened by what you said, and spoken defensively.
DAVID: Yes.

I asked David why he called home this afternoon. He said he doesn't know. I asked if it might have been to ask permission for what he is doing now, in essence, to get approval for starting to act autonomously. He thinks that is possible. I reminded him he has said, many times, he wants nothing at all to do with his parents, that he is a "bastard child." And yet, he called home again today. He says one thing and lives something else. (Earlier in the session he said, "I've been kicked so hard during the last four years, I'll say anything now.") We talked about how his calling home fits the pattern of his need for approval from his parents. At this point, David picked up and carried the ball, ticking off, once again, the major moves he has made since 1976: to Atlanta, to this city, to Chicago, and back here. He sees each move now as an attempt at reunion with someone or some place from his past at the expense of making an autonomous move of his own.

David was over his anger by the end of the session and appeared pleased by how things had gone.

February 6, 1984

David is having problems with the two courses he just started, one in French literature, the other in French history. According to him, they are being taught with a strong Freudian orientation. He feels this is getting in the way of the material being presented, because everything is seen in the light of Freudian constructs. "Why do I hold on to Freud?" he wanted to know. "I just read *Beyond the Pleasure Principal*, though it wasn't assigned." He feels his tie to Freud may be related to the years of work he did with Freudian analysts, most recently Harris and Stacey, and an attempt to recover experiences in his past that offered security and identity. "I know this is limiting, just as I knew Harris was limited by his Freudian training," he said. "But I hold on anyway."

David has criticized Harris before but not as strongly as he did today. He used the words "liar" and "cheat." "He wanted," David said, "an interminable case." Later, he added, "There was nothing therapeutic going on at all." I believe he can see this now because, in contrast, he senses something therapeutic happening between us. It surprised me today, as it has before, that his anger at Harris doesn't seem to go very deep. Perhaps he received so much comfort from fusing with Harris that he cannot turn on him fully now.

Several times this afternoon David asked, "Why can't I break this?" He sounded like he is really having a hard time understanding why he can't just let go of his illness. He has raised the question before, but this time I sensed he sees more clearly how serious his illness has been, and still is. I suggested he compare his situation now to what it was two years ago, just before he was hospitalized.

David spent the last fifteen minutes of the session making what appeared to be a formal statement of recommitment to seeing his illness through to the end. He sounded like he was taking a pledge. He wants to break all the bonds that have prevented him from becoming autonomous in the past. He says he wants no more excuses—his or anyone else's. He is willing to take full responsibility for what has happened to him. He wants to move out of the house where he lives now and find an apartment of his own. (His friend, the biophysicist-musician, is planning to move to New York in April. They are not as close now as they were two months ago. "He's beginning to separate," David said, meaning, I suppose, he has turned his sights toward New York.) David has also committed himself to seeing through the two courses he is taking, even though he does not like the way the material is being presented. He feels the discipline of going to class and writing the papers that will be assigned would be good for him now. He also, in effect, asked me to rededicate myself to what we are doing. "Don't let me defend," he said. "Point it out to me when I do." He wants to make sure I won't abandon him or sell him out. What struck me most in all this is that David sounds as if he means it. In contrast to a year, or even eight months ago, he seems behind his words now. He says of his illness, "I'm ready to break it."

David called home today, among other reasons to ask if my bills to his father are tax deductible. He also wanted to know something about the terms of his inheritance. His father told him to get well and they could talk about it then. Just a few days ago, David told me the inheritance means nothing to him. Obviously, he is split on this issue. He needs money, but it has both good and bad meanings to him that he cannot integrate.

Almost matter-of-factly, David mentioned something I was surprised he had not told me before. During the two years he worked for his father in Atlanta (1976–1978), he was not given a key to his father's office. I asked if he thinks this is because his father did not trust him. He thinks it is.

February 10, 1984

David relaxed, sat quietly in his chair and spoke in a low voice this afternoon. He was "in touch" for the entire hour.

"I'm breaking this down day by day," he said. "That's the way I have to do it. It's like starting all over." He said he could feel the old him dying.

During the last half of the session David said little. He was calm and meditative and sat relaxed in his chair. He smiled as if he liked what he was feeling, as if it was good to be where he was. "It feels good, doesn't it?" I asked. He said it does. For the last ten minutes, he said nothing. Neither did I.

February 14, 1984

David was "in flight" this afternoon, more so than I have seen him in a long time. "I have to get out of this country," he said. "The Europeans know how to pay the price. They know what's going on. I could work with someone over there. In a socialist country no one exploits anyone else." I asked if by "Europe" he means France, and he said he does. I did not remind him that he does not speak French.

And he came at me, too. I see everything from an elitist perspective; I am trying to put words in his mouth; I don't have contact with the real world and with real people, and so on. He was repeating the familiar complaints about me he trots out whenever he is defending.

I knew something had happened but didn't want to interrupt by asking what. After about forty minutes, he told me he received a letter from his father yesterday. "It was the same old thing," he said. "I hate that man." David said the letter was "mealy mouthed." As far as I can tell, this means his father is again asking him to conform, toe the line, and get a job. "He wants me to become part of the American dream," David said with contempt.

"How dare he write me a letter like that?" he went on. "I called him back immediately. I wrote him a three-page letter. I told him I wanted nothing to do with the inheritance. It's not important to me." I reminded him that about two weeks ago, he asked his father to be more specific about the terms of his inheritance. Essentially, his father told him to be patient. "He will never confront anything directly with me," David said. "I may contact a lawyer I know about starting the proceedings for disinheritance."

Clearly, David is trying to manipulate his father so he will give him more money now. David has split feelings about money. Today, in his disappointment about not getting an advance on his inheritance, he said he doesn't want any part of it. "I can live in a one-room apartment," he said. "Marx had very little money. He went for days without eating. He wouldn't compromise." I asked if money isn't a major concern for him now, as he said several times recently. "Not any more," he told me. "I got some from the underground." I sensed David was not eager to discuss what the "underground" is, and I did not press him. If I had to bet, I would bet he was talking about doing something illegal.

David had no good word for anyone or anything today. He criticized a young woman he had dinner with last week, the girlfriend of an acquaintance, because she has never had to fight for anything and has never been "unmasked." "Her father sent her to school, bought her a house, and will offer her a job in his firm when she finishes law school," he complained. "Her father's money is the reason she can spend eight hours a day in the library, reading." I pointed out that he has had many of the same privileges. He tried to deny this, saying he paid for some of his college tuition with money he won at poker. I believe David's real complaint here is that his father isn't giving him enough money now so *he* can spend eight hours a day in the library.

David interviewed for a job with the housing bureau this morning. When he told me he was going to do this two days ago, he said the work would be worthwhile because he could help find housing for underprivileged people. But today, he said the job would be all bureaucracy, that he knew what to expect, and none of it would be good.

His father's letter opened the old wound, and all the bitterness gushed out. And how did David try to deal with what he was feeling? By splitting and defending. The same reductions and simplifications, the same bad faith. For the first forty minutes, I doubt he could have admitted this. Then, suddenly, his mood changed, and he did. We laughed together, sharing the knowledge of what this means. He left more in laughter than in anger.

February 16, 1984

As soon as David started talking this evening I could see he was building toward something, that he was trying to make a point. He talked for about a half-hour, mentioning events and encounters during the last two days, as well as what came up in the French literature class he attended last night and the reading he did today. He wove the threads together, loosely. When he seemed to have said most of what he was going to say, I reflected a summary of his words back to him: "It sounds like you feel Harris was distorting your situation while you worked with him, that he really didn't understand what was going on, and that you didn't get any help from him." "That's right," he said. "He thought I was angry at him because of the transference, but I was really angry at how he was handling me. Nothing in the transference was therapeutic."

None of what David said surprised me because we have discussed these points again and again. What did surprise me is that he spoke *as if he was coming to see it for the first time.* He spoke with the tone of discovery. In a sense, I believe he is just discovering what he told me tonight. Earlier, he knew it cognitively—in his head—but this somehow did not quite reach him. As he spends more time "in touch," what he thinks and feels about himself are coming more into sync. Today, he "discovered" something about himself that he has "known" for at least two years.

Last night's French literature class and two books he is reading, one on psychoanalysis, the other on the poet-critic Yvor Winters, provided the clues for David's "discovery." In class, the teacher talked about Freud's *Interpretation of Dreams,* particularly the language Freud developed so he could make psychoanalysis a science. "Everything has a fixed meaning," David said as if he does not believe it. I sense he was reacting to (and objecting to) the reduction of lived experience to symbols and terms. The book on psychoanalysis he is reading deals largely with the aggressive instinct in families: mothers, fathers, and sons all out to get each other. One case history reminded David of how Harris was analyzing his situation with his parents. Suddenly, he said, he realized how ridiculous the whole thing is. In contrast, the book on Yvor Winters offers a vision for life that is not reductive or "ridiculous," one that allows for subtlety and ambiguity. Thus David "discovered" today what he has "known" for a long time.

David spoke calmly and evenly tonight. He was not angry and he did not appear to be defending. He looked better, too, less like the "wild man" he often seems. He was more likable. I have noted before the difference in David's personality when he is "in touch" and when he is "in flight." Tonight, I saw the "in touch" David. He talked about his parents with understanding and affection. He acknowledged that they have good qualities, something he rarely does. "I'm really surprised," he said, "that my father and mother haven't died from what I put them through during the last four years, considering their age."

February 18, 1984

David said he felt pretty good this afternoon, considering that he was up until 6 A.M. He wasn't in the mood to read last night and went to a neighborhood bar where he used to spend a good deal of time until about five months ago. He doesn't like the people who go there because, he says, they're off-the-wall types, and not stable. He has had trouble with some of these people before. It was clear from the way he spoke that he felt going back to this bar was a comedown for him. He needed company last night and went there to find it. He left with someone, and they went back to his house and played chess until 6 A.M. David said the guy didn't take it well when he started losing.

David sees his agitation last night as a reaction to the French literature course he is taking. "Reading Freud and listening to the lectures on Freud makes me think of the work I did with Harris and Stacey," he told me. He repeated the same objections to the way Harris dealt with him that he made two days ago. The criticism was fair and well thought out, and he was "in touch" as he spoke. He admitted again his complicity in continuing treatment with Harris, even after he "knew" it wasn't doing him any good. He seems to be working this issue through on deeper levels.

I pointed out that while he is angry at Harris, this anger is not paralyzing him, as his anger at his parents has and continues to. "They're bad people," he said, as soon as I mentioned them. "I don't want anything to do with them." When I pointed out that what he had just said is different from what he said two days ago — that his father and mother do have some good qualities — he replied, "That's over," as if to say it is no longer true. He began a tirade against his parents that lasted a half-hour. At the end of the session I pointed out that today he was again looking only at a part of what he sometimes admits is the truth about his parents. "Why do I do that?" he asked later, as if he really doesn't know, even though we have talked about this in detail many times. "I miss so much by doing this," he admitted. It seems that the David who can see the ambiguity in his parents ("in touch" David) and the David who sees them as all bad ("in flight" David) are not in touch with each other.

David talked again about moving out of the house where he lives. "The neighborhood isn't healthy," he said. "And there's nothing going on in the house now." He also talked about moving out of the city. "There's nothing for me here," he has said over and over. He wants to leave, but does not know where he wants to go. "I really don't want to go to the University of Texas," he told me this afternoon. "I really don't want to go to Austin." His friend in Houston has been encouraging him to move down there, but David is suspicious of his friend's reasons. Then, David said something about getting a job on Wall Street but backed off when I asked how he would go about it. When he returned from Houston, he said he was planning to apply to the University of Texas for a graduate program, but has apparently decided against that.

"We haven't been doing much good work during the last ten days," he said after the session ended. I told him I am not concerned about how things are going.

February 20, 1984

David began the session this afternoon with a good deal of vague talk about books and ideas. He was pontificating again, masturbating cognitively and boring me to tears. I had heard most of it before. I did not let on I was bored, but listened carefully, asking for a clarification now and then. This went on for perhaps fifteen minutes.

Gradually, David soared to new heights "in flight." He denied he is ill; and when I pointed out that he has acknowledged his illness many times, the contradiction did not appear to bother him. "You're no model of mental health," he told me. "How do you define mental illness?" I reminded him that on many occasions during the last four months, we have agreed on what his illness means. Being reminded made no apparent impression on him today.

"What does sick mean?" he wanted to know. "You can't do the things you say you want to and have the kind of life you say you want," I replied. He told me he would challenge me in swimming, tennis, seducing women, and reading books. "Then we'll see who's sick," he said. He was baiting me, strongly. "Even if you won in all categories," I said, "what would it prove?" That he is not ill, he said.

He attacked me directly, both as a person and a therapist. He also attacked the mental health profession. He said he feels art is more therapeutic than therapy. "I get more from listening to a half-hour of music than I get from therapy," he told me. I tried to point out that music is an aesthetic experience, that it does not directly address the meaning of his illness and will not in itself help him to get better. He was not convinced. "What can I learn from you?" he asked. I told him therapy is not education and that all I can do is extend an invitation to him to become more free, which he can accept or reject.

He spoke again today about getting money from the "underground." When I asked if that means he got it illegally, he implied strongly it does. "No one is getting hurt," he volunteered. He said he has lived hand to mouth for the last two years and sounded as though he feels he has a right to take something now. He glorified people in the ghetto who steal to survive, and it was clear he identifies with them and with their struggle. He said that public officials routinely steal and do other illegal things. And didn't Sartre glorify Jean Genet, who was a thief and served time in prison?

"To separate," he said, "I need financial independence." And, I said, there are three ways you can get it: (1) your father can give it to you; (2) you can get a job; and (3) you can do something illegal for it. David then implied his father had recently turned him down on a proposition he made. (Hence, the recent rebastardization of the "bastard child," along with the threat to change his name.) He is trying to get a job, he told me. But the "underground" has apparently come through in the meantime. I pointed out that people who break the law sometimes get caught. "I won't get caught," was his response.

It occurred to me this afternoon that David's recent feelings of guilt and his recent attacks on me could be related to whatever he has done to get money. To justify something illegal, he must remain convinced that American capitalistic culture is evil. To him, I am a part of the establishment and the status quo. If he can trash me, he can justify what he has done.

Clearly, David was grandiose this afternoon, running from his feelings and his real issues, defending himself, attacking me, his parents, and this culture. Near the end of the session, he began talking in the language of filmmaking, using words like camera, lens, and angle. He was seeing himself as the director of a film about his life. "It sounds like you want to make a movie out of this," I said. I pointed out that the notion of making such a movie seems an escape from his real issues, his ultimate fantasy gratification and justification. He agreed. "I can do it," he said in spite of the acknowledgment. "No problem. No one in America will understand it, but they'll understand it in Europe."

Phone call this evening:

DAVID: I was really flying this afternoon.

ME: That's where you were, and it's a part of what we're doing.

DAVID: But we have to get down to this illness.

ME: This afternoon, you said there is no illness.

DAVID: I know. I was flying then, but I'm on the ground now. It's good I can come down.

ME: Yes.

DAVID: This illness really *is* a drug.

ME: Yes.

David sounded like his "in touch" self tonight. During our two previous meetings, he has been fully "in flight." But when he called several hours after each meeting, he sounded grounded again and was also aware of how he had defended earlier. The "in touch" David acknowledges the "in flight" David, but the "in flight" David does not acknowledge the "in touch" David. This is probably a good indication of the strength of the lie he tells himself when he is "flying" and of how total his bad faith is as he defends.

February 21, 1984

David began the session tonight with a monologue on how things are for him these days. "I have about four hours a day of continuous feeling and activity," he said. During this time he reads, writes, walks, swims, and talks to other people. Then, he said, things begin to fragment, and he can't do anything useful. He has described this feeling several times before as "going in circles" and "coming off the wall." David is beginning to see the shape of his days now. He was "in touch" as he spoke, and behind what he said.

"It's been a good day," he told me. He ran into a woman he knows from Atlanta while crossing a street downtown. They went to a nearby coffee shop and talked for about an hour. She is teaching at a local women's college, married since David saw her last, and just had a baby. "She was a good fuck," he reported, recalling their past involvement.

I was with the "in touch" David tonight. I asked if he could distinguish how he was then from how he was when we met yesterday. He could. "I haven't raised my voice once tonight," he said.

February 23, 1984

As soon as David told me he felt good this afternoon, he began telling me how angry he is at me, and about the problems he is having working with me. He brought up the familiar complaints, which boil down to the fact that he and I are different in significant ways. This bothers him.

"I'm writing this all out," he said. "That's more helpful than therapy. What can I learn from you?" I pointed out again that I am not a teacher; and though he may be helped by keeping a journal of his days now, I can offer an invitation out of his situation he cannot provide himself. "My father can't deal with me directly," he said, repeating a familiar complaint. "He's paying you to act as an intermediary." It still bothers David that his father is paying me. To him, that I'm being paid by his father means I am being bought by him. I pointed out I am not acting as an intermediary and explained why doing so would be at odds with everything I believe therapy to be. I reminded him I've had no contact with his father since his visit here more than two months ago. He accepted what I said, and his objections collapsed. He admitted he was agitated and angry and was taking it out on me. David has attacked me broadly and often, but so far he has not questioned my competence as a therapist.

He was angry, he said, because it took him two hours to get started this morning. He was awake until 4 A.M., alone, just thinking about things. "I broke down some walls," he told me, meaning he was dealing with past issues that still have a hold on him. I asked if he was "going in circles" or "coming off the wall"—his expressions for those periods when he stops being concrete and present and lets the past overwhelm him—and he said he was not.

"I'm going to write a comical treatment of my experience with psychoanalysis based on Harris's letters to me," he said. "I have contacted a radical therapist and some academic people around the country about this." I told him I feel he has all the experience necessary for the project.

David said he is afraid of what lies ahead for him. "I want to move out of the house and find an apartment, so I can be by myself," he told me. I pointed out, again, that he is frustrated because he can't take the next step. He realizes he can't afford an apartment until he gets a job, and he has all kinds of conflicts about doing that. He called the brokerage house where he had an interview recently, and they told him there is no opening. "That leaves the job at the housing bureau," he said.

David is in a twilight zone now, somewhere between a serious illness and the world he wishes to rejoin and recover, even if only on his own terms. "I want the dawn," he said, evenly.

February 26, 1984

"This is going to be the last session for a week or a week and a half," were David's first words when we met this afternoon. "I have to start working this out for myself." I nodded, and he went on the attack. "I don't think there is such a thing as mental illness. It's a myth created by the dominant reality," by which he means the people in power. At this point I knew I was in for a rough hour.

"You therapists create a language to impose control on other people," he told me. I replied that many therapists do that, but I try very hard not to. He seemed willing to consider my point. He was totally "in flight," identifying with writers, books, and ideas—particularly revolutionary writers, books, and ideas—and out of touch with his situation. I reminded him of this. "Maybe it's true," he said softly, almost apologetically.

"Instead of struggling with your problems and fears concretely, you identify with the struggles of people like Marx, Sartre, and Laing," I suggested. This identification, which involves projection and introjection, is solely defensive and not lived out. David does not *do* anything "revolutionary," as he readily acknowledges. "This will always be a part of me," he said, meaning his interest in these writers. "But can you read them without at the same time backing away from your situation?" I asked. He sighed heavily, as he has done often when I point out he is "in flight" and he realizes he is avoiding what he knows he must do. "This is going to take a lot of work," he said.

"I came in here angry, and I'm taking it out on you," he admitted. "I think I'm really frightened of what is ahead for me." Earlier, David told me he is "looking for an identity."

About an hour after he left, David reappeared at my door. "I think we should talk about this," he said, standing in the hall. "I really don't think you know what's going on with me," he began. "I don't think you see things. When you read the paper, you don't read between the lines." I pointed out that his accusations were vague and that I was having trouble following him. I asked if he could give a specific instance of how I am misreading him. He said a few words, but they went nowhere. He couldn't put his angry feelings into a concrete charge against me. "I'm furious at you," he said. "I'm ready to take your head off." His face was flushed as he said this.

"What have you done for the revolution?" he wanted to know. I told him I try to do my job and help the people I work with. I got the impression he was willing to consider this as a reasonable contribution to the "revolution."

"What dues have you paid?" he wanted to know. "You haven't been through analysis." We talked about this for a while, and he seemed persuaded that analysis is not an absolute requirement for a therapist. I pointed out that he has been attacking me a good deal lately. "It's resistance," he said, "to use the Freudian term." I also pointed out that I have never complained about his being angry at me or fractious toward me. He agreed. "This is a part of your struggle to get through this," I said. "I expected it, and see it as an opportunity for growth. I suspect as you get further along and realize more fully where you have been for the last four years, you will be angrier still at how much you missed, and some of that anger will be directed toward me."

"I'm frightened of what I can do," he said. "But I'll make this commitment again: let's go all the way on this. I know we're on the right track." I do not doubt he means what he says, the "in touch" David, anyway. I also know he will attack me again, as he did today. "This illness is like a drug," he said. "Like Valium. It's like I'm going through withdrawal. It's like detoxing." Take away the drug (defense), and the anxiety and anger reappear.

David called tonight to make an appointment for the day after tomorrow. He sounded enthusiastic. "We're really on the way," he said. "Let's keep going. That's all that counts at this point."

February 29, 1984

David was in a tranquil, placid mood this afternoon. He sat relaxed in his chair for the entire hour. He spoke evenly and did not raise his voice. His face appeared less tight. His movements in the chair were more fluid than usual. He did not tie and untie his shoe laces, as he has been doing during our most difficult sessions recently.

He saw a movie last night — *Frances* — and liked it, though he thought it was "formulaic." He talked about film and filmmakers for perhaps a half-hour. He has been catching up on reading film journals. He said something about getting a job as a projectionist in a movie theater but then said that working at the ticket counter would be better because it would be easier to steal from there. He talked about the feminist filmmaker, Chantal Akerman, whose work he greatly admires.

One of his housemates, the biophysicist-musician, who is planning to move to New York next month, is encouraging David to move also. "I've written to NYU for a catalog," he said. He is interested in taking courses in film and liberal arts. "That would be the perfect environment for me," he continued. "There are people there who are open to new ideas. There's also an underground economy." I have come to recognize "underground economy" as David's codeword for illegal activity. He also told me his healing would not occur through swimming and therapy but by making films. As far as I know, David has never been behind a movie camera.

David dropped the French history course. He will get thirty percent of the tuition refunded. "It's not what the catalog says it is," he told someone in the Registrar's office about the course. He is upset it will take two weeks to get the refund.

He said he is trying to "check" himself when he begins to lose touch with concrete projects. "I have a good four or five hours a day now," he told me, meaning he feels relatively well and can be productive during that time.

March 1, 1984

"I feel much better away from therapy. I find this sterile. I can do more when I work things out by myself." This is how David began the session this afternoon. Here we go again, I thought.

ME: You seem angry.

DAVID: I'm in a war.

ME: It seems like you're saying we're on opposite sides now. Last night, when you called, I sensed you felt we were on the same side. Something has changed between then and now.

David told me he had just read a poem by Robert Pinsky that attacked psychiatrists and their profession. Apparently, this poem set him off against me and the work we are doing. It doesn't take much to change David's thinking — on anything. His lability is a consequence of the splitting defense he uses so often.

He was angry at me for the usual reasons for the first fifteen minutes or so. "Coming here has bad associations," he said. He means the neighborhood, which is in one of the nicest sections of the city, near the university. It is an upper-middle-class neighborhood that reminds David of his parents and of where he was brought up in Atlanta. My office, on the tenth floor of an elegant Tudor building, has a good view of the northeast section of the city, much of which is sky. Last week, he said something to the effect I was working "in the clouds," with the clear implication that this is not good. David's feelings about this area change, as do his feelings about everything else. Recently, he said he likes it here and would like to find an apartment nearby.

March 3, 1984

David came directly from the tennis court to our session. He seemed eager to talk about the match.

ME: How did you do?

DAVID: I was winning, but I clutched in the last set. I'm a better player. I hit fourteen winners, he hit two. I beat myself by making too many errors. Let's talk about this. I didn't follow through. It's like I do with a lot of other things. Let's get to the heart of this.

ME: How did it feel when you were ahead?

DAVID: Good but strange.

ME: Do you think it may be because you're not used to that feeling?

DAVID: Maybe. It's war on a tennis court. There's a winner and a loser. I didn't want to crush him.

ME: Why?

DAVID: I'm not sure.

ME: As you said, it's like that with other things, too. We've talked about this before.

DAVID: When I was playing, I saw an image of my mother's hand with a diamond ring going across my face. She hit me because I did something that made her mad. I was about seven. She used to tell me I was a "terror."

ME: Were you?

DAVID: I didn't burn buildings and shoot people. But I will.

ME: It sounds like you made things hard on your parents and generated a lot of static. What was your mother punishing when she hit you?

DAVID: My freedom. My autonomy.

ME: When your mother hit you, what were you trying to accomplish that offended her?

DAVID: I don't know.

ME: Would you be willing to consider the possibility she was punishing your wheel-spinning and acting out, rather than a truly autonomous move?

I could tell by the expression on David's face I had touched something with my question. Recently, he told me a woman he was involved with briefly several years ago said he had never been "socialized." I believe she meant David is not concerned enough about the "niceties" of life, such as manners, which finally comes down to being considerate of other people's feelings. I reminded him today what this former girlfriend said, and he seemed willing to consider her point. Then, as if he saw a connection, he repeated something his mother said to him many years ago: "The reason we didn't get into the country club is that you screwed everything in the neighborhood." David felt it was insensitive of his mother to say "every*thing*."

ME: When you were ahead this afternoon, you had the chance to beat this guy, but you didn't follow through, to use your words. Would you consider the possibility that when you worked for your father between 1976 and 1978, he may have seen your suggestions for restructuring the business as unrealistic? Could he really have felt you were not ready to take over the business, as he said when he was here in December? Could it be he was threatened, as you say he was, not by your ideas and talent, but by the noise you made and the static you generated? If someone started to break down my door, I'd be threatened, too. And I would try to defend myself.

David raised his voice for the first time this afternoon now. "You're lying," he shouted. I pointed out I could not be lying because I was not asserting anything, just asking a question. "My father was a dead man when I went back to Atlanta," David said. "He was finished."

ME: It sounds like, at sixty-five, your father was near the end of his career, unsure about what he should do with his business, and not convinced you were ready to take it over.

DAVID: I'm being defensive about this because there's something real to defend myself against.

But David's anger subsided more quickly than I would have expected if he felt I was completely off the mark on this. He settled down, and we talked more about how he has always been threatened by success, and how he pulls back whenever it is within reach. "I've done that with school, athletics, the stock market, and women," he said.

A most important question comes out of all this. Have David's mother and father failed to reward his genuine moves toward real autonomy, or did they react negatively and defensively (properly, to defend themselves) to his wheel-spinning and acting out? I raised the question, and I could tell David feels there is something to think about here, unpalatable as the thought might be.

Near the end of the session, this brief exchange occurred:

DAVID: I hate therapists. They put you to sleep.

ME: Do I do that?

DAVID: No. You're mean. I like that.

I think David means he knows now that he can't fool me.

March 5, 1984

David called last night and said, among other things, he wants to "speed up" therapy, so he can leave this city by May, and move somewhere else. He mentioned Austin and said he is thinking of applying to the University of Texas. Several weeks ago, he told me he had decided against going there.

David brought a writing pad with him to the session this afternoon. He sat back in his chair and seemed to be making notes. For perhaps a minute, he said nothing. I assumed he was putting the final touches on his schedule. Then, as he began to read, it was clear this was something else. He read a quotation he copied from a book by Simone de Beauvoir on women and men. The essence of the brief quotation is that women have been responsible for keeping the home fires burning and continuing the species, while men have run the world and made the discoveries.

Why is David so concerned now with feminine and masculine roles? I reminded him that during the last few months he has said that women are superior to men, emotionally stronger, and more "in touch." "The feminist revolution," he told me more than once, "is the most important revolution of the twentieth century." Is David "identifying" with women and their struggles? Is he asserting what he calls his "feminine side," that part of him that is passive and wants to be taken care of?

David often identifies with blacks, workers, prisoners, and others who, he feels, are not being treated fairly by American society, as well as with their struggles to win equality. "My father treated me like someone just off the boat," he says now and then about his experience in the family business. And in the same vein, he has said, "My father treated me like a nigger, like one of his workers in the warehouse."

David has spoken before about what he calls his "pathology toward women," and mentioned it again today. Last fall, he told me, "I think that's my main problem." We have talked about his situation with Sally many times. He goes all the way from being "in touch" on this, taking responsibility for the breakup of their relationship, to being "in flight" on it, blaming her for everything, saying he didn't care for her that much, anyway. One of David's "problems" with women now is that, as he says, he doesn't have any. Before his last breakdown nearly five years ago, he had women coming and going.

He talked again today about wanting to make films. "My illness," he said, "is a blocked work of art, a film I've never made." He says he wants to make this film, and doesn't seem to feel his lack of technical training would be an obstacle. "I'll learn how," he told me today. He regrets he didn't go to New York when he was in his twenties to study filmmaking. "I listened to the wrong people and played it safe," he said.

David is still trying to find a job. "There was nothing in the paper yesterday [Sunday]," he said. He saw ads for waiters and announcements for training programs for salesmen and executives, but he is not interested in doing this kind of work. When I suggested he has a dual problem — finding a job in a bad economy and dealing with a strong conflict about what having a job would mean for him — he denied there is any conflict and accused me of harping on the issue of work. "You told me you are almost out of money and have to find a job soon," I reminded him. "You have said money is a major issue for you now." He admitted this. Then I asked how he spent $4,000 in three months. (His father gave him $5,000 in December; he used $1,000 of it to pay off debts.) "I spent too much," he told me. "I'm not good at managing money now the way I used to be." This easy admission surprised me. During the last two months, David has been to Philadelphia and Houston, bought clothes, and spent money in restaurants and on taxi cabs.

At the end of the session, I told David it sounds like he isn't really interested in a career or even in being able to support himself for very long. "What you seem to be saying," I told him, "is that your father should give you more money, one way or another, until he dies, and then you can get your part of the inheritance and live off that." David did not deny this very vigorously.

March 7, 1984

Last night, David went with the biophysicist-musician and his girlfriend to see Chantal Akerman's film, *Jeanne Dielman*. The film is about a woman who has been widowed and supports herself and her young son by working as a prostitute. It covers three days in her life in great detail, at a slow pace. David admires Akerman, a feminist filmmaker from Belgium.

David was upset that his friend did not respond to the film as he had. "It's because he's only seen things from one perspective," David said. "He has never had to work for a living." I pointed out his friend did get a Ph.D., and that *is* work, and that during the last year he has worked hard preparing himself for a new career in music and dance. David admitted this is so.

David was also upset that his friend was not upset over a recent story in a local newspaper describing an incident in a black section of the city when a domestic argument led to murder. His friend said something like, "That's the way it goes in the ghetto." "He's never seen life on the other side of the tracks," David objected. "He doesn't know what it's like."

Two responses from his close friend, one to a film, the other to a murder in a black neighborhood: both made David angry. Why? "You probably identified with the pain of the woman in the film and with the violent feelings of the black man who murdered his girlfriend," I suggested. "And you were upset that your friend did not respond as you did." David admitted there may be something to this interpretation. Then he added, "If I don't break this [illness] soon, I'll take someone's head off." Not long ago, he told me he felt like taking *my* head off.

I suggested that in the film, the woman's pain and suffering became David's pain and suffering. "It's not only her pain," he said, "but the objects around her and the architecture. Everything shows the sterility and alienation of modern life. The buildings are like prisons." Because of his illness, David has lived in a jail of his own making during the last few years and feels now everyone else is in jail also. To him, the world is a jail.

March 19, 1984

This morning, I received a letter from David's father:

3/15/84

While David tells us that he is feeling better and healthier, he still appears to be quite bitter and resentful, and continues to bring up the past, blaming myself and the family for his medical illness — instead of forgetting the past and focusing on the future. Also, his life is not very structured, and he does not have a job — which, I believe, is most important. The financial support has stopped with the five-thousand dollars he received last December.

I would appreciate your assessment of David's progress and a short statement of how we should relate to him, and what position we should take with him — since David is a very hard and complex person to deal with, and his frequent phone calls are very upsetting.

This is the first communication, except for payment of bills, I have had from David's father since he was here in December. David has been very sensitive about any contact between his father and me because he feels I may become his father's agent against him. I have tried to reassure him this will not happen.

I showed the letter to David when we met today. He became somewhat agitated as he read it. "It's the same old thing," he said. "The same old mentality operating. It's so predictable. Get a job. That's all he thinks of." I told David I feel the letter is fair and even-tempered, reasonable, and not at all manipulative. He did not immediately agree, but his resistance collapsed gradually, and he had to admit his father was not being unfair.

I told David I feel the best way to answer his father's letter was by phone. He suggested I call while he was here. I agreed, realizing this would allay the worst of his fears about any "collusion" between his father and me.

Mr. Helbros was pleasant and agreeable. He asked if I had shown his letter to David and seemed pleased when I said I had. "That way, we keep everything in the open," he said. I told him I feel David is making good progress in therapy, working hard, and not complaining about what he has to go through; he is trying to find a job, but this is hard because he has been out of the work force for five years and because the employment picture in this city is grim. Mr. Helbros was sympathetic. He is willing to help support his son but wants me to understand he is retired now, working only part time, and has already spent several hundred thousand dollars on David's illness. He spoke calmly and without bitterness. I got the impression David's father is one hundred percent behind his son and willing to give him the benefit of every doubt. He feels David calls home too frequently for his budget and wishes he would not spend his money this way. He also said David is "up and down," by which he means David will suggest doing something one minute, only to back off and then suggest doing something very different the next.

Considering the sensitivity of the issues covered in my conversation with his father, David was unexpectedly composed for the rest of the session, as we went over once again his father's main concerns about his son.

"My father should give me $100,000, and let me do what I want with it," David told me several days ago. In other words, he wants his inheritance now. His father won't give it to him, and David is angry. "You really feel you have your father by the balls, don't you?" I asked. "Yes," he said, immediately.

Recently, David told me that the biophysicist-musician has a brother who lives at home with his parents and does not work. "They're not sure what he'll do if they don't take care of him, so they let him stay," David said. I sensed David sees some connection between his situation and that of his friend's brother. We have talked about how David wants to be taken care of. Today, he said he is going to look for a woman who can take care of him for the next few months.

March 23, 1984

David talked today about his first breakdown, when he was twenty-one. A woman he was involved with for two years developed a serious emotional problem and began to lean heavily on David for support. He pulled back, essentially telling her to get herself together. Eventually, she broke off the relationship. David tried to get her back, was not successful, and fell apart. "Everything was going my way before that," he said. "I was in school full time, on the dean's list, making money in the stock market, well connected with friends." Then, over a period of several months, he lost his girlfriend, his grandmother died, a close friend committed suicide, and his sister was hospitalized following a suicide attempt. He had a breakdown, and was hospitalized. He had another breakdown several years later, he told me, after the breakup of his marriage. He had not mentioned this before.

Then David changed the subject. "It's not that my father didn't trust me, or doubted my ability," he said. "He just wasn't sure I could commit myself to running the business." Is David finally coming to terms with the issue that precipitated his last breakdown?

Several days ago David asked, "Will you be strong enough for what we have to do during the next few months?" He was asking if I would stick by him as he tries to take the next step out of his illness. "This is going to be tough," he said again, as he has so many times since we began working together. I assured him I was strong enough and would stick by him.

March 25, 1984

Yesterday, David received a letter from his father. "It was the same old thing," he said. In the letter David's father spoke of his son's "behavior." "Reading this was like hitting a raw nerve," he said. David was upset and angry this afternoon. He spoke loudly, and tied and untied the lace of one shoe several times as he sat in his chair. He was tight and tried to work off the tension.

The letter set off a chain reaction of the familiar complaints and defenses. After he said his father had taken advantage of him when he worked in the family business, I reminded him that during the last session he admitted he was not sufficiently committed to the business to run it. "My commitment was obvious," he shouted today. There were the usual references to Marx and the political left. I pointed out that while he says he doesn't want any contact with his father, he still feels his father "owes" him. Today was reparations time again. David has said many times his father does not "owe" him. But as soon as the "raw nerve" was touched, he went into "flight," and his claim to support was reactivated.

David has another plan for supporting himself. "I'll steal it," he said. "I'm lighter on my feet now. It'll work. It worked this morning at the drugstore." I took this to mean he got away with shoplifting today. I did not comment. In the past, when he has talked about breaking the law, I have pointed out the consequences if he gets caught. David is well aware of these consequences.

Along with the familiar defenses, David's sociopathy seems to have been reactivated by his father's letter. He has what he calls "connections" with "people in the street," who, he told me, are small-time drug dealers. He talks occasionally about "putting something together" with them. About a week ago, he won $100 playing cards with some of these people.

Gradually, as I confronted him, David let go of his defenses and came back "in touch." He became more relaxed and spoke more quietly. Once again, he made the heavy sighing noise that means he is breaking another oscillation of "flight" to come back to being "in touch." The sigh probably means he knows he must get back to hard reality.

David told me he recently cleaned his house, that it looks good, and that he feels good about doing it. He checked through the classified ads today and said he would send out several résumés. "Job and apartment: that's the goal now," he asserted. When David left, he seemed at ease and drained of the anger he came with.

March 27, 1984
Afternoon

"I had a violent night," David said, but it did not show. He looked calm, at peace with himself, even pleased. "I'm breaking things down and working this through," he continued. "I felt delirious last night." As far as I could tell, "delirious" meant "in touch" to a very high degree. "I'm going to have to smoke," he said, taking out his cigarettes. I told him not smoking during our sessions was his rule and he has a right to break it.

Everything David said for the first twenty minutes seemed solid and without defensive distortion. I pointed this out, and he said he could sense it too. David was *feeling* this afternoon — his thoughts, his words, his body. From all indications, it felt good.

Somehow, David started talking about religion, which he despises. He has said, many times, that people use religion as a crutch and an escape. "But don't you do the same thing by taking up Marxist and revolutionary ideas as you do?" I asked. "Isn't that your religion of resentment? Don't you mystify your experience this way as an excuse for not making a place for yourself in this world? Isn't *this* a religion of excuse?"

David's calm left him now, and he sat eagerly at the edge of his chair as if he might move toward me. "I'm not doing it now," he insisted. "I'm in touch, and I'm not making excuses." I told him I recognize this but that I am certain he has used (and will probably use again) what he calls "revolutionary thinking" as an ideology on which to base his refusal of the world. "I'm not doing it now," he repeated, more insistently this time.

Again, I agreed with him. Then he attacked me for being "socially unconscious" and said he has problems with this. I pointed out he is having trouble being himself while allowing me to be me. He didn't think so. (In a session several hours later, he said he felt he was having trouble "separating" from me. I suggested this is another way of saying what he denied this afternoon, and he agreed.) I was defending, he said, and trying to make him think as I think. I pointed out he has never done anything about the revolutionary ideas he talks about and contrasted his fantasy rebellion to the activism of a Marxist professor at a university here. After I challenged him again several times about using revolutionary ideology as a religion of excuse, he said, "I didn't do it until four years ago."

David was agitated but not really angry with me as we sparred on this issue. There were times, several months ago, when we had the same discussion and he became enraged. His resistance was far less today, which makes me think he is more ready now to acknowledge this unpalatable truth and integrate it. He has acknowledged the issue before, but he seems to be owning it more now, and its truth seems to be touching him more deeply.

Before leaving, he asked if we could meet again this evening. "There are some things I want to work through," he said.

Chapter 2

ॐ

A Split Sexuality Revealed

March 27, 1984
Evening

We met again at 9 P.M. David was relaxed and not at all angry. He left his checkbook here this afternoon, and suggested doing so may have been a Freudian slip, a way of negating money and capitalism. I told him I feel the "slip" doesn't necessarily mean that, though he does trash capitalism often enough in other ways. He was agitated when he left, and his attention was probably scattered. Perhaps, as they say, the checkbook just slipped his mind. Even Freud had to admit that, sometimes, "a cigar is just a cigar." David allowed this might be so.

I'm not certain how he got to it, but David began speaking about bisexuality and said this is a part of his problem. I was not surprised because I have sensed for a while now that his current inhibitions with women owe something to a "split" sexuality. This issue has been a long time crystallizing, but there have been strong hints recently.

Several days ago, when he spoke about what he called his "pathology toward women," this was not the first time he used that phrase. A day or so later, he told me that his (and his father's) broker in Atlanta does not approve of homosexuality. His tone told me he was disappointed by the man's disapproval. About a week ago, he told me the biophysicist-musician, his housemate and close friend, was "working through his latency." (This friend is currently involved in what appears to be a serious relationship with a woman.) Several months ago, while we were discussing some aspect of sexuality, David asked, "Isn't everything sexual? Isn't therapy sexual?" David told me today that his former girlfriend Sally had women sexual partners during the time she and David were involved (1974–1976). David approved of Sally's sexual interest in women because, to him, it meant a fuller expression of sexuality. But when David brought this up in therapy with Harris, he disapproved. Clearly, David was disappointed by Harris's attitude and felt it spoke to some limitation in him.

Today, David said many of the best minds of the twentieth century have been bisexual or homosexual, adding that Michel Foucault, a French psychologist and philosopher, was diagnosed as schizophrenic and bisexual at the age of nine. David told me this with what I sensed as pride. He read a passage of several pages from a book by Foucault he had brought with him. "He sees everything," David said. I asked if he feels Foucault's being bisexual makes him a more sensitive seer and writer. It does, David felt. He also told me he had a woman over last night, that she is bisexual, and that this made it easier and more pleasurable for him to be with her.

Part of the problem he had living in Chicago in 1978 and 1979, David told me today, was that it is a masculine city: the Rockefeller money, the gothic (phallic?) architecture of the University of Chicago, the strong work ethic, Carl Sandberg's characterization of the city as having "broad shoulders." He contrasted the masculinity of Chicago with the bisexuality of San Francisco, where men — "clean, beautiful people," he described them, savoring each word — walk together openly. He also told me he has problems being close to his friend from Atlanta who teaches in Houston. He spoke about this problem for the first time several weeks ago, but he didn't want to discuss it then. He also told me today he feels bisexuality is a freer expression of sexuality because there is no "dominance" of one partner by the other. Many times, David has attacked what he calls the "dominant ideology" of capitalism. Dominating and being dominated appear to be sensitive issues for him.

I was getting ready to ask David more about his sexual feelings when he began a monologue on ideas, writers, and books that was interesting and did not seem escapist. I did not want to cut him off. Perhaps coming to terms with his latent bisexual feelings is what David had in mind several days ago when he asked if I feel I am strong enough for what is ahead.

April 1, 1984

There was a going-away party for the biophysicist-musician last night at the house he shares with David and several others. He will move to New York soon. David was pleased with the way the party turned out, but he was clearly displeased with what he sees as the limitations of the people who attended. They were, for the most part, friends of the biophysicist-musician, both from his graduate school days in science and from his more recent involvement with music and dance. David was disappointed with "the level of conversation." These people, he told me, don't see beyond the rational and the technical.

At first, when I pointed out he seemed very upset over the limitations of these people, he denied it, but he soon acknowledged this is so. I told him it sounds like he needs something from them they are unable to give him. After some further denial, he conceded this too is so. What it seems to come down to is that no one at the party was socially conscious to the point of being able to understand—"decode" is the word David used—this capitalistic society, and "see what is really going on." No one could "read between the lines."

April 2, 1984

David attacked again this afternoon—me, his parents, the country. His voice was low, and he did not seem behind his attacking words. He was "in flight," but did not fly as high or as fast. Once again, the "switch" was activated, but what was activated was not as strong. It was a replay of the "broken record," but at a lower volume, with the theme sung at a lower pitch.

"Isn't therapy surveillance?" "Aren't therapists the police?" "Isn't mental illness a social construct?" "Aren't mental hospitals prisons for those who don't conform?" All questions from the past asked again today, but paler now.

Most likely, this is David's "in flight" response to being "in touch" yesterday. Touching the painful truth "activates" the "switch" that brings the defense into play again. David recognizes this pattern now and sees it as part of the therapeutic process. Several days ago, he said something I found very encouraging. "One day, when this is over, we'll shake hands, and you'll wink at me and say, 'We did it.'" That's the day I'm working toward.

April 9, 1984

We met twice today. This afternoon, David started calmly enough, talking about his reading and writing. But about halfway into the session, he began attacking the country again, using Marxist ideology to trash capitalism. I pointed out that he was being defensive but did not try to cut him off. He was not angry, and was not defending as strongly as, say, two or three months ago. About an hour after the session ended, David called to ask that we meet again this evening.

He began the second session by talking about his work again. After about a half-hour, out of the blue he said the reason things didn't work out better in therapy with Harris is that he was blocking his feelings of sexual latency. (The latency issue came up last during our March 27 session. Since then, I have been waiting for him to bring it up again. He was doing so now.) "I couldn't open up to him," David said. From this point on, things became murky. "Harris told me I had sexual feelings for him," David said. But Harris isn't his type, David insisted. He prefers dark, Mediterranean men. He mentioned the actors Robert De Niro and Al Pacino.

I asked if Harris had pursued the question of his latency feelings further. David said he had not and added, "If he had opened it up, this could have been the case of the century." Then, David did an about-face. "I really did like Harris," he said. "We come from similar backgrounds." (Whatever similarities there are, Harris is not Mediterranean. David is Greek.) David said he didn't want to talk about this anymore. For five minutes or so, he spoke of other things. I waited for what seemed like an appropriate moment and asked if his latent sexual feelings have had a significant effect on his life. He was not embarrassed or offended by the question. He told me about an incident that occurred when he was sixteen, while he was in prep school in Connecticut. One of his teachers invited him for a weekend and then made a sexual advance, which David rejected. "It was very traumatic at that age," he said. In spite of this, he still feels Harris tried to make more of the incident than was warranted.

Several months ago, David told me that when he was in Chicago in 1979 he heard from a third party his closest friend had said David was "pathological toward women," and a misogynist. At the time, David was furious over this accusation. He was upset, but not furious, when he repeated his friend's remark tonight. "It's not true," he protested. "I'm not pathological toward women. I never hurt anyone. I had good feelings for all the women I slept with." Then I reminded him he has told me, several times, his main problem is what he called "my pathology toward women." He immediately admitted making the remark and did not seem embarrassed by the contradiction. I took this to mean, though he is reluctant to talk about his latent sexual feelings for men, he recognizes the issue is an important one for him and must be dealt with. He has spoken before about how uncomfortable he feels being close to his good friend from Atlanta who lives in Houston. At the time he first told me about this, he did not want to say anything more. He brought up the issue again tonight, adding the names of three other male friends from Atlanta he feels uncomfortable being close to. "It was very incestuous," he said. The dialogue drifted away from the issue and the hour ended soon after.

April 10, 1984

David got up at 5 A.M. He spent most of the day working in the library. At about 3:45 this afternoon, while he was walking through one of the university buildings, he experienced an intense heightened feeling that lasted for approximately five minutes. He felt out of touch—his feet did not seem to be touching the floor—and as if he were walking through a labyrinth. He had this feeling once before, just prior to his breakdown in 1970, but this time the feeling was less intense and did not last as long. He described the experience as "breaking through many levels."

I was struck by how calm David was as he told me about this. I asked if the sudden, uncanny feeling frightened him. He said it did not, that on the contrary it was liberating. "I need that kind of anxiety," he said. I also asked if he feels he could be having another breakdown. He does not.

I wanted to find out if he is ready to talk more about his latent sexual feelings for men. "Not really," he said, "I'd rather stay with the concrete present situation." Clearly, he was avoiding his concrete present situation. I could have confronted him, but I was reluctant to do so because this is obviously a highly sensitive issue and he did not seem ready to talk about it today. He will bring it up again when he is ready. By asking the question, I hoped to show him I am ready to talk about it. He did mention that when he was fourteen, his father walked into his bedroom while he was masturbating and made him feel this was "the worst thing in the world." David felt guilty. "I never had any privacy in that house," he said. "That's why I spent so much time away from there. I'd go out with friends in a car and pick up girls. It was right out of *American Graffiti.*"

Toward the end of the hour, David looked back wistfully over the last five years. "Dante couldn't have done a better job of making a hell than the one I made for myself," he told me.

Just before the session ended, David repeated something he has said a number of times: "You know, I really should have killed my father." When I pointed out he might have gone to jail if he did this, he replied, "They would have given me a psychologist there, and I would have made friends with people of my own kind." I told myself he did not mean what he was saying, that he was not behind his words. (Reconsidering this threat a year later, I was not so certain.)

April 11, 1984

"I didn't open up to Harris about my latent homosexuality because I didn't trust him," David told me about fifteen minutes into the session. He didn't trust Harris because Harris "hated" all left-wing and radical thought. I asked if he felt Harris was judgmental about his political and social views. Yes, he was. "Were you concerned that he might be judgmental about this kind of sexual feeling as well?" Yes. "He's middle class, and can't see anything else," David told me. "He was trying to rehabilitate me."

David was responding to my invitation yesterday to talk more about this issue. I want him to deal with it in his own way and at his own pace in our sessions. So, I said this: "We're in a good position to open this up now." He agreed, and seemed pleased I think so. Again, I wanted him to know I'm ready.

David moved away from this subject, and I made no effort to bring him back to it. He was more "in touch" this afternoon than I have ever seen him before. He spoke slowly and quietly. He took sole responsibility for becoming ill. "I did this to myself," he said. "I was hedging all the way between 1976 and 1979. I really didn't want the business, and I really didn't want the stock market either. And I didn't have it for graduate school then."

I pointed out that when I interpret to him now, he can use the insight as a base for working through. Six months ago, when we began therapy, he was intellectualizing to the point where insight didn't "touch" him very much. I explained that's why I insist on encountering his issues experientially, why I try as much as possible to deal with feelings and not ideas. He is beginning to realize what an evasion of himself and his real issues all that intellectualizing was and, to a considerable extent, still is. "I can't hide out in the library anymore," he said.

David went to bed at 1:30 this morning and got up at 9. He had trouble turning off his thoughts while trying to sleep. I suspect he was doing some working through. "I'm not blocking as much now," he said. "I had some good feelings about you last night."

David then started a long monologue on Sartre, not so much about his books as about the man. He liked his mind, but spoke more about his life — how free he was, optimistic, engaged, uncomplaining, not embittered by the failing health and blindness of his last years. "He broke all the codes," David said. "He didn't hold on to anything." David compared Sartre to Freud. "Freud," he said, "was a child in comparison. He didn't believe in freedom." Sartre versus Freud; freedom versus determinism; me versus Harris: these dichotomies play significantly in David's efforts to struggle with his illness. Is he responsible for what happened to him, or is his father? If he can make himself sick, he also has a shot at making himself well, or at least better. I believe he is coming to see this now.

April 12, 1984

David called just after 11 p.m. "There's a lot going on," he said. "Can we meet tonight?" He sounded anxious but in control.

"We are really at the iceberg," was the first thing he said when we met. "I would like to deal with this."

David was leaving the library this evening when he ran into a graduate student from the Spanish department he knows slightly. The young man is bisexual. David didn't want to go home, didn't want to be alone, and was eager to talk with him. He started a rambling conversation about movies, poetry, philosophy, literature. Everything ran together. "Do you like this?" he asked. "Do you like that?" When the student inquired how David supports himself, David told him he plays the stock market part time. He told me he "invented" this.

David felt out of touch as he talked with the student. "I was flying," he said. "Out of control. What I was saying didn't make sense." I asked if the encounter had sexual overtones. It did, he told me. Knowing that the student was bisexual made him appealing to David. Clearly, David wants to deal with this issue now. He does not understand these feelings but knows he has to. "Where is this coming from?" he asked.

I asked David if he could trace out a history of his sexual attraction for men. When he was in Atlanta in 1976 working for his father, a friend who was bisexual would visit him at his house. They talked. I asked if he had ever experienced this kind of attraction before 1976. He had not, he said. David recently told me that one of his housemates, the biophysicist-musician, is trying to come to terms with his latent homosexual feelings. (He moved to New York last week.) He and David became close friends and talked a good deal. David admitted feeling a sexual attraction for him as well. I asked if anything physical had ever come from any encounter with a man. "Never," David said unequivocally.

I then asked how Harris responded when David spoke about his latency. He had told me earlier he felt Harris had made too much of the incident in prep school when a teacher made an advance toward him, and he said so again tonight. He felt Harris was pushing a meaning on him that is not there. I got the impression that Harris made him feel sick and guilty about the incident. Is that why David didn't open up anymore to him about his sexual feelings for men? "He really did a number on me," David said.

"What does this mean?" he asked. "I'm a eunuch with women now. This started in 1976, when I was in Atlanta. I never had problems like this before."

This is the "iceberg" David spoke of at the beginning of the hour. The issue was a long time surfacing, though in retrospect he has dropped hints about his sexual feelings for men since we began working together. Clearly, David is relieved to get this out in the open. "We are at the core now," he said, as if he really feels he is there. "I have to work this through."

David seemed relieved, optimistic, and hopeful by the end of the hour. He left feeling good.

April 15, 1984

"I'm moving to Houston May 2," David said emphatically as soon as he settled into his chair. "I've had it with this place. There's nothing for me here. It's time to move on." He sounded upset. His voice was loud, and he spoke quickly. He was going to move to Houston and stay with his friend and his wife in their new house until he gets settled there, he said. I challenged him on his reasons for wanting to do this, reminding him this is not the first time he has "decided" to leave the city precipitously. I pointed out the obvious fact that if he moves to Houston, we could no longer work together. David attacked me vigorously, though not viciously, bringing up many of the familiar charges. When he called last night, he was ebullient about the progress he feels he is making and eager to continue our work.

David was fully "in flight" for the first fifteen minutes today, saying he was ready to fly, literally, to Houston, and away from our work. But he did not fly long, and he responded to my invitation to come back down and be concrete again. "What am I defending against?" he wanted to know. I asked what he thinks might have set this off. "I just read the classifieds," he said. "There's nothing there." Once he was back "in touch," his insight was on target. He dropped the defenses and admitted he is frustrated by not having a next step and, at the same time, frightened of what it would mean if a next step did materialize for him. The classified ads offered rejection *and* possibility, each holding a different kind of anxiety. Rather than work through this anxiety, he discharged it by calling up the familiar defenses.

David started the session today "in flight," but left "in touch." In between, he did some working through. He lived out another cycle of this familiar dyad.

David called tonight to set up a schedule of sessions for this week. "Boy, what an illness this has been," he said. "I'm just beginning to see how bad it is. I feel like I'm coming off a strange drug. But I'm also opening up a lot of doors. This has been a bad poem. Let's turn it around. We're on the way." At some point in this brief conversation, he said, "Thanks."

April 16, 1984

A messy session today. I asked David how long he can hold out with the money he has. About a week, he told me. He looked through the classifieds again this morning and again found nothing. "I'm not going back to the trenches," he said, meaning he won't take just any job. He won't work in sales or wait on people in a bar or restaurant, he said. "I'm going to keep reading and writing, so I can get back to the level I was on before I got sick," he told me, as if nothing else matters. I reminded him he acknowledges finding a job and supporting himself are "necessities." Then David got angry: "What am I supposed to do? I can't manufacture a job, or beg for one." He said he should be working. "It's not good to spend all my time in the library. It takes me four hours now to do what I used to do in one. I jump from one book to another, one author to another, one idea to another."

Suddenly, David turned on me. "Why do I fool around with therapists?" he wanted to know. "You're the wrong therapist," he continued. "There's no capital return on this." I pointed out that is a curious remark for a Marxist and asked what "capital return" he expects from therapy. He did not know.

We talked about why work is such a sensitive issue for him. "Not all my work experience has been bad," he admitted. He pointed to his job with the social services department in 1976 as a good experience, though not without problems. Then, as if he were touching a profound truth, he said,

"I know what's behind this: I can't make it in the system." That, I believe, is what terrifies David about work, any kind of work, whether it be business, the stock market, or academic work. His conflicts about work are deep, and he defends against doing it, often and hard. About ten minutes before the hour was up, he said, "This isn't going anywhere," and he walked toward the door half-heartedly, as if to leave. But he turned around, sat down again, and finished the session.

We talked for a while about David's anger at his father and his demands for reparations following the liquidation of the family business. "I took this up as a brat," he admitted. Yet, he still justifies not working now by the disappointment he felt when the family business was sold. David's lived attitude toward work goes something like this: Look, my father's a million-aire. He fucked me over. If he had any creativity, he would have set some-thing up for me. He could have written it off. But instead, he tried to make me middle class. Nine to five. And I got sick. That's his limited, immigrant imagination.

Some blood was spilled this afternoon. Some deep wounds were opened up. Again, David asked if I am up to what is ahead of us, meaning, I believe, he expects even more blood to be spilled as we go further into this.

April 20, 1984

David won $106 playing poker last night and felt good about it. "I didn't pull back, as I have done before with so many different things," he told me. He didn't feel guilty about winning. Several weeks ago, he won a comparable amount in a poker game and felt bad about it. "It's not worth it," he told me the following day. "I'm not going to do it again."

"Walking over here, I tried to think what kind of shit I'd throw at you today," he told me. But the session this afternoon was placid. David was "in touch," and, in contrast with the last few sessions, he threw nothing at me. I suggested that is because he didn't need to. He was not anxious today, and it was not necessary for him to defend. He seemed to carry the good feeling of winning last night into the session.

April 24, 1984

David played poker again last night. He won more than $100 from the same person he played several days ago. He has not received any of the money owed him yet. The agreement is that everything will be paid by Friday (April 27). David is not sure this person, the same one who assaulted him after losing to him at poker last fall, will pay up. He is angry and anxious in the face of this uncertainty.

It did not take long to become apparent David was back in what he calls his "strange world," the "swamp." He was "in flight" this afternoon. He was running from his present situation and what this is requiring of him now. The paper for the French literature course is due May 3. He still has not found a job, and he is almost out of money. He has agreed to move out of the house he is living in now sometime during the first week in June, which means he must find — and pay for — an apartment of his own. I pointed out that as long as he stays in the "strange world," he can forget about the demands of the concrete present.

Like an organist at the console, he pulled out one defensive stop after another. After about a half-hour, the crescendo he built seemed to all but bury the call he feels to come out of his illness and accept the world. Playing poker reminded him of playing the stock market, which, he says, he never liked; that was winning, and *that* was machismo, which is a joke. He tried to blame his troubles with women, now and in the past, on his involvement with the market. "My energy all went into trading stocks," he said. "My best times with women were when I didn't have anything to do with that. I wasn't in the market when I was dating Sally."

He reminded me again that women are more intuitive than men. David considers himself highly intuitive. He was feeling what he calls his "feminine side" this afternoon — passive, dependent, in need of nurturing and support. He should have listened to the women who warned him about some of his male friends, he said. He blamed the breakup of a relationship with a woman in 1970 on a fraternity initiation he went through at that time (more machismo gone wrong). "She warned me that if I did that, it would be over between us," he told me. (Several weeks ago, he gave a different account of why the relationship ended. The woman was having emotional problems and asked for David's help. He told her to get her life in order and pulled away from her. She dropped him soon after.)

As one of the final stops in his crescendo of defense, David said again he was thinking of moving to another city. "There's nothing for me here," he insisted, for what seemed like the hundredth time. "All the associations are bad." (Later, he said he really doesn't dislike the city and that only some of the associations are bad.) I asked if he feels the work we are doing is worth staying here for. "There are good therapists all over," he said. David's experience playing poker last night led to what seems like a concatenated recall of past experiences — bad experiences — all the way back to 1970.

David knows he may not get paid the money he won recently. If he doesn't, he will feel he has been taken again, just as his father "took" him when he liquidated the business. In the face of his anxiety over this situation, David went back into his "strange world." "It's awful there," David acknowledged. "I can feel the difference when I go back. I felt good for an hour and a half last night after swimming. I could feel my legs under me as I walked home." David can distinguish the two worlds now, and recognize when he is in one or the other. They are entirely different territories, with different contours, surfaces, and textures.

April 29, 1984

David's friend from Atlanta who teaches in Houston visited him yesterday. He came for a conference in a nearby city and spent the day here. David began the session by saying how much he enjoyed the visit. They played tennis in the afternoon, had dinner, and went out for drinks in the evening. But from the start of the hour, I could hear a good deal of resentment under the good feelings.

David postponed our meeting today for several hours to meet with the person who lost to him at poker. The guy didn't show, and David now feels he won't pay. He is angry and resentful about this and brought these feelings into the session. The anger and resentment were not directed toward the person who owes him money but toward his friend from Houston. David feels he gave more to the relationship over the years; he found women for him (he was not good at finding them on his own, according to David) and showed him how to have a good time. He listened to him when he broke up with his first wife and was almost nonfunctional for a year. "He paid for everything yesterday," David said, as if this was due him as reparations. David also feels his friend's urging that he come back to Atlanta in 1976 was one of the reasons he did come back, and he considers that a mistake now. He acknowledges this resentment is due to what he calls his "failure to separate," another admission of David's sexual feelings for his friend, which were most likely not reciprocal.

David beat his friend at tennis. He lost the first set because he choked. He got mad, saw "angry images," and hit the ball too hard, losing control. But he pulled himself together, and won the match. At some point, David began to feel "it was all right to win," and did.

David spent a good deal of time "in flight" today on many of the familiar issues. He would look through the classifieds, he told me, and find something better than the four-dollar-an-hour job he feels he has a good chance of getting at the library. "There are jobs in brokerage houses," he said. "I can't live on $160 a week." When I said his father might be willing to continue subsidizing him if he gets the library job, he said he is sick of being subsidized and left it there. He also told me he is thinking of leaving the city again, but not for Houston, which he sees as a "preppy town." I told him I feel the only unique thing for him here is the work we are doing. "I can do that anywhere," he said, as if he really didn't believe it.

May 1, 1984

I expected David would be calm and happy today, considering that his father called him this morning to say he would give him between $1,000 and $1,500 to pay for the move to his own apartment. I was looking forward to an easy session after the rough one yesterday. This was not the case. He started out smoothly enough, but it was soon clear he was very angry. "Obviously, my father needs an intermediary to deal with me," he said, referring to the call he and I agreed I would make to his parents last night. "I have never been able to talk to my father directly."

It went downhill from there. He attacked his father viciously for not being open with him about his plans for the family business between 1976 and 1978. "They wouldn't listen to any of my ideas," he said. "They weren't ready to hear what I had to say." He was in high "flight," and I challenged him vigorously. The higher he "flew," the harder I confronted him on his evasions and the angrier he became. When I reminded him he has said several times that he wasn't ready or "cut out" to run his father's business, he denied it bitterly and attacked me and my motives for saying so. He also denied his part in the breakup of his relationship with Sally. As I continued to challenge him, he became more verbally abusive. "You're just an American," he said as part of his attack. I was also "middle class."

At the end of the hour, David's anger was still peaking. He got out of his chair and walked to where I was sitting. "Get up," he said, his face contorting in anger. "This won't get us anywhere," I responded. I did get up with the expectation that I could calm him. He grabbed my hands tightly and pushed me hard several times. I believe he came very close to striking me. "Let's talk about this," I said. "Words are fists," he said. He put his face directly into mine as he spoke. I reminded him again he was denying everything he had acknowledged about his responsibility for his illness. "My only mistake was that I didn't learn how to lie well enough," he said.

His anger was spent within about five minutes. "Are you all right?" he asked. I told him I was. But my hands hurt from being twisted and there was a slight taste of blood in my mouth, which must have meant he hit me in the face during the brief scuffle.

"I'm very agitated," he said. He started to gather his things several times and walk toward the door but stopped to talk some more. "I have to calm down," he said. He wanted to stay in my office, but I had had enough of David for one afternoon. As he was leaving, I asked him to call me this evening.

About ten minutes later, I took a walk to work off some of the tension from this very rough session. Five blocks from my office, I saw David walking on the opposite side of the street. I crossed over. "I'd like to walk with you," he said. "You can charge me for it." We walked for about fifteen minutes. "What do you think set me off?" he wanted to know. "At what point did I lose it? Where did your surgeon's knife hit?" I told him I believe it hit the powder keg when I reminded him about his relationship with Sally. But I am certain the explosion was building all the time I was confronting him. He was defending, I suggested, because now, with his father's most recent bailout, something more will be expected of him. He has one less excuse now for not committing himself to something. And this scares him to death. I believe that's why he was "flying" this afternoon and probably why he exploded at the end of the session. David thought so too.

After we walked several blocks together, he headed toward home, having decided to walk all the way.

David called this evening. He apologized twice for his outburst. He was calm and cordial, his voice was low, and he was fully "in touch." "It was a great catharsis," he said. "It's not a setback. I pulled myself out of it." He admitted everything he had denied this afternoon, the whole coverup. "It's obvious I'm blocking and defending," he said. "I'm scared." Later, he added, "I give you my commitment I'll stay here until we get this licked."

May 10, 1984

David seemed relaxed and sat easily in his chair as he talked about the reading and writing he is doing. He laughed, now and then. After about ten minutes, I asked how he is feeling. "I feel fine," he said.

But something sinister soon grew out of the lightness and the laughter — an attack on me. "I get more out of talking to my painter friend than I do from talking to you," he informed me. David was referring to the young man he met here, who moved to Philadelphia last year to live and work. David visited him in January. "I don't like therapists," he continued. "Artists have a much richer life." And again, he complained about how much therapy is costing him: "I wouldn't have any problems if my father would pay me what he is paying you."

He continued his attack on me for about a half-hour and then started on the furniture in my office. "It's patrician," he said, without approval. David doesn't like anything or anyone he considers patrician. He often makes this a point of contention between us. The furniture in my office is Danish modern, and the colors are muted: beige, blue, and brown. "It's sterile," he said. He had one new arrow to shoot into me today. "Harris is smarter than you," he said coyly, as if unconvinced.

David has been through most of this critical litany before, but there was a difference this afternoon. He was laughing a good deal as he attacked me and was not angry or vicious as he has been on other occasions.

I asked what he thinks this attack is all about. "I'm defending," he said. He was going back into what he calls "that strange world" again. But not so far back this time, and he didn't stay there long. I asked if he has any idea what triggered this brief reentry into the "swamp." He told me he read an essay by Walker Percy in the *Southern Review* this afternoon. David admires Percy's writing and feels a strong affinity with his Southern themes. "Do you think the essay reminded you of the good old days in Atlanta?" I asked. "Did it stir up a desire for going back home?" David thought so. "I can't go back to that," he said. But thinking about this could have set him off against me, since I am challenging his fantasies about returning (home, at least symbolically) to a pathological dependency.

Again, I brought to David's attention how similar his attacks on me are to his attacks on his parents, sister, and friends. Last week, he referred to a stockbroker friend in Atlanta, with whom he has traded for many years, as a "cripple." The man was totally paralyzed by polio when he was in college and has lived since then in an iron lung. In spite of this, he has become very successful. David has spoken often of this man's courage in the face of his tragedy. Now, describing him as a "capitalist puppet," he was calling him a "cripple." "You must be getting desperate for ammunition if you have to sink that low," I said. He agreed.

"I'm going to try to have another good night like last night," he told me. "I broke down a lot of defenses. I did a lot of working through. My best hours for this are from eleven at night to two in the morning. I start peaking around eleven. But I'll have to change that schedule if I get a job or go back to school."

"I did a lot of flying this afternoon, didn't I?" were David's first words when he called this evening. I agreed but reminded him of his lighthearted mood. "I was laughing at myself," he told me. "Actually, I'm feeling pretty good. I have five to seven good hours a day now. But I don't have full continuity yet."

David called again about an hour later. He wanted to make an appointment for tomorrow. "I may just move to another city instead of getting an apartment here," he said. "All I need is a pool and some pretty women. There are good therapists in Houston and Atlanta." *Atlanta?* That's the first time I've heard him say he would consider moving back there. Walker Percy's essay must have really hit home.

There was a third call tonight. "Boy, I've really done it to myself with this illness," he said. "I didn't realize how bad this was when we started. This is going to be hard work. You'll have to confront me on this business of leaving here before I'm ready. Every time I think about taking a step ahead, the resistances come back and I block and defend. I have to keep breaking these circles."

May 12, 1984

David spent several hours last night at the neighborhood bar he recently resolved not to return to because of what he considers the destructive influence of people who hang out there. He saw the young man who owes him money from poker but did not receive any assurance he would be paid. This person said he lost David's watch, which David had given him as security on a postdated check. "How much more of this can I take?" David wanted to know. "I'm thinking of getting a hit-man to eliminate the guy. That's the best way to take care of him." He cited several historical examples.

David said he has spent more time in this bar during the last two weeks than in the preceding four months. "Why is that?" he asked. It was just two weeks ago that his father promised him the money to move out of the house and get an apartment of his own. Since then, he has stepped up his attacks on both his father and me and assaulted me physically. Given a shot at something better, a more autonomous life, David is backing off, covering up and going back into "that strange world" that is his illness. As he acknowledges readily, being in this bar plays into his regressive needs. It is also a place to meet people who live on the fringe of the law: gamblers, drug users, drug dealers, and a variety of deadbeats.

David was angry at his father this afternoon because he has not sent the balance of the money he promised for David's move ($1,000 to $1,500). He sent $500 last week. "Why doesn't he just come around with the check?" David asked. "It would be so easy to set this up. He could even make it tax deductible. But he's playing a game with me."

What David can't get from his father he will try to get from what he calls the "underground economy," which includes the gamblers, drug people, and petty thieves who hang around the bar where he spent time last night. But David has almost as much trouble dealing with the "underground" economy as he does with the capitalist economy. "I don't feel at home in that bar either," he told me. He's not confident enough to make any major deals with these people, though he has talked about doing so several times. "I'm not as fast on my feet as I used to be," he said more than once. "If I tried something now, I'd probably get caught."

David is still looking for an apartment, but ambivalently. He set the mechanics for the move in motion when he agreed to be out of the house he lives in now by June 1, but he is struggling with the consequences of the move: living alone again and having one less excuse for not taking the next step.

While talking about his mother this afternoon, David used the word "matricide." I asked what he means by this. "Let's open it up," he began. "It's killing all traces of the influence of my mother on me." I asked if this means becoming autonomous. He said it does. He seemed to be saying that "killing his mother" is killing the need to be passive, nurtured, and nonautonomous. How strong his dependence must be, in all its many forms, if it would take a symbolic murder to free him from it.

May 13, 1984

David began "in flight" today. He was thinking again of moving to Houston, for the same reasons as before. He complained again about how much therapy is costing him. "This is not economically feasible," he told me. "It's time to renegotiate the contract." He was trying to get me to reduce my fee. He was trying to manipulate me with another of his cons. I didn't fall for it. "If you're really serious about moving," I said, "you'd better make plans soon." He agreed. He said he may contact a friend in Houston, not his close friend who teaches there, about the therapist he is seeing. "Would you be willing to send your notes to him?" he wanted to know. I said I will do whatever would help him make this transition.

And, of course, he attacked me again. He questioned me and baited me, trying always to put me on the spot. He bullied and browbeat me, as he has done so often before. He spoke as if I were a part of all that is wrong with this culture. "I have trouble working with you because you're a patrician," he said. "This is a white, upper-middle class, WASP ambiance." But when I asked if he feels I'm judging him by my values or trying to make him into a patrician, he said I am not. That put my therapist's conscience at ease on this point.

"Why am I defending?" he asked about a half-hour into the session. He answered his question. "I'm exhausted. I had a rough night and didn't get much sleep." In spite of his fatigue, David did eighty laps in the pool this afternoon. Between defending and covering up, he often touched the truth of what he is doing, admitting his bad faith. "As a therapist, you have the ultimate subversive weapon," he said. "Let's use it." To David, using the "subversive weapon" means challenging the bad faith that underlies his illness. "You're ruthless," he told me, "and I admire that."

There were three phone calls from David tonight:

First

He wanted to know how I feel the session went this afternoon. I told him he did a lot of "flying" but recognized it and pulled himself down. "Every move toward bad faith I can feel in my body," he said.

Second

"I'm on shaky ground," were his opening words when he called the second time. "I want to open this up." He was breathing more heavily than usual, and I pointed this out. Clearly, he was agitated. "We did such good work for three or four months," he continued. "Now, I'm backing off. I'll look for an apartment tomorrow." I told him I do not see the rough time we have been having during the last two weeks as a sign of regression. Quite the contrary. It is because he is making progress toward taking the next step that he is defending and covering up so much now. It can be no other way. To go forward is to "activate" the coverup again. "Your vision is much healthier and more thorough than Harris's was," he said. He also said some other complimentary things about me.

Third

"I'm sorry to bother you again, but I just got some bad news," was the way the third phone conversation started. David just learned one of his former housemates, who had moved out in February, had killed himself.

He used his father's gun. He was twenty-seven. "It must be in the city," David said. He has called this city "sick" many times during the last few months, claiming everyone he knows here is depressed. "This is getting scary," he continued. "He seemed to be getting better." I asked David if he feels threatened by his friend's suicide. He said he does not and pointed to his physical strength and the suicide last December of his friend Martin, which did not effect him adversely. "I'm not a therapist," he told me. "I only have to look out for myself."

Mr. Helbros called me from Atlanta around 11:30 tonight. David called home twice today, once to talk to his father about sending the balance of the money for the move, once to talk to his mother (today is Mother's Day). He was nasty to her, Mr. Helbros said, and she hung up on him.

David's father called to ask my advice about sending the rest of the money he had promised David. He sent $800 a week or so ago—David said it was $500—and is ready to send another $1,200. He told me David has less than $200 left from the $800 check. I explained I feel David is at a critical point now and is anxious and ambivalent about the move he wants to make. It is not just moving he is afraid of, but everything the move implies. I believe he deserves the shot, I said. Mr. Helbros promised to send the check tomorrow. Without any sign of self-pity, he told me how much trouble David's illness has caused him. He once asked David what he would do if he had a son like him. "I'd send him straight to hell," was David's answer.

As when we had talked before, Mr. Helbros was calm and sympathetic to his son's situation. Toward the end of the conversation, he asked what could be expected from the therapy we are doing. I told him I hope David could heal to the point where his next major loss—which, as for everyone else in this world, is inevitable—will not send him back to a hospital; that he might eventually commit himself to some work he finds satisfying; and that he might have better relations with his parents, with friends, and with women.

May 14, 1984

"I had a violent night," was David's opening remark when we met this afternoon. "I was up until five this morning."

But we did not have a violent hour; quite the contrary. This must have been the calm after the storm. David often raises his voice during our sessions, but he did not do so today. His words came easily, because he was behind them. He was "in touch." He used most of the hour admitting the coverup that is his illness. "I alone am responsible for what happened," he said. "My father saw that the business couldn't be run the way I wanted to do it. I wanted to put in two hours a day and spend the rest of the time sitting in the sun and chasing young girls. He probably held on to the business two years longer than he should have, just to see if I could take it over. He dragged himself down doing this." Is this why David has said so many times, and always with scorn, that his father is "too nice"? Was he complaining that his father didn't tell him what he probably recognized soon after David started working in the business in the fall of 1976, instead of waiting two years? "You should have put me out of my misery right away," I believe I hear him saying whenever he mocks his father for being "too nice."

The question now is how long David can hold on to the truth of his situation before backing off and defending against it again. Even more important, how deeply is he touching the truth? At what level was the mask torn off this afternoon?

"I'm sick of being a baby," he continued. "My father doesn't owe me anything. I can't keep depending on him, and I can't keep calling you three or four times a night on weekends." He said that ninety percent of his anger at me is due to his blocking. He admitted he was taking out his anger on his mother when he called her yesterday. "When I act like a man, I'm treated like a man," he acknowledged. "When I act like a shit, I'm treated that way."

We talked about the suicide of his former housemate. "It scares the shit out of me," he said. "I wonder what will happen when I really put myself on the line." (David thought his friend was getting better.) I needed to know his worst thoughts about this. "Do you think about having another breakdown?" I asked. He said he does. I asked if he ever thinks about doing what Martin did, or what his former housemate just did. "No," he said. "I'm not suicidal."

There was one call from David tonight. And there were two memorable remarks: (1) "I *can* have my life"; (2) "From the outside, this illness would look like shit to me."

May 17, 1984

David called three times tonight. He sounded as much "in touch" as I have ever heard him. He is planning to sign the lease tomorrow for an apartment, which is near the university and one block from my office. He is both exhilarated and frightened by the prospect of moving. "I had a confrontational day," he told me. He is confronting the move, which appears imminent now, and all that the move implies—the next step out of his illness. "This is sickening," he said, talking of where he has been for the last five years. "I can feel it in my guts. It's going to take a lot more vomiting."

"Hold me to the fundamentals," he pleaded, meaning I should keep confronting him on the basic issues, uncovering his coverups. "Are you ready for this?" he wanted to know again. (David has asked this question many times, always when he is doing his hardest work. He wants to be sure I'll stay with him as he does it. Again, I assured him I would.) "I want to break this down," he continued. "I want an entirely new life at this point."

David began the second call by saying, "I'm breaking." His voice was firm, and he sounded more thrilled than frightened about what was happening. I asked what the breaking feels like. "It's like a motion picture, compared to a still life," he said. "It's a liberating feeling." I took this to mean that David was "in touch" at a deeper level tonight. He told me he could feel the tension draining out of his body. David is breaking through, not down.

"How could I have blocked out so much reality?" he asked, without expecting an answer. Seeing the "motion picture," David is comparing it to the "still life" of the last five years. He thanked me for what I have done. "You have a good invitation," he said, referring to my "therapeutic invitation," a term I introduced in our sessions some time ago.

David became lighter and more hopeful as he spoke. "Visit me in the sun," he said. I took this to mean that he is thinking about returning South after we finish our work. "We'll have a party."

May 18, 1984

"We really have to get down to work," David said before he sat in his chair. And work he did—on me. More specifically, he worked me over. "You're a WASP and a patrician," he said, clearly unhappy about the situation. "Why have I been wasting my time with you? You've been fooling me." I reminded him we both knew I was a WASP and a patrician when we began working together. "I'm not trying to convince you to be this way, or any other way," I reminded him. "You'd better not," he said, "or you'll find yourself hanging from a ceiling." He said he could wipe me out in a fistfight within five minutes. (I'm not so sure of this, but I kept quiet.) "You've never been into the revolution," he continued. "You don't know anything about the left." David went through the familiar litany of complaints against me, most of which have been recorded here already. When the hour was nearly up and while he was still attacking me, he suggested we "go a little longer." We went for three hours.

The first two hours were ninety-nine percent "flight." He touched ground three or four times, briefly acknowledging the coverup. But immediately he went back up in the air. After two hours, he came down to earth, and stayed there for the remainder of the session.

While trying to intimidate me about my lack of revolutionary consciousness, David asked if I have ever been taught by a Marxist. I told him I have not. "Haven't you ever been seduced by a teacher?" he wanted to know. "In what sense?" I asked. "Intellectually? Sexually?" He meant it in both senses. He told me about a teacher he had in prep school and how they became close. (He has mentioned this teacher before.) "That almost led to a sexual encounter," he said. "It's too bad it didn't," he added quickly, rushing the words. "It cost me Yale." (Almost certainly, David made a slip of the tongue here. I have never heard him utter a word about wanting to go to Yale. He seemed to imply if he had accepted the teacher's advance, the teacher would have gotten him into Yale, a somewhat dubious prospect. Here was a chance to probe further the bisexual feelings he has acknowledged. I should have taken it.)

I challenged David on his "flight" during the first two hours, but as already noted, he came down only momentarily. By the third hour, he was asking, "What am I defending against?" as if he wasn't sure.

This morning, he put down a deposit on an apartment not far from my office. "It's a WASP neighborhood," he told me during the first hour; and it's near the university, which he said again today is a CIA front. Clearly, David is anxious about where he is moving. He is wondering if he would be better off in an apartment closer to the heart of the city. "There's more to do downtown," he said, "but it's healthier up here. I'd be near the library, the pool, and the tennis courts."

Before coming to my office this afternoon, David spent some time with a man who teaches philosophy at a college in the city. "He said I might be able to get a job teaching there," David told me, "and promised to help." Several months ago, he told me he believed the man is gay and felt uncomfortable talking with him because of this.

David decided he was defending both against the move and all it implies and the prospect, vague as it is, of getting a job teaching. "I was shocked by the man's suggestion that I could do this," he told me. We talked for a long time about how what he was doing in the session today fits the pattern we have come to recognize: something (or someone) comes within David's reach, and he backs off and defends.

I asked David what he resents about me. "You remind me of my mother," he said. "That's it. I just realized it."

During the second hour, David made some negative and bitter remarks about upper-middle-class WASP women. I asked what he has against these women, and he said he has nothing against them. But why be so angry and bitter toward them, I inquired. "Has a woman from that class ever rejected you, or put you down?" David denied this had happened to him. But during the third hour, he brought up this issue again. His first serious girlfriend was a WASP, and her rejection was one of the factors that led to his first breakdown in 1970. His wife, too, was a WASP; and their divorce several years later was a factor in his second breakdown. He repeated my question: "Was I ever put down by a WASP?" His tone and expression suggested he had been.

"My mother could die at any time," he said during the third hour. (His mother has had two operations for cancer and received two years of chemotherapy.) "I'm blocking her death anxiety," David told me, meaning he is not coming to terms with the possibility she may die soon. Several days ago, he told me his mother had recently told him that she is planning to live another ten or fifteen years. But today, he told me she is walking with a cane now. When I asked why, he said this is due to a shattered knee cap she received after being thrown from a horse thirty years ago. When I asked if she is generally weaker from the cancer, he said she is.

"I'm going out of here feeling badly this afternoon," David said shortly before leaving. He was feeling tight this afternoon, particularly around his stomach. During the last half-hour, he fell into a reverie about his illness and what it had done to him. He moved from the chair to the couch. "Why do I do this over and over?" he asked himself and me. "Why can't I break it once and for all? We have to get to the core of this." I told him I believe we should continue to do what we have been doing.

May 19, 1984

David and I were scheduled to meet at five this afternoon, but he did not show and he did not call. I was concerned, because he has never missed an appointment before. (He has other, more inventive ways to take out his anger on me.) At about 6:30, I called his house. I spoke to a woman who lives there, and she told me David was not at home. About 10:30, David called. On the way to my office his cab was sideswiped at an intersection. The driver was seriously injured and was taken to the hospital in an ambulance. David rode with him. David was checked out in the emergency room and released. He had asked someone there to contact me, but I did not receive a call.

David looked at another apartment downtown today, in a section of the city he particularly likes. "It's in good condition, and it's a good place to write," he said with more enthusiasm than I have heard from him in some time. "It's close to stores and restaurants, and it's on the bus line uptown. It would be easier to meet women there. It's also eighty dollars a month cheaper." David said he will find out Monday if he can have this apartment.

David was "in touch" as we spoke. He felt tight but said he has felt this way for three weeks. He seemed more upset about his ongoing situation than about the accident. And he was very cordial to me. "You're a good therapist," he said. "I'm glad we're working together. We have to get to the core of this illness. I can't take this anymore."

May 28, 1984
Afternoon

David's father called me this morning from Atlanta. David has been calling home frequently to ask for more money. His father has sent him more than $2,000 this month, and David has only $300 left. Mr. Helbros wanted to know what David did with the money.

We talked about this for the first half-hour this afternoon. David told me he spent the money paying off old bills and debts for food, beer, and carfare from his house to my office and to the university. He had also bounced four checks and had to make good on them. I couldn't understand how this adds up to $2,000, and he seemed baffled as well. "I know I've been irresponsible about this," he said. I was concerned he could be buying and using cocaine or some other drug, but he assured me he is not doing this. I believe him. "I spend money trying to deal with my loneliness," he told me. "I go to that bar near my house, just so I don't have to be alone. They hate me there."

He has said before that he is throwing his father's money back at him. "That's pathological," he admitted today. And again today, he became very angry at his father for what happened with the family business. He raised his voice for long periods during the session. But his anger did not go as deep as it did three or four months ago. He didn't seem as convinced that his father had betrayed him.

May 28, 1984
Evening

We met for two hours this evening. For the first hour, David was as "in touch" as I have ever seen him. He came clean on every major point we have discussed for the last seven months. He sat comfortably in his chair, spoke slowly and evenly, without raising his voice once. He took full responsibility for his illness and discussed it with great insight. He acknowledged that he must have caused his parents "incredible amounts of pain" during the last five years. "Going back to Atlanta in 1976 was my Vietnam," he said.

After about an hour, one I wish I had on tape, David told me he used to "dance around" situations as they came up each day, implying this is a healthy way to do things. He was talking about a period of several years before his last breakdown in 1979. I recognized this as his first hedge away from being fully "in touch," and challenged him on it. Suddenly, he became angry. His voice became loud, and he sat upright, stiffly, in his chair. "I feel lighter when I'm with some of my friends than I do around you," he told me, naming his friend who teaches in Houston and the biophysicist-musician. He mounted a medium-size attack on me that went on for about fifteen minutes. I told him I am not here to make him feel good but to help him come to terms with his illness. Necessarily, this means that I will often make him feel bad.

Then, as suddenly as he went into "flight," he came down and was fully "in touch" again. I pointed out how, after being defenseless and vulnerable for an hour, he recalled a defensive maneuver—the "dance"—denied it was a defense, and tried to cover up the denial. We talked about how when David comes clean and faces up to his situation, this unmasking is soon followed by another coverup. David acknowledges this is the pattern.

May 31, 1984

"I'm anxious about my future," David said as he settled into his chair this afternoon. He repeated these words several times during the hour. Once he added, "I really am in despair."

David will sign the lease for his apartment tomorrow morning (he chose the downtown one) and begin moving tomorrow afternoon. As much as he wants to get out of the house, he is anxious about being by himself in his own place. He must become accustomed to the new neighborhood, finish the paper for the French literature course, find a job, and start thinking about his future. A year ago, he was living so far in the past that he wasn't ready to think about the future. Now it's staring him in the face.

David told me today he is not comfortable in masculine roles, which I took to mean doing the things men normally do. "I'm in touch with my feelings," he added, as if being so is not compatible with being a man. David's sexual identity is not as strong or as clear as it was prior to his last breakdown in 1979. He has told me that bisexuals have a richer life than heterosexuals. He has also spoken critically of several people who do not approve of homosexuality. Several weeks ago, he expressed admiration for Mick Jagger *because* he is bisexual. I am fairly certain he has had dissociated homosexual feelings for at least two men in the past and has them now for a former housemate, the biophysicist-musician who recently moved to New York. Not long ago, he told me that gays live in the neighborhood where he is moving. Several days later, he said with what I took to be disappointment that the neighborhood had a number of "burned out gays."

June 1, 1984

"Back in touch," were David's first words this afternoon. He sounded glad to be there. He stayed up until 3 A.M., talking about philosophy with a male acquaintance. "It was awful," he said. "I did it out of loneliness. I couldn't get to sleep, thinking about the move."

He signed the lease for the apartment this morning and moved about half his possessions earlier this afternoon. The apartment will not be ready until Monday (three days from now), so David will spend the weekend at the house.

"I don't know why moving is so difficult for me now," he said. "When I moved from Atlanta to Chicago in 1978, I had everything ready to go in one day. Now, I think about each step." I told him it sounds like he is walking through the move with lead shoes. He agreed. "You're dragging the past with you at every step," I suggested. "Everything you are doing now is weighed down by associations with the past, as well as your anxiety about the future." He thought so, too.

David was having second thoughts this afternoon about the downtown neighborhood he is moving into. "It's not healthy," he said. "I was in a drugstore across the street from my apartment today, and saw several junkies waiting for their fix. There are a lot of deadbeats in that neighborhood." Several days ago he looked at another apartment in the area where I have my office, and liked it. "It's the best deal in town," he said. "Just $130 more a month than what I'll be paying. It's healthier up here. I always did well here." He lived in this area from 1974 to 1976 while he was involved with Sally, and again from the fall of 1979 after he returned from Chicago, to March 1982 when he was hospitalized. I pointed out he decided about two weeks ago he would be more comfortable downtown because, as he put it, that part of the city is more "open-ended," and he could meet more people there. Today, he said he could meet more people up here. David is constituting both locations alternately as desirable and undesirable, denying the ambiguity in each by splitting the meaning (advantages and disadvantages) one time this way, another that.

David reviewed the history of his illness, starting with his first breakdown in 1971. He sees the pattern now clearly: a major possibility in his life turns into a major disappointment and he falls apart. We talked about how in each case the disappointment was precipitated when he pulled back from an ongoing successful or potentially successful situation. "I could never follow through on anything," he admitted.

About ten minutes before the session ended, David suddenly stiffened in his chair, and his voice became loud, clear signs he was defending now, and "in flight." He said that I and his close stockbroker friend from Atlanta were from the "silent generation of the fifties" that cared only about their careers. Ten years younger, he was part of the generation that protested the Vietnam war and tried to change "the system." "I wonder about some of what goes on in here," he said, meaning in my office, as if he really did wonder—and worry—about it. "Isn't therapy surveillance? Isn't it like the CIA?" I told him I have no connection with the CIA and that I am not keeping him under surveillance. He protested, but ineffectively, and let the issue drop after several minutes.

Again, David was following disclosure with coverup. Again, the "mechanism" of retreat in the face of advance was being activated, but not very strongly, compared to several months ago. During the first few months we worked together, David attacked me viciously more than once for what he saw as my connection to and sympathy with the CIA and the establishment. Then, his attack was a bang. Today, it was a whimper. Is he starting to have serious doubts about my "CIA connections?" Is he starting to see that my being a "patrician" does not have to interfere with the work we are doing?

June 4, 1984

When David didn't show up for his appointment at 5 P.M. and did not call during the next hour, I was concerned because this has happened only once before, several weeks ago, when he was in an automobile accident en route to my office. I left for dinner just after 6; and when I returned about 9:15, there was a message that he had called. Within five minutes, he was at the door. "I got mugged this afternoon," he told me. "On the way up here. It was in an alley. There were three of them. One had a stick. They got around twenty-five dollars. I tried to fight back. Then, I called the police. It won't do any good, because they won't catch them. It's really rough out there."

The first thing I noticed was how solid David looked and sounded. He was somewhat shaken but not panicked. "I must give off signs of vulnerability," he said. "I must be setting myself up for this. I'm going to take a course in self-defense." This is the third time in a year David has been mugged.

After ten minutes, David finished telling me about the mugging and wanted to talk about other things. The remainder of the session was very much like our session yesterday. "I'm pleased with what we've done," he said. "I'm not as angry and resentful now. It should be fun for you to see this through. You'll learn something." He was "in touch" for the entire hour. "I have to start shaking," he told me. "I have to get off this drug." He has often spoken of his illness as an addiction and said he has been a "junkie" for the last five years. When he lets go of his defenses and is "in touch," he experiences something very much like what an addict feels when he goes cold turkey on drugs: symptoms of withdrawal. This emotional withdrawal "activates" the "switch" that sends him temporarily back into what he calls "that strange world."

David finished moving today but will spend tonight in the house because the gas and electricity will not be turned on until tomorrow.

He left feeling good this evening. "I have to get some clothes for the summer," he said as he walked out the door. Yesterday, he told me he was once "the best-dressed man in Atlanta."

June 6, 1984

"I'm going to file a report with the police," were David's first words this afternoon. "That's the only way to handle this." Last night, he went to the bar near his house where he has had several bad experiences and played chess for ten dollars a game with someone who works for a local TV station. After David won the last game, his partner, without any provocation, threw the chess board in David's face then hit him. David fought back, getting off three good punches before being restrained by some bystanders. At the same bar several weeks ago, this person struck him in the mouth, but later apologized. Last night, David gave him another chance, to his regret. "The guy's a loser," David said. "He took his frustrations out on me. Everybody in this city is bitter. Three months more. That's all I'm giving it, and then I'm out of here. People in this city think they're doing you a favor if they look at you."

David was upset but fully in control this afternoon. He was angry as he told me about what happened last night. Many of the old resentments came up again, not so much toward his father but toward the country. Today is the fortieth anniversary of D-Day. David is offended by the front-page coverage the story has been given by a local newspaper during the last few days. He takes offense at anything even remotely connected with the military. He says this country is going the way Germany went during the 1930s, when Hitler was building his power. "It's all fascism," he has said often. To him, disco music is militaristic. So is the current interest in physical fitness and body building. David is also convinced that the government is encouraging—"programming"—all these activities to get Americans ready for war. He feels it's all part of the masculine, machismo stance of this country, and he hates it. David is having trouble with his identity as a man. Overt masculinity, in certain forms, threatens him.

David was resentful this afternoon, but he did not use the resentment to cover his anxiety or as an excuse for not doing the work he knows he must do. He was distracted from his main issues because of what happened last night, but was not "in flight." "I guess this was a wasted hour," he said as he walked out the door.

David called this evening from the house where he has been living. He is still there because the refrigerator in his apartment hasn't been repaired yet. "When I got home tonight," he told me, "the house was full of dope." Several of David's housemates routinely use drugs. David does not.

He was calm as he spoke. He took responsibility for putting himself in the situation that led to the fight last night. I suggested this afternoon that he seeks out the kind of people who hang around that bar—gamblers, petty thieves, drug users and dealers, dropouts, and deadbeats—and seems to have a special affinity for them, in spite of the abuse they often inflict on him. He acknowledged this. Tonight, he also acknowledged he is looking for what he calls "male bonding relationships" and admitted what he usually finds are "destructive people." I did not pursue what he means by "male bonding relationships," but I feel he was trying to say something more about his attraction for and need to be with men. This afternoon, he told me his backsliding these last two or three months is due, in part, to the problems he is having "separating," as he put it, from the biophysicist-musician, who moved out of the house in April and now lives in New York.

June 14, 1984

I was several minutes late for the session this afternoon. "What's going on?" David wanted to know. I apologized for not being on time and told him it was unavoidable.

For the first twenty minutes, David spoke with anger about his father for all the familiar reasons and then referred to him as a "closet fag." When

I asked what he means by this, he said his father has "never dealt with these feelings," clearly meaning his sexual feelings for men. David gave no reason for believing his father has these feelings. Clearly, he is projecting and identifying with the projection.

When David's anger subsided, I asked how he likes his apartment and the neighborhood. There is still some work to be completed, but he seems comfortable where he is living now. "There's a lot of noise at night," he told me. This noise is caused by the male prostitution that goes on at David's doorstep. Men wait there to be picked up by other men driving by. David told me this without any hint of disapproval. "There are a lot of crazies in the neighborhood," he continued, "and that gives me someone to talk to."

David made several comments this afternoon that led me to believe he wants to explore further his sexual feelings for men. He mentioned with admiration Pasolini's film, *The 120 Days of Sodom,* and said that every father wants to sleep with his daughter, every mother with her son. "Sure," he continued. "What do you think is going on?" After telling me how insensitive his father is and how much he, David, is like his mother, he said, "I'm my mother with a penis." I reminded him he has said several times that gay and bisexual men are more open and sensuous than heterosexual men. Again this afternoon, he told me with pride that Sally had been bisexual during the two years they were together and that he had taken part in a ménage à trois with her several times. David told me his friend from Atlanta who lives in Houston was "very sensuous." More than once during the last few months, he said their friendship between 1976 and 1978 had become "incestuous." This closeness frightened him.

When I reminded him that during the last two or three months he has told me, sometimes directly, sometimes indirectly, about his sexual feelings for men, he acknowledged this without embarrassment and seemed grateful I had brought it up. I asked if some of his anger toward me for being upper middle class and a WASP has anything to do with what he may see as my inability or unwillingness to help him deal with his sexual feelings. He told me this is so, again without embarrassment and with apparent relief. Earlier in the session today, David said he feels "a sense of morality" about what goes on between us in therapy, and mentioned I disapprove of drugs. But I sensed by "morality" he means more than drugs, that he fears I may be judgmental about his sexual ambivalence. I assured him I would not.

I now believe David chose to live downtown rather than in the area near the university at least partly because this is a gay neighborhood. Today when I said it seems that the neighborhood where I live is predominantly heterosexual, he said it is, with what I took to be disapproval. I also believe David's dislike of upper-middle-class WASPs that occasionally flares into hatred owes something to the fact that upper-middle-class WASPs are, for the most part, heterosexual, and do not socialize easily with bisexuals and homosexuals.

Last winter, David told me his father said he hoped David would produce a grandson soon. David scoffed at the idea, insisting he is not interested in getting married. When he said today his father is a "closet fag," I felt he was projecting his own situation onto his father. When he talks about what he calls his father's sexual repression, as he does often, is he really saying *he* has repressed sexual feelings—for men? David most likely feels his father, not having accepted his son as a promiscuous heterosexual, would never accept him as a bisexual. "My father never accepted me as I was," David says often with anger and pain.

"Women come on to me now," he said, "but I don't respond." Nothing in David's tone made me believe he regrets his lack of interest. He started turning away from women in Chicago in 1979, he told me. "I was frozen there," he said. He has had very little to do with women sexually since then, in contrast to the very active sexual life he had prior to 1976, when he left here to go back to Atlanta.

"Good session today," David said as he was leaving.

June 20, 1984

David had five good hours yesterday, he said. After swimming late in the afternoon, he went back to his apartment and listened to music. Later, he read and wrote in his journal. The apartment is pretty much in order now. He has become friendly with a man and a woman who live together in another apartment in the building. They invited him over several times and took him to a party last Saturday night. The woman works in a medical library in the city. She told David about an opening for a serials cataloger there. She promised to set up an appointment for an interview. I asked if he feels he could tolerate doing that kind of work. He said he believes he could.

The five good hours David had yesterday were followed by several bad hours, and he could not sleep last night. I asked if he has any idea what brought on his insomnia. He said it might have been because he was reading René Char, a French poet who was a friend of Camus. I asked where the anger he felt was directed. He was angry at his father, but more angry at himself, he told me. This morning, David received a check from his father, along with a note that included, as David put it, "the same old clichés." Mr. Helbros is upset because David still does not have a job and continues to cost him a good deal of money. Several days ago, David told me that his parents "aren't off the hook yet," as if he wasn't certain when he would let them off.

Near the end of the hour, David began an attack on the upper middle class. I asked if he has to hate people with this background—his background—and suggested his response was like that of a racist. He became furious. He got out of his chair and walked toward the door. "I think we should call this off," he said. "I'm going to call Stacey." He left. Last week, David saw Stacey walking on the street near his office, which is not far from David's new apartment. He said he is thinking of calling him to ask for an appointment. I said it would be interesting to get his view on how David is now. He stopped therapy with Stacey about nine months ago.

Several minutes later, David was back. "I think you should get in touch with my father and tell him I want to stop," he said. "You're being well paid. You're under contract." I told him if he wants to discontinue therapy, *he* should break the news to his father.

June 22, 1984

I began the session this afternoon. I told David I see him now on the horns of a dilemma: He can take the next step by getting a job and letting his father "off the hook," but by doing this he would be living the admission that his father no longer "owes him." "Why not?" he asked. "What do I have to lose?" I pointed out that he has a good deal to lose. He would have to let go of an old identity (as badly as it is serving him) and then open himself up to the prospects of both failure and success. That is the "psychoeconomics" of his situation. That is his dilemma. I pointed out when he says, "I really *am* the bastard child," a thirty-five-year-old man is saying first, he is a child; second, he is an abandoned child; and third, he feels being an abandoned child is an outrage. David still feels his father owes him a living. Sometimes he acknowledges it, sometimes he denies it.

After about ten minutes, David's mood became ugly. "We'd better break this [the illness], or I'll take your head off," he said. "There's an incredible amount of violence underneath this," he continued, showing me his forearm, which was bulging with tension. His face was contorted in anger.

"I want to see the notes you're taking," he demanded. I told him I do not feel this is a good idea. "On whose authority do you base that?" he wanted to know. I told him it is not a question of authority but of care, my therapeutic care — caring — for him. "I want to keep what we're doing open ended," I said. "Reading the notes would interfere with that." He accepted my explanation.

Then he began a strong verbal attack on me, repeating many of the familiar accusations but adding some new ones as well. I was surprised by his inventiveness and at how low he would stoop for ammunition. "How do you think you would do in a physical confrontation with me?" he wanted to know. I asked if he was thinking about tennis. He wasn't. "What, then?" I asked. "I don't know," he said. He left his chair, walked toward me, and sat on the arm of the sofa, which is near my chair. Sitting there, he was a foot or two above me, and seemed to enjoy the advantage that position gave him. He was becoming more agitated, and his body was tightening. I thought of that day, several months ago, when he angrily grabbed my hands. My left hand still has not healed, and there are times when the index finger gives me considerable pain. I was concerned he might assault me again. "Maybe I should find a woman therapist," he said. "You're just like my mother." As the verbal attack continued, I stood my ground and tried to answer his accusations. After about five minutes, he returned to his chair, considerably less agitated.

David said he had a "violent" night. He tossed in bed, unable to sleep. He got up at 3 A.M. and did some exercises to work off the tension. He was angry at me last night, but would not say why.

A woman who lives in David's apartment building has arranged an interview for him on Monday for a serials-cataloging job at the medical library where she works. The woman who will interview him is thirty-five, divorced, and has a Spanish last name, he told me. "That's the kind of woman you like," I said. "I don't like Mediterranean women that much," he replied. "It depends on the season." David's remark surprised me, because he has said many times he prefers Mediterranean women with dark skin and dark hair. He considers blondes superficial and WASPy, his ultimate put-down. Is he anxious because the woman might attract him? Is he concerned about what demands that attraction would make on him?

The hour was nearly up, and as I looked at the clock David said, "Let's go another fifteen minutes." I told him I had to make a phone call first. He left, and returned about ten minutes later. "I want you to know I've always respected you," he said as he walked in. He shook my hand. "But that's not consistent with so much of what you said during the last hour," I replied. "I know," he continued. "There's been a lot of bad faith." "Not on my side," I said. "On mine," he acknowledged.

David's anxiety and anger today may be due to the job interview scheduled for Monday. "Every time I get close to something, this happens," he said. "It's the pattern." He had what he considers a rather good day. He read for a while, wrote in his journal, and took his typewriter to be fixed.

During the second hour, David made two remarks that surprised me. I cannot recall the context of the first one, but it came down to this: "I don't have trouble with . . .; I have trouble with fags with small sticks." When I asked what he meant by this, he said, "I don't know." The second remark came out of the following dialogue:

DAVID: Why am I stuck in this city?

ME: Why do you think?

DAVID: To settle accounts.

ME: With whom?

DAVID: With you.

ME: In what sense?

DAVID: I don't know.

I believe both remarks have sexual overtones: the first explicit, the second implicit. David wouldn't (or couldn't) tell me who "the fags with small sticks" are. Is he asking me again to discuss his homosexual feelings with him? I was ready, but he backed off. During the first hour we met this afternoon, when he was sitting on the arm of the sofa near my chair, he said, "Maybe I should discuss this [unspecified] with a woman therapist." Does he mean it may be easier for him to talk about his sexual feelings for men with a woman than with me? During the second hour, I reminded him he said this, and he replied, "Oh, that's just bullshit."

What does the second remark mean? What accounts need to be settled? I told him I sense he wants something more from me than I am giving him and that not getting it makes him angry. "It's nurturance," he admitted. "That's not my job," I replied, and he agreed. He said his friend from Atlanta who teaches in Houston gives him this. "He's like a brother," David told me.

Is David trying to say he has sexual feelings for me? Is he angry because I am not responding? Toward the end of the session, he told me he likes my gray hair. Earlier, he made a complimentary remark about my right arm, which is larger than the left arm because I play tennis and am right-handed. During the first hour we met this afternoon, what did he mean when he asked how I feel I would do in a "physical confrontation" with him? Is something sexual suggested here?

I cannot recall what provoked it, but David left his chair again and sat on the arm of the sofa near my chair. He was angry and agitated, as when he did this earlier. "Are you scared?" he wanted to know, glaring down at me. "No," I answered truthfully. He became calm soon after, returned to his chair, and later left my office without anger but with a good deal of nervous energy.

June 25, 1984

David began the session this afternoon by saying he has been masochistic during the last five years. He recognizes that his rage, directed outward toward everyone and everything, has been most destructive to him. Whatever he has put his parents through — and it has been a great deal — it does not come close to what he has done to himself.

Last night, David spent some time at a bar near his apartment. As soon as he told me he picked up a woman there, he reversed himself and said she picked him up. They went back to his apartment and talked, but David didn't like the way things were going and nothing sexual occurred between them.

About twenty minutes into the session, David became quarrelsome. "For fifty dollars an hour I can get the best prostitute in town and heal up that way," he insisted. "That's why people go to prostitutes. That's what it's all about." In other words, for what he is paying me he could have a prostitute and get better that way. I said if he really wants a woman, he could probably find one without having to pay her. (I believe David still has the skill to attract a woman for a night but is either too anxious to do so or not sufficiently interested.) It was clear he did not want to talk about this. He made some remark about misogyny that I did not hear. When I asked him to repeat it, he said, "Let's let that hang."

"Maybe I should see a woman therapist," he said for the second time in several days. When I asked what the advantage would be, he replied, "So I can act out my feelings about women on her." I am not certain, but I believe he added, "instead of you."

This morning, David interviewed for the serials cataloger position. He considers it a "minimal" job. He would have to work eight hours a day, five days a week, and would earn $8,000 a year. He was nervous and not at his best, he felt. He said the woman who interviewed him is "burned out," and wore too much mascara. He also said that "she was dressed for penis envy," meaning she wore a business suit. The most difficult part of the interview was a typing test. The typewriter was an IBM Selectric, which he is not used to. The touch is lighter than that of his electric portable. "Isn't that an example of the feminization of America?" he asked. "How clitoral." Is David themetizing the world—in this case, the country—as he feels himself these days, more feminine than masculine? The woman promised to call him about the job in two or three days.

Just before the hour ended, David shifted ground and said, "It all comes down to the fact I can't trust women." I asked if this is the basis for all his problems. "Ninety-nine percent," he replied. I wanted to pursue this, but there was no time. I believe David is ready to open up on this issue now. For several months, he has been dancing around it and giving off very strong signals that he has more to say about his sexual feelings for women *and* men.

June 27, 1984

When David called this afternoon to make an appointment, he said last night was one of the worst nights he has had in a long time. He did not get to sleep until 7 A.M. "I was going all the way down," he told me when we met tonight. "I was letting go of prejudices and my anger toward my father. It felt good."

David seemed more calm when we met this afternoon than he has been in some time. He may have let go of his anger toward his father last night, but he was obviously holding on to it when he said, "If my father had croaked in 1979, I wouldn't have any problems now." I asked if this means he would have made the changes in the business he suggested to his father and if making them would have saved the business, giving him financial independence. He said yes but then changed his tack: "I would have sold the business and gotten out," he told me emphatically. "What I should do now," he continued, "is convince my father I want to go to business school. I'd have to talk baby talk to him for a while. Then, I'd take the money and run. That's what all sons of the upper middle class do." I pointed out that it seems he still feels his father "owes" him. He agreed.

"I also have my doubts about you," he said. Several days ago, he told me it would make more sense to work with Stacey again because his office is just a ten-minute walk from his new apartment. (My office is about twenty minutes by cab, which is the way David usually gets here.) When I asked if he was saying the time to get to our respective offices should determine which therapist he would do best with, he said, "That's right. It all comes down to time." I thought this a bizarre response, but did not pursue it. I took it as a below-the-belt punch at me, one of the many imaginative and resourceful punches he has delivered recently. He spoke vaguely about working with other therapists and said he had called Stacey. Speaking of these "other therapists," he said, "They're busy." I don't know if he has made an appointment with Stacey. I let him know that would be all right with me.

David spent about half the hour tonight talking about himself and where he is now and the other half lecturing me on philosophy and literature. Again, I pointed out how he uses ideas and books to avoid his issues and browbeat me. He admits doing this.

About ten minutes after he left my office, he came back and asked that we meet again. "When I was outside, I was thinking, 'This isn't me,'" he said. He was speaking of the half-hour—half of the session just completed—he had spent defending. "The closer I get, the more I defend," he continued. I told him I consider that a hopeful sign. "The really hopeful sign is that I was willing to spend another fifty dollars to come back up here," was the way he looked at it. As much as David claims to hate capitalism, the dollar is never far out of his consciousness. "The best capitalists are Marxists," he has told me several times. "That's why I'm a Marxist."

"This isn't me." Is David saying he is identifying more strongly now with his "in touch" self than with his "in flight" self? He recognizes the difference and implies a preference. I told him I have been able to recognize "two Davids" for some time. They live in very different worlds, talk differently, even look different.

David was "in touch" for the entire hour. "I want to get through this illness," he said. "I've had it. There is a battle going on between you and me. Don't let up. Keep uncovering my coverups. I gave you a commitment I would see this through with you, and I will." Once again, he took responsibility for everything that has happened to him during the last five years. He does this periodically, only to back off and return to the "shoulds" and the "oughts"—his and his father's—he believes would have made him financially comfortable for life.

He left feeling good about himself and what we are doing.

David called at around 12:30 A.M. from a phone booth near his apartment. He does not have a phone yet because he can't afford one. "I'm at ground zero," he said. "It feels good. I feel like I'm at a breakthrough point. I feel a rough night coming on, but I'm in touch with it." He sounded exhilarated and expectant.

"You're right," he said. "Most of the reading I do is defensive. It's total bullshit. This must be very frustrating for you. It's unbelievable." I reminded him he spent half the last session lecturing me. He admitted it. "This is the best move I've made in four years," he continued. "What's that?" I asked. "Working with you," he replied. "You were on top of it from the start."

Chapter 3

ε&

Implicit Violence Becomes Explicit

June 28, 1984
Afternoon

David ripped into me this afternoon, using much of the familiar ammunition. He said what we are doing isn't working and told me he has made an appointment with Stacey. He feels I'm not "subversive enough," that I'm too much a part of the system. He complained again about how much working with me is costing his father. Actually, he feels his father should give him the money he pays me. He said I am taking advantage of him and that he wants to cut back on our sessions. He also tried to convince me that ninety percent of his illness comes from how I am constituting him. In other words, most of his problems are in *my* head.

He had a rough night and didn't get out of bed until 1 P.M. He was angry, mostly at his mother. "I gritted my teeth for the first time in a long time," he told me. When I pointed out what he had just said about me is the exact opposite of what he said last night when he called, he agreed. When I asked what he makes of this, he said he doesn't know. The contradiction didn't seem to disturb him. I asked what set off this attack on me. He is almost out of money, and this frustrates him. He resents me because I'm upper middle class and because I'm costing him money. I asked if the working through he did last night made him anxious. He said it did. "I'm frightened of what's ahead," he added. He called the woman about the library cataloging job, but she wasn't in. He will call again tomorrow.

"Doesn't it come down to being what you call a 'bastard child' and what that would mean to you?" I asked. "What it would mean to be abandoned by your parents, if they no longer supported you." "I *am* abandoned," he said as if this is not all right with him.

"I don't have a masculine trait in me," he volunteered. "That's why I have so much trouble with you." I took this remark as the latest indication that David is having trouble seeing himself and feeling himself as a man. Is he saying he has trouble with me because he has the sexual feelings of a woman, and I am a man?

David's anger came and went during the rest of the session. He left feeling very angry.

June 28, 1984
Evening

David asked that we meet again this evening, as he has done many times after a rough afternoon session. He began our meeting tonight with a sentence that was most likely rehearsed: "I want you to write a letter to my father saying you feel I should work with Stacey now." I said that considering he had worked with Stacey for a year with what he admits were no good results, I could not in good conscience recommend this to his father. I pointed out he is free to stop working with me at any time and could continue with anyone he chooses. He let the issue drop there.

David lectured me and badgered me for most of the session. He told me I couldn't "read beneath the text" and that I "don't sense certain things." Then, as so many times before, David suddenly changed ground. "Actually, you're sharper than Harris on this," he continued. "He couldn't deal with it." Then, he told me he was more attracted to Harris and to Stacey than he is to me. "Their offices are nicer than yours," he said, quickly scanning mine. He gave reasons for this preference, but I cannot recall them. Then he added, "Everybody has these [sexual] feelings. Therapy is sexual." Later he said, "Maybe I should work with a woman on this."

I had no idea David has sexual feelings for men when we started working together eight months ago. I began to see it slowly, two or three months ago. My first clue was the way he spoke about the biophysicist-musician. When his friend moved to New York about three months ago, David said he felt he had been "abandoned." He also mentioned that his friend was "trying to work through his latency feelings." David claims he started "backsliding" just after his friend left this city. He spent more time in the bar near his house and less time in the library and at the pool. I also noticed he was making casual negative remarks about women and heterosexual sex, while speaking with great admiration about certain bisexual and homosexual men. Often, too, he has spoken negatively of families, the product of heterosexual unions.

At the end of the hour, David went to the telephone on the desk and, without saying anything, dialed a number. As he held the receiver impatiently, he said, "You're sharper on this than Harris was," repeating what he said earlier, clearly meaning that I recognize his sexual feelings for men. He seemed to resent my being "sharp" about this. After what seemed like three or four rings, he slammed the receiver down angrily. He walked toward the door. I followed him.

He was about to leave when he turned around and said he would like to talk some more. Suddenly, he slammed the book he was carrying, which was open, into my chest. He grabbed me by the arms and hands, and pushed me. I asked him to stop and tried to convince him that whatever he was trying to work out, this was not the way to do it. He was not interested in what I had to say. He used abusive language, some of it suggesting sexual feelings. During the scuffle, his glasses fell to the floor. He hit me in the face at least twice and slammed me against a wall. I tried to tell him one of my teeth may have been loosened. "See a dentist," he sneered at me. I defended myself by blocking his moves against me but did not take any offensive action. I saw the possibility of having to call an ambulance for a bloodied patient. I didn't like what I saw. I told him I would call the police if he didn't leave. "So therapy *is* the police," he replied triumphantly. After what seemed like three or four minutes, I maneuvered him into the hall and out the door, which I had previously opened. I closed it, and told him to call me tomorrow.

A mirror told me my shirt was covered with blood, most of which came from a gash above my right eye. My nose was bleeding slightly. The smallest finger on my left hand was bruised and swollen. Both hands hurt badly. The damage was serious, but it could have been far worse.

About a half-hour later, David called. I assumed he was in a bar because I could hear music and voices. He apologized. "I responded to you that way because that's the way my father related to me," he said. I knew this was nonsense but let it go. He wanted his book back, the one he slammed into my chest. I told him I would leave it at the desk in the lobby tomorrow. He said he hoped we could still work together. I said I had my doubts and asked him to call me tomorrow afternoon.

June 29, 1984

David called around 1 P.M. His voice was low, and he sounded apologetic. "I was up all night thinking about this," he said. "I'm disgusted with my behavior." I cut in, saying, "I really don't think it will be possible for us to work together anymore." I gave three reasons: first, there is a question of whether we have reached a therapeutic impasse because of what happened last night. I must ask myself, in view of his feelings for me—attraction and hatred—and the violent way he has acted on these feelings, is it possible for therapeutic work to continue? I have my doubts. Second, I am concerned about my physical safety. David's attack on me last night was the third, and he was far more vicious than before. What would the next attack be like? Third, there were complaints about the noise last night. Several people were frightened by what they heard (probably scandalized, as well), and contacted the night man at the desk, who then phoned me. Out of consideration for others in the building, I do not want this to happen again.

"Can't we work it out?" he wanted to know. I said I don't think this is possible. "You seem to be headed in the direction of another therapist anyway," I reminded him. "That's not really true," he said. I suspected he may have been trying to manipulate me when he said he was going to call Stacey. It sounded like he was admitting it now. But I told him again that I don't think we can work together any longer. He wanted to know if I think what happened last night was the result of long repressed feelings. I said that seems likely.

July 1, 1984

David has called four or five times since we last met Thursday evening (June 28). He wanted to meet yesterday afternoon, but I declined. I told him I would never again put myself in a position where I could be the target of his violence.

"Boy, I really do it to myself," David said. I had to agree. He said he feels "abandoned." I told him I expect him to feel this way. He became very manipulative as he tried to convince me to continue working with him. He promised he would never be violent again. "I'll put it in writing," he said. "I'll sign a contract." I reminded him he has put things in writing before only to back off. When David's father came here in December, he showed me a letter David wrote more than a year earlier, promising he would be less resentful toward his parents and that he would get a job. He put that in writing more than a year and a half ago! David seems no more behind what he writes than what he says. Twice, his voice dissolved into tears. He said we could settle this over a drink. I told him we could not. "Now I know how vicious you are," he said later. I told him he does not seem to understand that something fundamental changed after he assaulted me Thursday evening. Some time ago, while describing how angry he was, David told me a psychological test he took during one of his hospitalizations showed he is a "potential mass murderer." Now that I have seen his rage face to face, I can imagine how this could happen. Would he try to kill me? I can't be sure he wouldn't. Several days ago he said, "If this [therapy] doesn't work, I'll take your head off." Does this constitute a threat? Maybe.

The events of the last few days have underscored something I knew when we started working together and understand better now. David's fundamental project is to do nothing and be supported — fed — by his parents. To commit himself to something, to get a job and earn his own living, would be tantamount to being *abandoned* by them. He would rather suffer from his illness than act autonomously and feel abandoned. He is furious at his father because he will not recognize David's right to be fed. "My father is trying to make me middle class, nine-to-five," he often says. "You're his agent," he tells me. "He's paying you to make me a part of the system."

David's only projects are fantasy projects that have no chance of coming to fruition. He says he wants to make a film, but he does not know how to make a film and is not willing to learn how. The contradictions do not appear to bother him.

David called this evening. "I feel awful about what happened," he said. He told me he became violent in response to "the issue you brought up," which clearly is his sexual feelings for men. "Maybe we pushed too fast," he continued. "We took this issue at your pace," I reminded him, "over a period of three months. If I hadn't addressed it directly on Thursday night, I would have felt negligent."

"I'm thinking of leaving the city," he said. "It's becoming more frustrating." Several minutes later, when I asked if he thinks he would really leave, he said he is not sure. "I've been under a lot of stress lately," he replied. He reminded me he has been mugged three times this year and assaulted several times. I believe he is exaggerating how stressful these events actually were for him. As a sociopath, David may possibly have a good deal of sympathy for his attackers—blacks and people on the fringes of society—and identify strongly with them. He probably sees these people as other con men doing their thing. It's not his attackers he's enraged at but his father and, obviously, me.

Periodically, he still says that while he was working in the family business he should have stolen his father blind. When he last said this about a week ago, I asked how much he feels he could have stolen and how he would have done it. He said he could have taken about $1,000 a week by writing false orders. "Don't you think your father would have found out about it eventually?" I asked. "I don't know," he replied, "maybe." It didn't sound like a very realistic plan. "Anyhow," he said, as if trying to save face, "I stole $20,000 from him." He did not give any further details.

David asked if I had filed assault charges against him with the police. I told him I had not but I would immediately if anything like that ever happened again. "Do you know what a vulnerable position I'm in?" he asked. I said I do. "I'll have to be one of the toughest individuals around," he added.

He said he would call Stacey and ask for an appointment. He wanted to know if I would be willing to meet with both of them to discuss what happened Thursday evening. (I suggested doing this several days ago.) I said I would be glad to. It will be interesting to see if David contacts Stacey. Obviously, it would be a difficult meeting for him.

July 5, 1984

David did meet with Stacey. They agreed I should call him.

Stacey seemed overly cautious when I called. I got the impression he was trying to say as little as possible. His only concrete comment was that he felt the frequency of our sessions had something to do with David's violent outburst. I told him I do not believe this was the primary reason and that David was most likely reacting to my confronting him on an issue that had been unfolding for several months. I did not mention that the issue is David's bisexuality. I said I believe I can still work with David, in spite of what happened. I also told him I have the impression David feels he can benefit further from working with me. Stacey agreed.

David called this afternoon, wanting to know if we could meet later today. Several days ago, he said he would be willing to go to a lawyer and make his promise not to assault me a "legal document." What an irony. A sociopath, who hates this country and believes its laws are fascistic, wants to use the law he despises to assure me he will not be violent toward me again.

Once again, David denied he has sexual feelings for men then said if he does have these feelings they are no more than most men have. He admitted "missing" the biophysicist-musician after he moved to New York but claimed nothing was unusual about that. And he talked again about having what he calls "heightened feelings" when he is around intelligent men. But he denied any of this poses a problem for him. I told him I feel it does and that the issue needs to be opened up and addressed. "I never did anything," he told me tentatively. I took this to mean he has never taken part in any homosexual act. Again, I told David he is denying this issue. Then came a remark *de profundis,* the slip of slips: "If there are no more denials, there's nothing left." I did not point out this obvious slip and doubt he recognized it. I only said that working through the denials properly *would* leave him with solid ground to stand on. He accepted this.

Today, a week after he assaulted me, David said that what happened isn't all that unusual. "Patients assault their therapists all the time," he told me. "There's violence in the paper everyday," he continued. "I know," I said. I could have added, "That's what worries me." For the first few days after the assault, David was apologetic and seemed ashamed. Now, he feels what he did isn't unusual or execrable. Who am I dealing with? A sociopathic borderline with global rage, who tests out as a potential mass murderer, who has dissociated homosexual feelings he is blocking, and who acts out violently. Should I really let this person back into my office?

July 11, 1984

With some reservations, I have agreed to meet with David. I have assured him if he strikes me again, I will call the police, he will be arrested, I will press charges, and our therapeutic relationship will end. He said the terms sounded "fair." I doubt he believes so. In fact, I believe very little of what he says, and I do not trust him. I don't think he has any consistent notion of what "fair" is. But I will take the risk of meeting with him again, so we can continue the work we began in October. I have also considered the possibility he could experience a serious abandonment depression if I terminate with him now.

David has called several times during the last week. I asked if he feels he is in any danger, whether he might harm himself or anyone else. He does not. He told me with pride he is definitely not falling apart.

David was turned down for the job at the medical library. The woman who interviewed him hired someone with more experience and told him he would have been bored working there. This leaves him nowhere as far as a job is concerned. I reminded him today it has been two full years since he left the hospital. I pointed out that he refuses to take what he considers a "menial" job, such as bartending or driving a taxi but knows he is not ready or willing to work in a brokerage house at what he calls an "entry-level" job either. He has been doing an elaborate dance around the issue of getting a job for two years, sporadically making halfhearted attempts and regularly calling his father in Atlanta for more money.

David oscillates between two extreme positions on whether his parents should support him. Most of the time, he acts as if they owe him a living. Then, when his father complains about how much money supporting David is costing him, David says, "They should have cut me off years ago. Then I would have had to make my own way." When he is in this mode, he talks what he calls "baby talk": "I *have* to find a job this week; it's the top priority now; I *need* to work to structure my day and have self-respect." But he soon returns to the "they owe me" mode.

David alternates between the fantasy that his father should die so he can get his inheritance as quickly as possible and saying he doesn't want the inheritance, that he wants to be independent. More than once he has said he is thinking of changing his name. Doing this would be in line with his sometime view of himself as what he calls the "bastard child," i.e., a child (at thirty-five) who has no parents. And just before he moved about five weeks ago, he said he was thinking of not giving his father his new address and cutting off all communication with him. I wanted to ask how, if he did this, his father could continue to send the money that keeps him going. But I restrained myself.

David's father told David that the bills he has been receiving are too high for his bank account and that we should meet less often. When I suggested that we cut back to three sessions a week, David objected, saying that we need to continue working at the present intensity. Later, he agreed to reduce the number of sessions.

July 13, 1984

We met for the first time in two weeks this afternoon, the first time since David assaulted me on June 28. It was a low-key session. The hour passed slowly.

David spent most of yesterday looking for a job, without success. He met with someone he knows at the state employment office, sat through a lecture on the man's philosophy of employment, and was told there is nothing for him there. A woman he knows told him about a bartending job that just opened up. David went to the bar and left his name. He has changed his mind about doing this kind of work. He says he will take the job if it is offered to him. He also called a brokerage house downtown to ask about working in their research department. They said they would let him know.

David is having money problems again. "I'm seventy-one dollars overdrawn at the bank, with no check on the way," he told me. "I'll just have to keep writing checks." He has overdrawn his checking account several times recently. Not having enough money is one of David's greatest frustrations now. This frustration and the anger that comes with it was one of the reasons he assaulted me, he said. "It was the end of the month, and I was broke," he explained. Now and then David says if his father paid him the money he pays me, he wouldn't have any problems.

Almost matter-of-factly, David told me he believes his latent attraction for men has something to do with his first relationship with a man—his father. He was not clear why he thinks this is so, and I told him I could not follow his thinking. He talked about "taking up my father's repression," by which he means sexual repression. Again, he is projecting and identifying with the projection. He acknowledged his relationship with his father is heavily narcissistic. Several times since we started working together, while he was talking about how badly his father treated him when he worked in the family business between 1976 and 1978, David has said, "What my father really wanted to do was fuck me in the ass." I don't know what to make of David's assertion that his father has something to do with his sexual feelings for men, but I was pleased he acknowledges this is an issue for him and is willing to talk to me about it.

He spoke briefly again about leaving the city, but he has no plans about where he would go or what he would do when he got there. "I should have gone to Europe in 1978," he said. "Everything pointed in that direction." In Europe, David expects he would find "people who think like I do," and who could "cross-fertilize" his thinking. "All I want to do is read, write, and think," he said again today. He has been keeping a journal for years and considers this his "writing." I doubt he has plans to publish any of it. David has not published anything or even submitted anything for publication, as far as I know. When I asked if he has considered writing for a living, he said he has not. Writing for magazines and newspapers? He's not interested in that sort of thing, he said. "Writing" is one of David's fantasy gratifications. He has read me excerpts from his journal. There are some good insights in what he writes, but much of it is self-indulgent and self-referential.

During one of his recent, and frequent, calls to his parents, his mother told him he could probably get a job working for his long-time stockbroker friend in Atlanta. But David is not interested. "I don't want any part of Atlanta," he said. "I feel numb when I'm in his [the stockbroker's] office," he added. "I don't like office buildings." Earlier in the session, he asked if I knew how many women he has lost because he worked in the stock market. "Women don't like brokers," he said, "because what they do is only about money. Women go for the poets." Is he saying that if he trades on the market and makes money, he will be less a man, or less successful with women for doing so?

July 17, 1984

When David called this afternoon to ask that we meet today, he said he had some fundamental issues he wants to work through. But fifteen minutes into the session, it became clear there were no new issues being addressed, just a runaround on an old one—getting a job.

David went to the state employment office again this morning and found nothing that interested him. "It's all high school stuff," he said. He has an interview tomorrow with someone who runs a business, just what business David was not told. A mutual acquaintance arranged the meeting. While talking about his prospects for finding a suitable job (he realizes they are not good), he shifted ground suddenly and said he would go to graduate school. "The only time I was happy was when I was in school," he told me again today. He hasn't, however, made any moves toward applying. Then, shifting ground again, he attacked capitalism, saying that its contradictions (as seen by Marx) are destroying this country and that the end would come soon. He was clearly joyous at the prospect. "They're laughing in the Kremlin now," he says often when he makes this criticism of the United States, though he did not repeat this remark today. When I pointed out he was using his attack on capitalism to discharge the tension that dealing with the issues of job and graduate school generate, he immediately agreed. He acknowledged again he must find a job.

I sensed a good deal of submerged hostility in David this afternoon. "If I'm going to jail, it won't be for punching someone out," he said looking at me intensely through a sneering smile. Because I do not remember the context of this remark, I am not sure what he meant. I can imagine two possibilities. First, he may be thinking of doing something illegal to make money when, as he has said, "I'm fast enough on my feet again." Second, he may be threatening me with something more serious than assault and battery. "I wouldn't mind going to jail," David continued. I believe this means he is considering trading the global pain of his situation now for the specific, concrete pain of being in prison. He has said, many times, that if he had killed his parents years ago and gone to jail for doing this, he would be out by now. He often speaks of prisoners with admiration, pointing out that Samuel Beckett chooses to live opposite a prison in Paris. Later, he told me a friend from Atlanta, a poet, has been involved in thirty-five cases of assault and battery and never gone to jail. "A good lawyer can get you off," he told me through what I took to be a threatening smile.

During the sessions we have had since David assaulted me, I have sensed feelings of violence underneath the almost constant forced smile he has shown me. Is there some love–hate dynamic directed at me? Possibly. Could this erupt into violence again? I believe it could. From what he says about being willing to go to jail, he may just be willing to pay the price.

David is putting on a friendlier face for the world these days. Talking about approaching people for a job, he said he is "killing them with kindness." Several weeks ago, he told me the person he knows at the state employment office who has been trying to help him find a job thinks he's just a nice guy down on his luck, who's looking for some honest work. "That's what he thinks," David said, "but I'm really getting ready to steal this country blind." As he said this, his face was contorted in anger.

David wrote a conciliatory letter to his father several days ago saying the anger they express for each other during their phone conversations isn't good for either. I believe this may not be a move toward reconciliation, which David repeatedly says he will have no part of, but another pose to get more money from his father. Using what he calls "baby talk," he is trying to convince his father and other people he is ready to make some kind of accommodation to this society. I doubt he has any intention of doing so.

July 20, 1984

Violence lurked beneath the surface of everything David said this afternoon. "Philosophers want war," he told me, naming Nietzsche, Marx, and Sartre. He was equating the violence of ideas — the thoughts of revolutionary thinkers — with guns and bombs. "How else will change occur?" he asked.

David has been spending a good deal of time recently looking for a job. So far, he has been turned down on everything. I asked if this rejection has anything to do with his mood now. "You're damn right I'm angry," he said. I tried to get him to talk about these feelings, but he went right back into his attack on this country and everything it stands for. He did not want to discuss his feelings today. When he said this city is dead and there is no one here for him to talk to, I reminded him that the work we are doing now will, if we succeed, allow him to leave here eventually and move someplace more to his liking. But he didn't want to talk about this prospect either. He continued his vicious attack on this country. While talking about the necessity of working and making money to keep himself going, he said, "I'll just have to steal." I believe to the extent David sees himself supporting himself in the future he imagines doing so in some illegal way.

He mentioned his family only once this afternoon. "Do you think it's possible I may just hate my father, my mother, and my sister?" he asked with what seemed like complete sincerity. "I'm against everything they and their class stand for."

Just before meeting with David this afternoon, I read a newspaper story about a man who killed twenty-one people yesterday at a McDonald's restaurant in San Diego. I was struck by certain similarities between this man and David. The murderer, too, hated this country, was unemployed, and spoke often of violence. David told me again today I do not understand fully how capitalism oppresses people because I am too much a part of the system. There are moments when he seems to focus all his anger and resentment on me. I have some concern if he decides to act on his violent feelings, I may be the first person he goes for. I believe if he does act violently, he would be more likely to hurt someone other than himself.

Just a few minutes before the end of the hour, while he was still expressing his rage, David shifted ground suddenly and said his assault on me had something to do with his friend, the biophysicist-musician, leaving the city and moving to New York. At the beginning of the hour, he told me he had just received a letter from him. Clearly, he was pleased by this. "You're right," David said, "I was attracted to his energy. I have been attracted to other men with energy, too." He abandoned the issue as quickly as he raised it. Because we were running out of time, I was not in a position to encourage him to talk more about this. He has told me, more than once, I do not have this "energy" the biophysicist-musician and some of his other male acquaintances have. I believe he considers this a deficiency on my part and resents me for it. Was his resentment one of the reasons behind the June 28 assault?

Several days ago, I asked David if he is meeting any interesting people in the bars he frequents near his apartment. "They're all 1950s types," he said, clearly disapproving. "They're not in touch with what's going on." And what about the women he meets there, I asked. "At thirty-five," he told me, "it's not appropriate to pick up women in bars. That was all right when I was twenty-five." David doesn't seem interested in pursuing women now. Not long ago, he told me one of the reasons he is reluctant to become involved with a woman is because he is self-conscious about not having a job and a career. There is probably something to this, but I doubt as much as he claims. David's gratification with women these days is strictly fantasy gratification. When a woman approaches him and speaks to him, he imagines she is coming on to him; but he doesn't test out her intention by following through. He leaves it at the level of fantasy.

David has said little about his marriage and divorce. He was married approximately thirteen years ago, but the marriage lasted less than two years. His wife was an alcoholic, and her drinking caused major problems. She was hospitalized three times for alcoholism before they were divorced. "I didn't know what I was doing when I married her," David told me recently, clearly meaning he was confused about everything in his life then, not only the woman in question. He also said his best friends were getting married at the time, among them his close friend who teaches in Houston, who was marrying then for the first time.

Just over two years ago, while David was still hospitalized, this friend was married again, to a woman seven or eight years younger (he's thirty-five, the same age as David). At that time, David said he gave the marriage five years. Several times recently, he said he considers going with younger women a sign of immaturity and even illness and became critical of his friend for becoming involved with what he called "a young girl." He said this with at least disapproval, and possibly repugnance. He admits he has developed what he calls a "moralistic" attitude toward women and claims he has internalized this feeling from his father and from Harris, both of whom have tried to make him feel guilty about being involved sexually with numerous women in the past. David told me recently that when he resumed therapy with Harris in the fall of 1979, Harris told him he should feel guilty about "the women you ruined."

Taken together, David's remarks about women and sex during the time we have worked together have a certain flavor and texture. He seems to be turned off by women now. At the same time, he feels "heightened" in the presence of certain men who have "energy," such as the biophysicist-musician. But he is also conflicted and frustrated about what to do with these feelings. "It's easy to tell who the bisexuals in the gym are," he told me several weeks ago, as if he was on the lookout for them and felt they were better persons for being bisexual.

Not long after we began working together, while David was talking about his reasons for returning here in the summer of 1978, just before he moved to Chicago, I suggested one reason may have been because he had still not resolved his feelings for Sally, though they had ended their relationship at least a year and a half earlier. He denied this, angrily. But last week, without any prompting from me, he acknowledged it was so. Later, he told me something even more revealing about his relationship with Sally that says a good deal about how he relates to women. He admitted loving her while they were going together, but had reservations about marrying her because, as he put it, "No one came around with a check." Sally's parents have a good deal of money, but apparently they were not offering any of it to David.

July 22, 1984

David began the session by asking if I have a tape recorder — I do not — presumably, because he wanted a record of what he was about to say. His voice cracked often during the first fifteen minutes he spoke. "I'm tired of living in the fantasy world I have made for myself," he said. He went into great detail about how everything he does now is "off the wall," and about how he doesn't follow through on anything he plans or starts. His self-description was accurate and penetrating. He admitted playing "intellectual academic games," where "I let one writer take me to Paris, another to San Francisco." He said he is not cut out for academic life because he is too free-spirited. David was doing his I-hate-this-illness-and-I-want-out-of-it routine this afternoon. I've heard it before. Does he mean it? As much as he means anything else now, I suppose.

David met a woman in a bar last night. They left together, went to another bar to listen to music and then went back to his apartment. David said he was nervous and self-conscious. He talked incessantly, jumping from one topic to another. The woman, too, was nervous. They listened to records and talked, but nothing sexual happened between them. He seemed troubled by this. Here is yet another instance of his not being able to get anything going with a woman now. My gut feeling is he does not want a woman but is too conflicted about his sexual feelings for men to follow through. Sexually, he seems to be in limbo now.

David spoke about what he called the "solid work" we did from October to April, when "every day was a concrete experience" for him. What happened in April to change this? The biophysicist-musician left town. "I felt abandoned," David admitted. I suggested we look more closely at his feelings when his friend left. He was willing to talk about this but was not comfortable doing so. "He brought structure and order to the house," David told me. "He knew what was going on. I could talk to him at one in the morning. He would come into my room, too." I asked how he feels about having "heightened" feelings for men who have "energy." The question surprised him, and he fumbled for words, which he does not often do. "How does anyone feel about that?" he asked, avoiding the question. "How do you feel?" I inquired. After some further fumbling with words, he said he feels "all right" about having these feelings, but I am not so sure. "It's all intellectual," he said about his relationship with the biophysicist-musician, as if trying to reassure both himself and me.

David said he was also "abandoned" by a woman in the Italian department who left for Europe after the spring term ended. I asked which abandonment was more painful for him. He said the woman's leaving was worse. I doubt this but did not challenge him. Clearly, at this point he is minimizing the issue of his sexual feelings for men. I don't want to push too fast on this. The issue should unfold at his pace.

He was "in touch" for most of the hour. "What can I do to get well?" he wanted to know. I pointed out how differently he was talking today, compared to the last time we met—two days ago, when he was angry and spoke of violence. He acknowledged the difference and said he recognizes he was "in flight" then. I pointed out again how he uses his defenses when things get rough. "I have to stay concrete," he said, "every minute of the day." I also pointed out that by going into "flight," he subverts what we are working toward.

About five minutes before the hour ended, while he was discussing his relationships with Sally and other women, I said it seems he is either too close to a woman or too far from her, and he has trouble being close in a way that fulfills his needs. We have talked about this before, and David agreed it is a problem for him. So, I was surprised when he became angry and hostile at my remark. "That's your psychological way of looking at it," he said, in effect denying the problem. Earlier in the session, he admitted one reason he came back here during the summer of 1978 was because of Sally. Now, he was saying it had been all over with her by the time he left in 1976. "I made the decision to leave," he said. Yes, I told him, but the consequences were not satisfactory to you. With some reluctance, he agreed. For about five minutes, he had gone back "in flight" again, trying to deny an issue he had already acknowledged.

David told me again today the neighborhood where he lives now is "not healthy." "I'm approached many times a day by people asking for money," he said. "The area is full of drug addicts and people who are burned out." He did not mention the area is also full of gay men and male prostitutes. "It was another bad move," he said. I reminded him he knew what the area was like before he took the apartment. He readily admitted this. He deliberately chose not to live near the university, with its pool and tennis courts, a neighborhood he considers "healthy." He had even put down a deposit on an apartment there, but then chose to live downtown instead. I believe he did this because of something he expected to find in this gay neighborhood. He says he regrets the decision now. But what does he "regret" about it? And for how long?

David called later this afternoon. He said he feels we had a good session, and thanked me for my part. "You're good at this," he said. He sounded grateful. I believe he was thanking me for helping him confront his confused, conflicted, and ambivalent sexuality that is causing him much trouble and pain now.

July 28, 1984

David and I have worked together for nine months. The time seems appropriate to pause and attempt some estimate of his capacity for benefiting from the work we are doing. To what extent is he capable of responding to my therapeutic invitation?

David is caught between a multiplicity of worlds. He lives fragments of each world, not fully *in* any of them. Instead, he lives in the cracks. Somewhat arbitrarily, we can imagine him caught between these eight worlds:

Autonomous world ↔ Infantalized world
Idea world ↔ Business world
Legal world ↔ Criminal world
Heterosexual world ↔ Homosexual world

David cannot take root anywhere in this multiplicity of worlds. There is no ground from which he can draw continuous nourishment. To him, the world is a kaleidoscope of meanings, often changing from minute to minute. He is a chameleon, changing necessarily as he changes the constitution of his world, as he wanders in the cracks. No one, including himself, or nothing, is constant in this changing coconstitution. Perceiving and living himself, others, and the world this way suits his purpose because it allows him to live partially and temporarily in each of the eight polarized worlds without taking the risk of committing himself to any of them. It is a fancy piece of footwork. It is no accidental choice of words when David says he "dances around" things.

Caught as he is in this multiplicity of worlds, David has weak ego boundaries. He's not sure where he stops and others begin. To shore up his "split," weak ego, he projects, identifies with his projections, and makes narcissistic mirroring demands on others, particularly his parents and close friends. Not surprisingly, being unrooted in the world, his reality testing is poor. His breakdown five years ago occurred after his father liquidated the family business David had plans for reorganizing. That these plans were unrealistic, unworkable, and in some instances involved illegalities did not—and, in retrospect, still does not—diminish his demands they be put into practice. As noted often, most of David's gratification is fantasy gratification.

The main question is in what world will David eventually live? Will he live autonomously, or as an infant? In the world of ideas or the world of business? Within the law or outside it? As a heterosexual or a homosexual? The conflicts that originate in his unrootedness are tearing him to pieces now.

I believe the greatest crisis David has faced since we began working together is the ending (or at least the attenuation) of his relationship with the biophysicist-musician, when he moved to New York in April. He admits "missing" his friend and having trouble "separating" from him. When he talks about their relationship, he does so with strong sexual overtones. Apparently David has had sexual feelings for men since he was an adolescent; but, I believe, this is the closest he has come to having a "relationship" with a man, though he says nothing physical has occurred between them. In spite of denying he does not feel bad about having these feelings, I believe they are clearly and strongly ego-dystonic.

At the end of a session several days ago, David told me he believes his last hospitalization, in March 1982, owed something to the fact his close friend from Atlanta who teaches in Houston was about to be married. He took this as another abandonment. Before leaving Atlanta for Chicago in the fall of 1978, David was upset by the closeness of their relationship — "I was afraid of the intimacy," he told me — and felt their friendship had become "incestuous." I believe it is significant that perhaps a half-dozen times in the last few months David has waited until the end of the hour to say something about his sexual feelings for men. He talks about these feelings reluctantly and self-consciously.

Through his friendship with the biophysicist-musician, David has been confronted with a sexual attraction to a man that, it seems, remains unresolved. How will he deal with this? He brings up the issue often in therapy now, more implicitly than explicitly. In addition to whatever guilt he may feel about living out his latent bisexuality, David, because of his underlying borderline structure, will have all the problems associated with trust and commitment with men he has always had with women. What seems to be his rapidly unfolding bisexuality is a new and dangerous issue for him. The "abandonment" he has been experiencing since the biophysicist-musician left in April has, as he recognizes, added a new complication to the work we are doing. Several times, David said his friend's leaving is a key factor in what he sees as a "setback" in our work and to his progress out of his illness.

And what will become of David's sociopathic inclinations, which he has acted out sporadically since early adolescence? Is he a sociopath who has been hampered in his illegal undertakings by his borderline structure? Has he not had a "career" as a criminal for the same reasons he has not had one in the stock market or in academia? (After initially saying he felt bad about assaulting me, he now feels it was not such a bad thing to do.) Could his sociopathic inclinations be so deep-seated that therapy will not be effective? Is he equal to the task of working through? And if he does integrate somewhat through therapy, will he use his new strength to make his way by breaking the law? Am I helping to rehabilitate a potential criminal?

August 6, 1984

The biophysicist-musician was back in town this weekend. He and the woman he was involved with while he lived here have broken up. "He doesn't have it for women," David said, noting his friend will begin psychoanalysis soon in New York. "It will take him four or five years to get himself together," David thought. He seemed somewhat disillusioned with his friend, and feels he is not free because he was totally conditioned by his environment. "He won't take any real risks," David said. He was disappointed the biophysicist-musician would not join him in doing something clearly illegal (I cannot recall just what it was). They also had a yard sale this weekend at the house where they had lived, selling furniture they no longer needed. "We made out like bandits," David told me with satisfaction.

David still has no job prospects. "I have to find a way to make some money," he said. "How?" I asked. "I have connections in the underworld," he replied. In other words, he is thinking of breaking the law.

David "lectured" to me a good deal this afternoon. Literature, philosophy, the arts, politics—the same material he has glossed before, pitting one thinker against another, building one up, putting down another. Freud, Heidegger, Sartre; freedom, determinism. A familiar lecture, delivered with bitterness and resentment. David is deeply resentful his father is sending him only enough money to get along, instead of enough for him to be comfortable. "He's sent me $8,000 since December," David told me. "What's the big deal?"

As he has done before, he attacked the medical profession today. "Who are they curing?" he wanted to know. "Everybody knows they kill people in hospitals." He mentioned a story in today's newspaper about a young physician, considered brilliant by his teachers and colleagues, who was indicted for first-degree murder. "Doesn't it make you wonder if there are any competent doctors coming up?" he asked.

There was a paranoid tone to much of David's lecturing this afternoon. He sees conspiracy everywhere. "The game is fixed," he says often, trying to explain how the country works. And clearly, he does not see himself as having a stake in the game. David, the outsider, despises the insiders. "It's becoming fascism," he said during a session last week, referring to American capitalism, "and when fascism comes, the first victims are communists and homosexuals." He said this as if he had a good deal to lose if fascism does come. David is a Marxist and a strong supporter, at least in words, of many communist governments. He is also trying to come to terms with his sexual feelings for men.

August 7, 1984

A roller coaster session this afternoon. David was up and down, and all over the place. He didn't get to sleep until 6 A.M. "I opened up a lot last night," he said. "It felt good." He was alternately defensive and open to his feelings today. He attacked me, using the familiar ammunition. But the attacks were only brief skirmishes, and he admitted he is not sure why my being different from him would have to interfere with the work we are doing. He told me Harris and Stacey were better therapists than I. When I asked why, he seemed lost for words but then said their silences were better than mine. Earlier in the session, he told me that Harris was "incompetent."

David hinted he has a plan to make some money but refused to discuss it. "That's nobody's business but mine," he said. I believe he does have something in mind. Just before leaving, he said everyone would soon realize what a mistake it had been for him to come back here in 1979. Walking out the door, he said with a coy smile, "The question now is, what does David have up his sleeve?"

August 10, 1984

"I have to break this insomnia," David said early in the session today. "I didn't get to sleep until four this morning." This has been a frequent complaint recently. David has been, in his words, "trying to straighten out my sleeping pattern" since we started working together. The hot, humid nights lately don't help. It's hotter downtown, where David lives, than here; and David doesn't have an air conditioner. He does not look well. His face shows considerable strain and is often twisted into a sneer. His eyes dart and roll. He occasionally tells me he is not eating properly.

During these late nights and early mornings, David reads and writes in his journal. He also does a good deal of "thinking," some of which seems to be, from what he tells me, working through. During these hours he spends alone, he seems closest to himself and to his situation. But he also realizes much of the reading he does now takes him away from the concrete issues he is trying to work through. "My library is a pharmacy," he said, meaning he uses books to drug himself against his real pain. He is always hoping he will read something that will make the "connection" for the "breakthrough" he feels he needs to get better. It is as if he expects some thinker to save him. We have talked about this, and he says he knows it cannot happen this way, but then he slips back again into that false hope.

David said again today it was a mistake to move into the neighborhood where he lives. "I like the apartment," he told me, "but there's no life in that area. I get hit on four or five times a day for money, sometimes from male prostitutes. I shouldn't be there." I was struck by David saying he "shouldn't" be there. He did not say he finds males soliciting sex at his doorstep distasteful or repugnant. In some way he can't quite acknowledge, I believe he finds the neighborhood agreeable, though he feels he shouldn't. "If I get a job, I'll move," he said.

David has told me many times he does not like the English language. "It's not as rich and precise as German," he insists. Today, he was questioning the value of our therapeutic dialogue because it is in English. Not long ago, he accused me of not talking to him in "new words," by which I believe he meant our dialogue is not what he considers "poetic." To David, English is the language of capitalism, the language of the WASP, in other words, the language of what he hates most. He implied he should have a therapist who could work with him in another language. When I asked if he is fluent in any other language, he said he speaks Greek, which he learned from his family. I told him he might have difficulty finding a Greek therapist. "Not necessarily," he said, as if not really convinced. I also told him it sounds as though he doesn't trust me. He said he has problems with that but hesitated saying why. (At other times, he has been very specific about why he does not trust me.) "I guess I should trust you after all the shit I put you through," he said.

David has bounced a number of checks lately and continues to do so. "It's all because my father doesn't send the money on time," he told me. When I asked if he feels bad about putting the bank through all that trouble, he seemed astonished by the question. "Offend the bank?" he said incredulously. He did not say how he feels about inconveniencing the people he writes bad checks to. I didn't get the impression this causes him any pain either.

David told me again today his father has never been able to relate to him in any way except through money. "He never liked anything about me," he said. "Not my hair, not my clothes, not my friends." He recalled when he was a child his father would give him money and then send him away. Taking out several bills he had folded in his pocket, he peeled off two or three, imitating his father and repeating his words: "What do you need, David? Will twenty do? Go on now."

August 25, 1984

While walking downtown yesterday, David met a woman from Atlanta he has known for some time. She is married now and teaches in a women's college here. She told him a former boyfriend, with whom she had been involved for five years, was shot to death by his father last week in Atlanta. The man also shot his wife, then killed himself. The murdered son was twenty-eight, a graduate of Stanford, a chemical engineer, bright but unable to make anything work for him. David sees a good deal of himself in this young man. "He went back to Atlanta to be taken care of," David told me. (As he said this, I wondered if he was aware that's why *he* went back to Atlanta in 1976.) I noted, with some relief, David was identifying with the murdered son, not with the murdering father.

"Why is this taking so long?" David asked yesterday, meaning why isn't he making more progress in therapy. Almost immediately, he answered his question: "I can't play it straight." Is this David's admission he doesn't want to be part of what he considers the "system?" Several days ago, he told me he had read a case history by the French psychoanalyst Jacques Lacan, where Lacan describes a patient he could not help. "He [the patient] just couldn't do it," David said emphatically. "Some people are just lifers." "Did you see yourself in that patient?" I asked. He said he did not, but I was not fully convinced. David knows he is stuck, and in spite of all he says about wanting to break his illness, I believe the prospect of "playing it straight" is so repulsive to him he is sabotaging his best efforts to get well.

Violent thoughts and feelings are always with David. Yesterday, he told me the natives in the film *Burn* killed the revolutionary leader played by Marlon Brando when they realized he supported what David calls the "dominant ideology." As he told me this, his face was twisted into a self-satisfied sneer. "Is that remark directed at me?" I asked, remembering he has accused me often of being part of the "dominant ideology." "Not really," he said, as if not fully convinced.

August 29, 1984

David still does not have a job. Several days ago, a woman in her early forties who is going back to college paid him $100 to write a three-page paper on Homer's *Odyssey*. She asked David to tutor her in literature and agreed to pay him fifty dollars an hour. He seemed thrilled about the money he earned. "I've been rich and I've been poor," he told me, "and rich is better." This woman is very neurotic, David says. "It's obvious she's looking for a tutor, a friend, and a lover." Clearly, he is threatened by some of what he feels she is looking for. "I have to be careful," he continued. "I have to keep this professional." I was somewhat surprised to hear this, considering he has often said he is looking for a woman who will pay him for sex.

David seems increasingly incapable of managing his money. Last week, he spent $250. "I squandered it," he told me. He is still bouncing checks — "all over town," as he puts it — and this doesn't seem to bother him. Today, his gas and electricity were cut off because he hasn't paid the bill. Two months ago, his mother started sending the check for his rent directly to his landlord because David had not paid the previous month's rent, though his father sent him money specifically for that purpose. David considers this direct payment of his rent an "insult." He says he has decided to move to another neighborhood, closer to the university which, he told me today, is his "center of activity." "There's nothing for me where I am now," he said. "It's noisy, particularly in the morning. Moving there was a mistake."

As David was leaving, I reminded him we are scheduled to meet again tomorrow. "Actually, I feel better away from therapy," he told me.

August 30, 1984

David's father called me this afternoon from Atlanta. He was disturbed because David hasn't found a job, and is still asking him for money. He sent David a money order for $150 this morning, in response to David's call last night about having his gas and electricity cut off. "I don't know how to deal with my son," Mr. Helbros said. I had little new to tell him, except that I would continue working with David. "A psychiatrist here told me I should cut him off," he continued. I told Mr. Helbros I would be concerned about what might happen if he did this now.

David called soon after I finished talking with his father. I told him about the call, and as always he wanted to know what was said. I told him his father is very concerned David does not have a job, is financially dependent on him, and can't manage the money he sends him. Mr. Helbros feels David should take any job that would pay him something. Either that or go on welfare and get food stamps. "I'm not working for three dollars and fifty cents an hour," David said angrily. "He [my father] and Ronald Reagan can go to hell. They can both sing in the choir." Several months ago, while calling his parents from my office, he suggested his mother "take her mink coat into heaven."

September 10, 1984

Several days ago, David told me he was in a bookstore downtown recently when the young woman at the cash register winked at him and gave him the books he had selected—free. He seemed elated about this. "You're damn right I like to rip off the boss man," he said. "Do you know how many books Sartre stole?" This is how David relates most happily to capitalism— by, as he would say, "subverting" it. "I'm a thief," he told me several months ago. He seemed proud to be one.

David has not paid his overdue gas and electric bill, and he is still without gas and electricity. It has been almost two weeks since these services were cut off. He has tutored the woman he wrote the paper for at least once and hopes to continue doing so, though he has some qualms about it. "She wants to go to bed with me," he told me several days ago, with the clear implication he is not interested.

David called this afternoon, about two hours after he left my office. "I want to break this [therapy] off," he said. "It all comes down to getting a job and having financial stability. It's up to me. When everything becomes reductive, it's no good." In other words, when his situation is "reduced" to the truth, when the coverup is uncovered for what it is, when he is faced with the prospect of doing something instead of just talking about doing it, it's time to run. I did not say any of this to him. "Call me if you want to meet again," is all I said.

October 2, 1984

"I went to a bar Saturday night. I had four beers and an order of mussels. I talked to the woman who was waiting on me. She is still in school, studying piano. When I went to pay the check, she said I didn't owe her anything." As David told me this today, he was flushed with victory and seemed completely satisfied with himself. He smiled as he did when he told me last month that a woman in a bookstore downtown gave him several books free. "Guys don't do that sort of thing," he noted with a twinkle in his eye, "unless they're gay." He said the woman who let him out of paying his check was attractive, but this didn't seem to interest him.

"It felt good," David continued. "That's the way it was in Atlanta. I lived on sixty dollars a week and spent the rest on books. I never had to pay for anyone. The ladies paid for me. I don't know why I should feel guilty about taking money from my father. It gives me the freedom to create. Marx was supported by friends all his life."

"I've hated my father since I was seven," David continued. "He's an idiot. A nice person, who played by the rules. He never realized you could do better by breaking them. All he knows is hard work and repression. He did what his father told him to do. He became an uptown chamber-of-commerce guy. I'm not that way. I'm Greek." David often contemptuously refers to his father as an "American" and a "preppy."

"Sally was nice, too," he added. "That's one of the reasons I broke up with her. She was becoming middle class." Several times, David has talked disparagingly about the work Sally does now (she is an interior designer). "I hate nice people," he says often. "They're phony."

David is acknowledging once again he "can't play it straight." He wants no part of "the system," or of anyone who does. I pointed out why this is making it so difficult for him to find a job. He too sees this.

"What will you do now?" I asked. "Go to graduate school," he replied. He is particularly interested in the New School for Social Research because it is in New York City, which he sees as the center of intellectual and cultural life in this country, and because it is what he calls a "subversive university," by which he means a center for revolutionary thinking. He is planning a trip to New York to talk to some people at the school. He will stay with the biophysicist-musician, who is living and working there now.

I received a letter from David's father last week. Mr. Helbros is upset because David still does not have a job and is still almost totally dependent on him for support. Because of the expense, he asked us to limit the therapy sessions to ten each month. I showed the letter to David today. He read it through cheerfully and remarked only that he is not spending $1,000 to $1,200 a month, as his father claimed in the letter. Whenever I have shown David letters from his father to me before, his response has been anger; but not today. He seems flooded with joy because this young woman gave him something for nothing at a restaurant last Saturday night. Momentarily, he glimpses a future for himself. "Oh boy!" he exclaimed at one point.

October 11, 1984

David wanted to talk about what he calls his "blocked feelings toward women." "I've had many opportunities during the last two years," he told me. "There were a lot of offers from attractive women. Why am I holding back? This is keeping me from doing my work."

He had several explanations for why he has not been following through with women: he couldn't open up to a woman he knew when he was in Chicago because he was too angry and depressed; his bad relationship with his mother prevents him from trusting women now; he's being moralistic, picking this up from his father and from Harris; women have always been too easy for him; it's not appropriate for him at thirty-five to have a woman for just one night, particularly if she is drunk.

I told David I have sensed for some time he has turned away from women and is not really interested in them now. I said this slowly, and I was careful not to sound as if I were making an interpretative breakthrough. I told him I can hear his lack of interest behind his words (or, as I like to think of it, underneath the text). I could see David stiffen in his chair as I spoke. He did not like what he was hearing. He made a number of defensive remarks and then added, "I don't like men physically." *He* made the jump from talking about being blocked with women and me suggesting he is uninterested in them to denying he is interested in men physically. Is this another of David's slips? I believe so, but I did not call it to his attention. Later, as part of a continuing diatribe against this country, he said, "I can't stand American men with no meat on their chests." He was angry as he said this and smashed both hands against his chest so hard I could hear them striking his breastbone.

"I've tried the macho thing," he said later as if this had failed. He did not elaborate, but it occurred to me he might be referring to the 500 women he claims to have had intercourse with since he lost his virginity in Greece when he was thirteen. Has he, by being "macho," tried to beat down the sexual feelings he has had for men for much of this time? Perhaps this defense is no longer working for him. David told me once that of all the women he has slept with, he actually enjoyed sex with only three of them—his ex-wife, Sally, and one other woman. This does suggest a certain sexual compulsiveness.

David told me he is thinking of switching to a Freudian therapist, because "they're good at these things." "I'm not sure of you," he said. He questioned my credentials. Again, he said my language is not "poetic" enough and that Harris and Stacey have nicer offices. "Maybe I should work with someone who has more experience," he continued. "If you had the choice of working with someone who went through five years of analytical training and someone who didn't, what would you do?" I told him I would choose the person I feel would do me the most good. He seemed satisfied with this response. I didn't remind him he decided to work with me after becoming disenchanted with the last two therapists he worked with, both M.D.-psychoanalysts. He talked more than usual this afternoon. I sensed he needed to and said as little as possible. There were no awkward silences.

"I think we should terminate," he said, as he was walking toward the door at the end of the session. While standing in the hallway, he made some additional uncomplimentary remarks about me. But as he was walking out the door, he stopped, and asked, "Could we meet for another half-hour? I have something to discuss." I told him I had other obligations this afternoon.

David's tone was defensive for much of the hour today. During the last ten minutes, it became threatening. His face was twisted in resentment toward me. The first time we opened up the issue of his sexuality to this depth (June 28), David opened up my forehead with his fist. I was concerned he might turn violent again, and I was relieved when I closed the door behind him.

Within fifteen minutes, he called. "I was defensive, tight, and I smoked five cigarettes," he said. His tone was cordial now, and he asked if we could meet tomorrow. I was unable to. "I have to open this up," he continued. "There's no other way. Right? This really is like cancer.

"How are your other patients doing?" he wanted to know. "Are they making progress?" And then he added, "You're doing your part."

October 25, 1984

Mr. Helbros called me from Atlanta yesterday. David has called him each day for the last four days. "David is angrier at me than ever," his father said. "He asked for more money. I don't know what to do about him. I can't keep supporting him indefinitely. [It is still not clear what David is doing with the money his parents send him.] He twists and distorts everything I say. He's up and down. He vacillates so much. Several weeks ago, he called his mother, and spoke very nicely to her for an hour. Three days later, he called again and was ugly to her. It's like he's two different persons."

David is angrier with me now, too. I sense he is building toward something, some kind of explosion. What he can't (or will not) work through, he seems to want to act out. As much as he says he admires men who are bisexual, he doesn't seem to accept *his* sexual feelings for men. David is living his homosexual feelings as ego dystonic. His guilt is fueling his rage, and this rage is growing.

He has said many times all he really needs to do to break his illness is sit down at a bar with a few close friends and, as he put it, "open it up." "Why not?" he asks. He repeated this claim today, snapping his fingers as he said he could get well "just like that." I asked how this would happen, what change would occur. He had no answer, but I sensed he knew more than he was willing to say. Does "open it up" mean admitting openly, and perhaps acting on, his sexual feelings for the male friends who would be with him at this hypothetical bar?

David has spent a good deal of time during the last few days with a young man he recently met who teaches philosophy at the university. He is in his mid-thirties and married. "He and his wife are having a lot of problems," David reported with obvious satisfaction. David is spending more time with

men than with women now, particularly this philosophy teacher and a philosophy Ph.D. candidate who manages the university bookstore. He told
me today they have just started reading Heidegger's *Being and Time* together. Several days ago, David said he "really should" take out a woman he
met recently. "She's attractive, and she likes me," he added. But he spoke
as if taking her out would be a chore.

David considers Ronald Reagan a fascist, and spoke viciously about him
today. The election is less than two weeks off. He doesn't think Walter
Mondale is any better. "It's another four years of Reagan," he said bitterly,
adding, "When fascists come to power, the first people they go after are
gypsies and communists." He has said this several times before, but each
time added homosexuals to the list. Today he did not, but I would bet he
had this group on his mind. Among other things, Ronald Reagan, Republicans, and the moral majority represent to David a strong disapproval of
homosexual sex. He considers all Republicans—including his father, particularly his father—to be "repressed." Is David projecting his repressed
homosexual feelings onto them and identifying with these projected feelings? I believe so.

November 9, 1984

David has moved to an apartment in a building directly across the street
from my office. He was due to move November 1, but the apartment wasn't
ready then; and later, he wasn't sure he wanted to make the change. "I'm
ambivalent about this," he told me last week. "Actually, the neighborhood
where I am now is all right," he explained. "It's the apartment. There's too
much noise, particularly in the morning, and they're fixing the floor in the
apartment above mine." David has changed his mind. Previously, the apartment was fine, but the neighborhood was "degenerate." Now, the "degenerate" neighborhood is all right.

David seemed agitated when we met this afternoon. He spent the first
ten minutes reading the tribute Hannah Arendt wrote for Heidegger's
eightieth birthday. He had gotten a Xerox copy somewhere. He then went
into a long, rambling monologue about philosophy, literature, and the history of ideas, fueled no doubt by recent discussions with his philosopher
friends. He made very negative comments about several professors at the
university, basically that they were one-sided, and didn't see the "whole
picture."

Again, he said he is thinking of stopping therapy because I am not "in-
venting any new language" in our sessions and because he can think of better ways to spend the money this is costing his father. Apparently he has
talked to Stacey about working with him again. "Stacey told me he wouldn't
work with me unless I had a job," David said, letting me know that I am ex-
pendable. (Several months ago, David said "Harris really knew what he was

doing when he sent me to Stacey. He's in charge of the film program for the Psychoanalytic Institute." David attributes magical healing powers to film. When I asked if he feels *he* could get well by watching the right movies, he replied, "Sure. Why not? That's how Kate [a character in Walker Percy's novel, *The Moviegoer*] got well.")

David told me this afternoon, with animation and satisfaction, he had just found out a book he greatly admires was written in prison. Several times, he has said he admires prisoners and pointed out with obvious satisfaction that Samuel Beckett chooses to live across the street from a prison. He feels the best books of the twentieth century were written in jail. I believe he can imagine (project) himself imprisoned for some fantasized crime, and as an extension of this fantasy picture himself writing a book in his cell. Obviously, the book would be the ultimate put-down of capitalistic society. At times, I believe David will not be "satisfied" with his illness until he commits some major crime against the society he despises. To him, that would be "healthy," because it would be "subverting" what he considers evil. Committing such a crime would be living what he believes.

"I've learned my lesson," David said during a phone conversation last week. "I'm keeping my real feelings to myself." He has spent a good deal of time recently with his friend who teaches philosophy at the university and his wife. To make and keep friends, David realizes he cannot reveal his "real feelings" because doing so would alienate the people he needs for companionship. To have any kind of social life, he must hide these feelings, play a role, and act "nice." He must not let on how much he hates this country and how he would like to act against it. He feels he lost his chance to inherit the family business because he told his father what he planned to do when he took over, a good deal of which was against the law.

December 7, 1984

Near the end of the session today, after David talked once more about what a mistake it had been to go back to Atlanta in 1976 to work for his father, I asked: "Isn't five years of regretting that move sufficient? Hasn't your resentment taken enough of your time and energy?" He seemed to agree some kind of resolution was due because he replied, "I'm coming out with guns and knives nobody ever saw." David was saying again when he does finally get around to doing something to resolve this conflict, it will be violent. Later, as if to underscore his intention, he added, "Harris asked me how it felt when I almost killed someone when I was seventeen. It felt good. Every man has some of that in him." As he said this, his eyes darted and fired in their sockets. His body was rigid, and he appeared to be seething with a violence that was looking for a way to express itself. From the way David looked at me, I suspected some of the violence he was fantasizing about had me as its object. I was relieved when he left my office.

During a session earlier this week, while insisting revolution is the only way to change American capitalistic society and that this change will come soon, David said "blood will have to flow. Red. That's the brightest color of all," he insisted through a sneer, as if flowing blood would solve his problems. "Everyone in this country is co-opted," he said again today. "They're bought off." David means most people eventually find a place in "the system."

Earlier this week, while talking about his father's business, David admitted, "I never really wanted any part of it." It has become clear to me over the last few months David wasn't interested in his father's business for what it was—a wholesale grocery operation—but wanted it as a base for "revolutionary" and illegal operations. He has talked about setting up an "alternative" press and film studio in the warehouse and of using it as a front for prostitution and selling drugs. David told his father about his plans, and eventually Mr. Helbros sold the business rather than see it go in that direction. "You're crazy," his father told him after David explained what he wanted to do. David has often complained bitterly that his father holds his history of mental illness and hospitalization against him. "I've lost credibility with him," David exclaims now and then, as if he cannot understand why. "I was honest. I should have never told him what I had in mind. Next time I'll know better. I'll keep my mouth shut."

David considers his father a "fool" because he wouldn't back his plans for the business. "How much imagination does it take to see you can do those things?" he asks frequently, as if he can't understand how his father could be so naive. "He's repressed," David offers as a partial explanation for his father's unwillingness to break the law. Did David feel repressed when he was "pressed" into staying within the law because his father wouldn't provide the opportunity for him to break it? It seems so.

David says he will apply to the university here for graduate school. He oscillates back and forth about whether he can do the kind of work he wants to there. He sees the institution as right wing and CIA-dominated. "The word is out on this place," he says often. "No one wants to come here." But he still talks about applying. "The students here are dead," he insisted earlier this week. "They don't know anything about the streets. Where I went to school, girls turned tricks in their rooms to help put themselves through school. The guys dealt drugs. They really knew what was going on. Who do you admire more?" It was clear who he admired.

December 17, 1984

When I arrived at my office five minutes early for our appointment this afternoon, David was sitting on the floor in the hall going over his bank statement. Later, as he sat in his chair, he continued to look at the checks, turning them over, one by one. He seemed very pleased. I suspect some of those checks had been returned for insufficient funds. Is that why he looked so pleased? To him, bouncing checks is one way of striking out against the bank, a pillar of capitalism. Last summer, I asked if he felt bad about the checks he was bouncing then. "What?" he replied in amazement. "Feel sorry for the bank?" Recently, I asked if, at ten dollars a returned check, this kind of banking isn't getting expensive. "What do you expect me to do," he answered, "starve to death while I wait for my father's checks?"

David attacked me verbally for most of the hour. He used the familiar taunts, bringing them back one after the other, reviving accusations and complaints he had "resolved" many times before. When he complained again about the money therapy is costing him—and how this money is being wasted—he said he could have used it to keep his body in shape. I reminded him he goes to the gym nearly every day to swim and lift weights. "But I could be taking ballet lessons," he insisted. "That would involve other people. It would be a social activity." His friend the biophysicist-musician dances and composes music for the dance. He moved to New York last spring to continue his work there.

"It was a mistake to work with you," he told me. "You're too direct. I should have stuck with Harris." Later, he added, "I felt better during the summer of 1983 [before he started working with me] than last summer." He implied this is my fault. After making several highly negative remarks about me, he concluded his barrage with this one: "You're not a socialist. I need a role model."

I can feel the "temperature" of the sessions rising. Some of the same points are coming up now that came up just before he assaulted me on June 28. Today, as then, David demanded to see the notes I am keeping on our sessions. "I have a right to by law," he said (this is not so). During a phone call this evening, he again mentioned the notes and said if I didn't give them to him the authorities would come to my office and make me hand them over. But then, during a second call, he said he would be willing to wait until after we finish our work. "We can talk about it then," I said. He was enraged. "What are you defending against?" he demanded to know. "Why won't you show them to me? You're treating me like an infant." I told him I have doubts about showing him my notes because he often mystifies and distorts written texts. He did not take this well.

December 18, 1984

David called twice today, in the afternoon and in the evening. When he called first, he said he had to meet with me today. I told him this was impossible because of other commitments. "I think the best thing for me is not to see a therapist," were his next words. From saying he wanted to see me immediately to saying there is no need to see me at all, he made a 180-degree turn. The half-pirouette didn't seem to bother him. The call was brief, and he shot some familiar arrows in my direction.

The evening call was longer and bloodier. "I think I should break this off," he said. We talked for perhaps forty minutes. He cut fast from one subject to another, faster than ever before, splitting every issue he touched, deeply and relentlessly. He was fully "in flight." He asked that I review what we have done during the last year. He accepted most of what I said but flared when I talked about his sexual feelings for men. He denied them totally. "You didn't hear what I said," he insisted in a tone that seemed desperate.

"I'm suffering terribly," he told me. I acknowledged that I recognize this. "Are you suffering?" he asked as though he feels I should be. I told him that I'm concerned about his situation but I am not agonizing over it as he is.

David spoke the whole time through a barely controlled rage. Though he didn't threaten me directly, his tone was threatening. I reminded him again if he becomes violent toward me, I will call the police and press charges. I also reminded him he seriously injured the smallest finger on my left hand (the finger was broken), and I am not about to tolerate another injury. He responded contemptuously. "That's nothing," he said. "It happens all the time." Since June 28, he has made this comment several times.

I told him I feel we have reached an impasse now and that he should go it alone for a while or look for someone else to work with. I encouraged him to complete his graduate school applications. He said he would.

December 19, 1984

David called about 11:45 this morning. He spoke one sentence, and hung up: "I've decided we're going to terminate, and I'll see you on the rebound." He sounded bitter and spiteful.

I was surprised he called so early, because I'm pretty sure he was up most of the night. Usually, after a late night he sleeps late. It occurred to me he may not have slept at all.

December 20, 1984

David called late this morning. "I'm going to New York for about a week," he said. "I'm going to think things over and talk to some people at the New School." He said he would also visit the biophysicist-musician. His tone was cordial, and he seemed to be in control.

Mr. Helbros called from Atlanta this afternoon. He wanted to know how things are going with David. "Rough," I told him, and he was not surprised. David still calls home three or four times a week, mostly to ask for money. He begins the conversations pleasantly enough but soon becomes abusive, combative, and demanding.

"I want to do the right thing," Mr. Helbros said. "I'm not sure I am." He mentioned again that during the last fifteen years, David's illness has cost between $300,000 and $400,000. "Maybe I should have cut him off, so he'd have to do something on his own," he continued. "That's what I was advised to do by a psychiatrist David worked with here." I replied there's no telling what David might do now if he didn't have any money.

I told Mr. Helbros there is a good chance David may not be willing or able to support himself and perhaps the most he could hope for would be to stay out of the hospital and out of trouble with the law. David's father did not receive this news with any apparent surprise. "I'd like to do something for him," he said. "I have a building I could put in his name that's worth between $180,000 and $200,000. I could set it up so he would get an annuity of, say, $10,000 a year for so many years. But I'd rather see him do something for himself. He doesn't have to earn $25,000 a year. Even if he earned just $10,000, I'd be willing to subsidize him."

I did not tell Mr. Helbros that David said he wants to stop therapy. I'll leave this to David.

December 28, 1984

While I was away for Christmas, my thoughts returned time and again to David and to the ominous new turn our work has taken: his increasing resistance to the therapeutic project, his growing anger at and resentment toward me, his veiled threats of violence against me, and his notice last week that he wants to stop therapy. Before returning from vacation, I wrote this brief summary of the thoughts and reflections I could not shake.

"I've always felt better away from therapists," the "in flight" David has said often. "Therapy for me is contraindicated. It always was. It takes away my creativity." Many times during our sessions, David would associate his illness with being creative. This puzzled me, and I asked each time what he feels he has "created" with it. "Nothing," he readily acknowledged each time. Still, he continues to insist therapy is interfering with his creative powers. Only after I began to understand how deeply sociopathic David is did I see what he means: to challenge his illness in therapy is to challenge (and thus undermine) the criminal fantasy plans for sabotaging and subverting this country and its laws he is making for a time when, as he puts it, "I'm light on my feet again."

I am a direct threat to David's future. My therapeutic invitation is at odds with the deepest needs he is attempting to express and live. I am a part of what he hates — "the system," as he calls it. That's why he accuses me of being "the authorities" and "the police." "All therapy in this country is that way," he insists, quoting a prominent European thinker.

So why does David continue working with me? Because, as I came to see soon after we began therapy, there are "two Davids": the one who is "in flight," who "splits," denies he is ill, hates his parents and this country, and wants to strike out against both; and the one who is "in touch," knows he is ill, can discuss his situation without defenses and with great insight (however briefly), realizes his parents and this country are flawed but hardly hateful, talks about getting a job and going to graduate school, and says he wants to get well. The "in touch" David wants to work through his illness and wants my help doing so. The "in flight" David, on the other hand, wants to sabotage and subvert this country (though as a conflicted borderline, he can't bring himself to do it in a systematic and effective way), and resents my therapeutic invitation because it does not encourage him to do this. Once, after stating with strong disapproval that I am not a socialist, he added immediately, "I need a role model. Everybody does."

David tends to fuse his notion of what it means to be a socialist with what it means to be a criminal. Often, he uses "socialist" as a code word for socio-path because he can't look this word, and its consequences, straight in the eye. "Neutrality isn't good enough," he said more than once after I assured him I have no "blueprint" or master plan for his life and am not trying to change his political, social, or economic views. To David, it seems that if someone isn't against "the system" he's one of the enemy. David wants a therapist who will show him how to fight "the system" he hates and join him in the fight. I believe this is the basis for his telling me recently that I should have responded to his assault on me on June 28 with "one good punch." "That would have settled everything," he insisted. Outside the law, of course. He was asking that I, his therapist, should violate the thera-peutic discipline as he had done. Then, we would have been partners in crime. But instead, I told him I would call the police if he assaulted me again. By saying I would bring in "the authorities," I was acting outside his code, the code of the criminal.

"Words really are fists," David told me last spring. Not long after, while we talked about his latent homosexual feelings for the first time in depth, he reacted to my words with swinging fists. He told me recently as soon as he gets on his feet again he is "coming out with guns and knives nobody ever saw." I can't help wondering if some of these weapons will be directed toward me. Is he warning me again now?

December 30, 1984

David called early this morning. I had not heard from him since Decem-ber 20, just before he left for New York. "I had a good time in New York," he said. "I felt a lot of energy there." He spoke with two people at the New School for Social Research and seemed pleased with what he heard. "They're in a different league," he said, obviously comparing them to professors he knows at the university here. He was told he could start taking courses there in January but would have to pay his own way. When I reminded him his father has offered to help him financially if he does go back to school, he sounded unenthusiastic and said there would be problems taking money from his father for school. I didn't point out he doesn't seem to have any problems taking money from him for other purposes.

We met later this afternoon. David told me he had just returned from two days "in the country," but did not offer any details. He seemed somber. Soon after he sat in his chair, he rolled up the sleeves of his wool shirt to his elbows. He did this slowly and deliberately. Trying to read his body language, I was not reassured by what I saw: the muscles of his forearms were tensed and his face was twisted into a sneer. It occurred to me baring his forearms might be a sign of the violence he seems to be barely controlling these days.

I noticed his jacket was hanging from a corner of his chair, so the pockets were accessible to his right hand. He has never used the chair as a coat rack before, always putting whatever outer garment he wore on a nearby couch. It occurred to me he might have a weapon in his jacket. I remembered that in October David told me I am like a cub scout who could never figure out what you can do with a knife. Implicitly, I assumed David was saying he had figured this out, and that's what worried me this afternoon.

David seemed to be speaking through clenched teeth. I've heard it all before: the familiar complaints about the country, the familiar complaints about me. When I asked a brief question, he flared and cut me off. It seems he wanted complete control. He went on this way for most of the hour. "What was learned from Vietnam?" he demanded. "How are things different now? It's the same mentality as twenty years ago. Reagan is getting the country ready for war again. They're bringing back the draft." (During earlier sessions, David asked several times in the same tone, "What did my parents learn [from my breakdowns]? Nothing ever changed with them. They still don't hear what I was saying.") He talked about getting a job and complained again about how much money therapy is costing him. "I could have bought a job with the money I've paid you," he said bitterly. When I asked how he would have done this, he let the question drop.

I said very little. I noticed I was perspiring. I could feel my shirt beginning to adhere to my shoulders and back.

David said he is thinking of moving to New York in a week or two. But when I tried to get him to talk more about his plans, he did not elaborate. Nor did he seem enthusiastic about his planned move. I asked if he feels he could be happy in New York. "What does that mean?" he shot back angrily. "Could you do the work you want to do there?" I explained. With great satisfaction he told me certain teachers at the New School were "revolutionary thinkers." He was particularly impressed by a woman faculty member he spoke with who had taken part in the Hungarian Revolution. He heard her speak at a university here recently. During their meeting they talked, among other things, about the ego psychologists (one of David's chief targets these days), and David indicated the woman had sided with him against them. Momentarily, he seemed heightened at the prospect of being around these "revolutionary thinkers" in New York. He also met several graduate students from the New School. "They seemed jaded," he said a little sadly, "just like students at most schools."

David was in New York for four days. He spent two days with his cousin who moved there from Atlanta to work with computers. "He's finished," David told me with apparent satisfaction. "He's on drugs. Cocaine, Quaalude. He can't complete a sentence." He spent the next two days with the biophysicist-musician, who has a one-room apartment on the Upper West Side and plays a record of static to block out the street noise. When I asked if his friend is happy in New York, David said, "He's not really doing that well." David also mentioned he spoke to several psychoanalysts in New York. He said this in a way that made me feel I was supposed to be upset by the news. "Why are the best psychoanalysts in the country Marxists?" he asked. I said I have no way of knowing if this is so.

Almost parenthetically, David insisted he could look at my notes on our sessions any time he wanted. "I checked with the authorities," he said, but did not specify which authorities and let the issue drop there. He didn't seem to want to talk about the notes at any length today.

Near the end of the hour, when I sensed his anger and resentment toward me were winding down, I reminded David when he called to ask for this meeting he said he wanted to talk about his plans for moving to New York. He is thinking of staying at the Y, he told me. He didn't say what he would do with his furniture and books. "I have to find a job," he added insistently. "Financial independence is essential at this point. It always was." I felt David was talking about himself now as if he were someone else or as if he were speaking for his father. He didn't seem comfortable discussing the planned move to New York, or his hopes of going to graduate school there. Everything he said sounded tentative.

But he was calmer now, and it was clear the hour would not end in violence as I felt it might earlier. Just before he left, he said he is thinking of visiting Atlanta in four or five months. This surprised me. He hasn't been back there in over five years.

January 2, 1985

It is becoming clearer all the time that during the last few months I have replaced David's parents (particularly his father) as the principal focus and object of his hatred. Where he once spent the better part of most sessions verbally attacking his father, David now spends this time verbally attacking me.

I don't know if this deadlock can be resolved in the context of therapy. I am concerned he may try to "resolve" it violently by assaulting me again. Many times in sessions during the last few months, I felt he was considering doing just that, weighing the pros and cons, barely able to keep his feelings of rage under control. I also sense he takes sadistic satisfaction from his implicit threat, realizing as he does that I know he is capable of further violence. Soon after we started working together, while David was talking about how his parents had mistreated him all his life, he said: "I should have killed them a long time ago. I'd be out of jail by now." If he considered killing his parents, could he be considering killing me now that I have replaced them as his main object of hatred?

David sees no place for himself in the social order. He is in a no-man's land now, living between the cracks of the various worlds he oscillates between. Striking out against me would put him squarely outside the social order, firmly in the criminal world, and in prison. Doing this would give him a solid identity, a "negative" one from the perspective of the "legal" world, but an identity nonetheless. In Erikson's terms, David's painful identity diffusion would, through violence, become solidified into a negative identity. Finally, he could become what he has half intended becoming most of his life: a criminal. I have speculated before if David wasn't a borderline he might well have become a master criminal, considering his strong antisocial personality, his great cunning, and his ability to deceive others.

Acting violently against me would be a pseudoresolution of David's frustration and hatred. It would be a further magical transformation of the world he is already magically transforming through splitting and other related defenses. David isn't "together" enough now to subvert and sabotage American capitalistic society systematically (instrumentally), as he fantasizes doing. Violence against me, whom he sees as a paradigm of that society, would be a magical short-cut, giving him instantaneous "resolution" and gratification.

Hardly a month goes by without a story appearing in the newspaper about someone, usually a male, who explodes violently without any warning, killing one or more persons, often family members or coworkers. The stunned disbelief expressed by friends, neighbors, and relatives always takes the same form: "He was quiet, polite, and kept to himself. He was always friendly and helpful. He never caused any trouble." This is most likely how David's casual friends and neighbors would describe him now, because this is how he presents himself. David, I believe, is a bomb who could go off at any time.

David called yesterday (New Year's) to ask if we could meet in the afternoon. When I told him this was impossible because I had other plans, he suggested we meet today. After our last meeting three days ago, I seriously considered taking David up on his suggestion we terminate. I asked why he is so angry at me now. "It's probably because I'm blocking the next move," he acknowledged. When I told him I believe our sessions have become antitherapeutic recently, he replied, "Suppose I just drop it," referring to his rage. He sounded as if he was talking about someone else dropping it, not him. I suggested we not meet for at least a week, so he could try to put the energy he has been using to attack me into completing his graduate school applications. He agreed.

I asked if he is still considering moving to New York any time soon. He said he is. "It's a big decision," he replied, as if he was feeling the weight of the world on his shoulders, "and obviously I'm scared." He said he could still be there in time to start classes at the New School for the coming term, which begins at the end of January. He spoke to a teacher at a college here about making the move. "He said I've gone back and forth on this, but he still feels I belong in New York," David told me. His tone was meek, as if the project hinged on the approval of this man.

January 3, 1985

"I have problems living in this neighborhood," David told me during a session shortly before Christmas. As he spoke, he turned his face slightly to the side, glowering at me as if to say I was a part of both the neighborhood and of his "problem" with it. I started to ask why he is having trouble living here, but he cut me off. Clearly, he did not want to say why.

David lives on the ninth floor of a ten-story brick apartment building directly across from my office. On one side, the building faces the university. There is a drugstore on the ground level. It is an elegant Edwardian building, at least fifty years old, in an elegant neighborhood. Many of the residents are older people who moved from large houses nearby after losing a husband or wife or after retiring. For the most part, these people are upper middle class and well off. The building is also home to a number of professional people, including several professors at the university. There are also students from the university who share large apartments. David told me that one of his neighbors is a man in his thirties who teaches at a prep school here.

Who does David encounter in this neighborhood on any given day? Retired members of the city's "aristocracy," whom he despises because of the privilege of their social class; their friends and relatives who, for the most part, are from the same social class; professors and students from the university he despises because he feels it is "elitist," "science dominated," and a "CIA factory."

In the drugstore, where David shops now and then, makes calls from the pay telephone, and writes checks (some of which are returned because of insufficient funds), he comes into contact with the residents of the building, mostly older women, as they have prescriptions filled and buy newspapers, magazines, and various small items. In the late afternoons during the week, girls in blue or green uniforms from the nearby private schools stop by for sodas or candy bars (often both), carrying, besides their books, hockey sticks or lacrosse sticks, depending on the season. On the sidewalks and streets outside, all day and late into the night, students go to and from the university, to and from classes, the gym, apartments, and fraternity houses.

Almost everyone David encounters as he comes and goes in this neighborhood is white, WASP, upper middle class, and affluent —either a part of "the system," retired from it, or preparing to enter it. In short, David is living amidst American heterosexual respectability. Is it any wonder he has "problems" doing so?

January 6, 1985

David called late this afternoon. He was cordial, but there was an ominous undertone to much of what he said.

He is still planning to move to New York soon and will go there sometime within the next week to ten days to look for an apartment. He said he could stay with the biophysicist-musician for two days and would then most likely move to the Y.

David referred briefly and obliquely to the work we have done, reminding me again he and I have different perspectives and views. "What you didn't realize," he said without rancor, "is that at bottom we're all animals." Shortly after, he added, "Kid gloves weren't necessary." I recognized the code: he was talking in symbols, in undertones of violence.

"There's strength in unity," he said out of nowhere. He spoke of "my groups, my networks." He mentioned these before, several months ago, while telling me why he had been better off in Chicago during 1978 and 1979 than he is here. "There are networks of people there who think the way I do," he told me hopefully. "There's nothing like that in this city." At the time, he said New York also has these "networks." I am sure David was referring to leftist and underground ("revolutionary") groups. He attended the meetings of at least one such group while he was in Chicago. He believes he was put under surveillance by "the authorities" because of this and claims his phone was tapped.

January 8, 1985

When David called to make an appointment last night, he said he wanted to leave all his resentment behind and "keep himself open ended." But when we met this afternoon, he did a replay of our last session (December 30), which is hardly what I would call leaving his resentment behind.

He verbally abused me as much as he did nine days ago, though not as viciously. "One thing you never figured out," he said. *"There's another way of doing this—subverting it."* Here it is, at last, out in the open! David is making the implicit explicit now, saying directly what he has been saying indirectly for so many months: that he wants to be a criminal, that I won't help him, that he can't be one without my help, and that this situation is intolerable to him.

"It's all been co-opted," he said about the work we have been doing. "I made a mistake working with you." A short time later he added, "Your language is imperialistic. You support the status quo. You're a fascist." When

I asked why he feels he has to be co-opted by my perspective and values, which he occasionally will acknowledge I am not trying to force on him, he said with what I took to be genuine puzzlement, "I don't know."

He criticized me for being "afraid of violence" and again insisted, "That sort of thing [his assault on me] happens all the time." "I won every argument in here," he continued as if trying to defend himself. Once again, he seemed on the verge of violence. I recalled now that before sitting down he hung his jacket on the corner of his chair, as he did the last time we met. But it slipped off, and he picked it up from the floor more gently than I would pick up any jacket of mine, and hung it on the corner of the chair a second time. Is there a knife in one of the pockets, I asked myself? As at our last meeting, I felt the perspiration building. I wondered, as I have during so many sessions recently, if he would suddenly snap, and if I would be defending myself shortly against his fists or some other weapon.

As he does so often, David talked a good deal about philosophy and literature today. His "scholarly" talk is becoming less grounded (ultimately, in reality) and more bizarre. He is twisting the thinkers and their thoughts more to suit his growing pathological needs.

What David didn't want to talk about today is his plan to move to New York. I brought this up three or four times; and each time, after some perfunctory remark, he went right back to his monologue of resentment. Just before he left he said, "I think my problem is I'm afraid of traveling. I must have picked this up from my father, as he stayed behind his desk all those years."

David called this evening, as I expected he would. "How do you think it went today," he asked smugly? I hesitated, and the silence was uncomfortable. "I think it went well," he continued as if he had no recollection of how he trashed me this afternoon. But perhaps he did recall and was taking satisfaction from another fifty minutes of trying to intimidate me and threaten me, obliquely, with violence.

He talked about moving to New York. "It will be expensive," he said, "but maybe that's the price I'll have to pay." He plans to go there at the end of the week to look for an apartment. The question David must be living now is whether he will pay that price.

Chapter 4

Therapeutic Impasse and Termination

January 10, 1985

David called twice this afternoon. The first call was cordial. He had something to discuss and wanted to meet today. I told him I do not believe this would be the best thing for him, considering how the last two sessions went. I reminded him he spent most of these two hours verbally attacking me and not dealing at all with his issues. "It will be different," he said. "I want to talk about this face to face." I told him again I feel he has been using our meetings during the last month or so as a way of not following through on what he says he wants to do now, and I would in effect do him a disservice by meeting with him.

But David persisted. He said he wanted to meet one more time. I suspected his motive. Why one more time? Later, after some further attempts to change my mind failed, he said he wanted to drop off his copy of Theodor Adorno's *The Jargon of Authenticity*. As the title implies, the book is a critique of existential thought. "You should read it," David told me many times while attacking the existentialists, particularly their notions of authenticity and freedom. Whenever he mentions this book, I know he is splitting and polarizing the freedom–nonfreedom question on the side of nonfreedom.

After more discussion and consideration, David agreed the time has come for him to act on his own. He said he is going to New York soon to look for an apartment.

I have known for some time the work David and I have been doing for nearly fifteen months is coming to an end. Today, I know it is over; I will not meet with him again. I asked him to call me when he gets back from New York.

January 11, 1985

To the degree he rejected my therapeutic invitation, David rejected the world itself, which I came to represent. As he moved toward the instrumental world through the work we did, it repelled him because its values are, for the most part, so very different from his values. David came face to face with the instrumental world—the world as "it is," the world constituted without large-scale, long-term magical transformation, what is sometimes called the "consensually validated" world—and he did not like what he saw. He pulled back, reinvoking his defenses (denial, splitting, projective identification, idealization, devaluation) and resented me bitterly for showing him this world. To put it another way, David met the enemy, and it is him.

Is the incongruity of David's values with those of the instrumental world the reason he complained so often and so bitterly about the money working with me was costing him, why he would repeatedly say that the work we were doing is not "cost-effective?" If he doesn't want any part of the instrumental world, at least while he is splitting and polarizing it negatively, why should he pay for what he doesn't really want? Clearly, that *isn't* cost-effective.

When he was "in touch" in our sessions and (tentatively) accepting my therapeutic invitation, David would talk about regaining the freedom he lost through his illness. He praised the existential philosophers Heidegger and Sartre, whose work he read and reread. He complimented me on my skill as a therapist and said he realized Harris had misled him. But when he was "in flight," splitting and defending, he would deny even the possibility of human freedom. He would claim that Heidegger and Sartre are "second-rate thinkers," and idealize Freud, a determinist, as "the greatest mind of the twentieth century." He would minimize my therapeutic skill and effusively praise Harris, a Freudian analyst. During the last months we worked together, as David came close to the deadline for applying to graduate school, he spent more time in our sessions "in flight," denying the possibility of acting freely, trashing me, and allying himself with the determinism of Freud.

Sometime during the last few months, I wondered whether David may be a "lifer." Kernberg sees "lifers" as "patients who need to remain in treatment over many years because they cannot relinquish external support nor increase sufficiently their capacity for autonomous functioning" (1975, p. 188). And, Kernberg adds, in what could serve as a somber footnote to David's case, "This syndrome is sometimes iatrogenic." David substitutes therapy for life. He uses it as a crutch to sustain himself at a certain level, far below what could be considered true autonomy, and to prepare himself for the time when he can use his inheritance to, as he puts it, "subvert this country twenty-four hours a day." He also derives considerable instinctual gratification by acting out his anger. These moments of rage may be his most intense moments, the moments when he feels most alive.

January 28, 1985

David called last night from New York, the third time since going there. He is looking for a job and a permanent place to live. As planned, he stayed with the biophysicist-musician for two days and then moved to the Y. He will keep his apartment here for now.

"I was attacked," he told me during the first call. Immediately, I imagined him being mugged. "A woman in a bar in the Village jumped all over me," he explained. "She was ready to do it right there. The bartender told me to take her into the bathroom." Clearly, David was not pleased by this woman's attention. "Her father is in jail," he told me. "He's a white collar criminal." The woman is twenty-four.

David talked to several faculty members and graduate students at the New School. His enthusiasm for the school seems to have waned somewhat. "I didn't feel much energy there," he said. David is also looking into Columbia. He is impressed by several graduate programs they offer, particularly comparative literature; and he likes the campus. He has looked at apartments all over the city, and is most interested in the Upper West Side, which is where the biophysicist-musician lives. When I asked if it wouldn't be more convenient for him to live downtown, he said commuting to the New School would be no problem, since he would have classes only two days a week.

He had several job interviews, one for an editorial assistant's position in a small publishing house. "It was routine work," he said as if he isn't interested in doing it, "and it didn't pay enough." At another interview he took a typing test but didn't do well. "I'm not going to ruin my health typing in an office," he insisted. Someone he spoke to at an employment agency told him he would probably have a rough time finding a job. He estimates it would cost between $17,000 and $20,000 a year to live in New York. When I reminded him his father has offered to help financially if he is accepted into a graduate program, David said he wouldn't take the money because of the strings attached. If David can't earn the money he needs and if he won't accept it from his father (or, if his father won't give it to him), he can't live in New York. But this reality doesn't appear to be interfering with the plans he is making. "I'm coming back on Wednesday to clear things up at that end," he told me last night as if everything is settled. Classes at the New School, which he says he is "into," start the first week in February.

Each time David called, he spoke more softly than he usually does, more deliberately, as if he was trying to hold back his rage. He complained each time, as he has so often before, about how much money working with me has cost him. And there were other complaints. "The emphasis was always on Do, Do, Do," he said as if this was not the right emphasis. "I should have moved to New York nine months ago," he told me as if working with me had interfered with him doing so. There was more than a touch of resentment in his voice. The biophysicist-musician moved to New York nine months ago. Was David saying he should have gone with him?

I can't recall his exact words, but David said something about eventually coming back here, presumably after succeeding in New York, to take his revenge on this city. Is he looking for a way to make some fast money illegally in New York? I would not be surprised.

Just before concluding the call last night, David asked if we could meet when he gets back here. I told him again I feel there is no point in our continuing therapy because he is using his relationship with me now as a source of reasons for not making his next move. He didn't deny this. I said if he wants to talk he should call me, and we could talk on the phone.

February 7, 1985

David called tonight. He has been back for about a week. "I might as well do it," he said meaning move to New York. "I felt 'up' there. I wasn't distracted." He hasn't found a job or an apartment. He said he will keep his apartment here and commute. When I asked where he will live in New York, he said he could stay for a while with the biophysicist-musician. "I made a couple of other connections while I was there," he added.

David told me he has a tuition waiver from the New School. Classes there begin February 12. "It's time to renegotiate and get out of here," he insisted. I asked if his father will help him financially with school. "He's not interested," David said as if not fully convinced.

David was cordial as he told me about his plans for moving. He did not seem angry at me, or at anyone or anything else. But his tone changed as soon as he changed the subject. "It would be helpful to have a photostat of the notes," he said bringing up this issue again. He said he spoke to several people in New York, implying they also feel I should give him the notes. I told him again I am concerned he would take anything in writing about the work we did as a distorting objectification of him and of his situation. "That's called censorship," he replied. He argued tenaciously, trying to get me to change my mind. Finally, he said he would settle for a written summary of what we did. I told him I would give him a verbal summary but not a written one. Though he continued to press the point, he never became strident or threatening as he had when we discussed this earlier. "We'll see in the end," he said cryptically, "about the wise old men."

April 3, 1985

Early this evening, while walking several blocks from my office, I ran into David. I have not seen or heard from him since February 7, just before he left for New York.

He looked scruffy and needed a haircut, but he appeared more relaxed than when I last saw him. His face didn't seem as deeply creased, but I couldn't really tell in the dim street light. He was not wearing glasses (he is fairly nearsighted), and it occurred to me he might have gotten contact lenses.

David is on spring break from the New School. He told me about one class he is taking and seemed satisfied with it. The department where he is studying is being reorganized and is in some disarray. The students don't seem all that happy, he said.

David told me the New School would take him as a graduate student, but he would have to pay tuition; and this is making him think again about going there. A professor he talked to suggested he might study at one of several universities in Germany. He said he is also considering going to a state school, where the tuition is low. He mentioned the University of Texas (Austin). David told me all this when I asked what his long-range plans are. I inquired if he is thinking of moving to New York permanently. He said he is but didn't seem very sure about it. He then mentioned something about "winding things up here," adding that the manager of the building where he has his apartment told him he could get out of his lease.

I did not ask but I got the impression that David does not have a job. Nor did I ask where he is living or who has been paying his bills, and he did not tell me. He did say that finding an apartment in New York would be hard. He seems to like living there but feels that the city is becoming "gentrified." He mentioned that the biophysicist-musician has a job at Columbia and is working there twenty hours a week. He also told me that his long-time friend from Atlanta who is teaching at a university in Houston just got tenure.

David was cordial and a bit self-conscious as we spoke. He asked what I have been doing. He smoked a cigarette, inhaling it nervously and deeply as if for sustenance. He did not mention his parents. When I tried to end the conversation he asked again for a written summary of the work we did. He said this might be "helpful," and insisted he has a right to it by law. I told him it would be easy to write several pages summarizing what I feel our work means, but my professional conscience tells me not to do this. He told me again my refusal amounts to "censorship." He pushed his point tenaciously, but did not threaten me as he has before when we discussed this issue. Each time I tried to end the conversation he came up with another reason why I should do what he wanted. Finally, I excused myself politely and walked on.

May 10, 1985

While walking back to my office this afternoon, I spotted David about to cross a street I had just crossed. I had to look several times before I could be sure it was him. He has new aviator-style glasses. His hair is long, stringy, and disheveled. In spite of the heat, he was wearing bulky khaki pants, a heavy long-sleeved khaki shirt, and thick-soled, Wallabee-type shoes.

I asked how long he has been back, and he told me he came in from New York last night. He has just gotten an apartment there on the Upper East Side, in the eighties. A woman he met at the New School found it for him. She has been in analysis for six years but wants to terminate and become an analyst herself. I did not get the impression David is romantically involved with this woman.

He has not had a regular job but said he worked for a while in the Village without giving any details. He also tutored a young woman in philosophy briefly. "There's been no regular cash flow," he acknowledged somewhat sadly. I did not ask how he has been supporting himself. He did tell me he has been moving around a good deal. "It's hard to do things when you don't have a place of your own," he said. He has been staying for short periods with people he knows in Manhattan and Queens.

I tried to get some feeling for how things are going for him at the New School. When I asked if he plans to get a graduate degree, he was evasive and said there are some good points and some bad points about the philosophy department there. "They don't encourage cross-fertilization between philosophy, literature, and psychoanalysis," he told me as if this failure makes it impossible for him to do anything in that department. "They want me," he insisted, "but I'm also thinking about NYU."

I asked how his parents are doing. "My father is pretty depressed about my situation," he replied. And then he added, as if this is still a major impediment to his life, "We still don't see things in the same way." David said his mother seems to be doing well and is not letting her illness (cancer) get in the way. She just returned from a trip to San Francisco and she plans to go to Europe this summer.

David told me one of his friends from the New School was operated on recently for throat cancer. He is thirty-six, the same age as David. "Society is to blame for that," he said with some bitterness. "The New York analysts understand these things," he added cryptically. I did not ask if he is working with another therapist now.

I tried to read the expression on David's heavily creased face. I believe anger and bitterness lay just under his cordiality. He resents me deeply, among other more profound reasons, for not giving him my notes on our sessions. He did not bring this up today, but I am sure it is still very much on his mind.

We talked for about twenty minutes. I told him I had some phone calls to make and tried to end the conversation. At that instant, he saw a young man he obviously knows approaching, said good-by to me, and segued easily into a new conversation.

September 6, 1985

David called late this afternoon from New York. I have not seen or heard from him since May 10, when we talked briefly on the street near my office after a chance meeting.

He is still living in New York. He gave up his apartment here several months ago and seems glad he left. "It's been pretty good in New York," he told me. He has an apartment on the Upper East Side but plans to move to the East Village soon.

David said he is getting ready for the fall semester at the New School. He is disappointed with the students and the faculty there. When I asked what he doesn't like about the school, he said it was the lack of historical studies. "It speaks to the general malaise," he added. I take this to mean the New School and its students aren't revolutionary enough for him. To David, history, Marx, and revolution are equivalent and ultimately stand for the subversion of American capitalistic society. He plans to stick it out there another year to get an M.A., then go to Europe.

"I had a good relationship this summer with a woman in the philosophy department," he volunteered. "She's a budding psychoanalyst," he added with what sounded like pride. David mentioned this woman the last time we spoke. She helped him find the apartment where he lives now. He said he is also seeing a woman from the political science department.

I asked how his parents are. "I don't have much to do with them," he replied, obviously wanting to let the subject drop.

When I asked David if he is working, his answer was: "I made a few dollars with various projects." Later, he told me he had enough money to go to Europe last summer and wished now he had gone. I did not ask what the "various projects" were, and he did not tell me.

After about fifteen minutes, David again asked about the notes from our therapy sessions. I told him my feelings haven't changed, that I do not believe it would be in his interest to receive now a written record or synopsis of the work we did. He referred to the notes I took on our sessions as a "suppressed document." "I want to get a fix on what was going on during this period," he explained. He said the notes are "a reconstruction of what I [he] was doing." He mentioned a law requiring me to provide him with copies of his records (the law does not include notes on therapy sessions). "Eventually, I'll need to contact someone [another therapist] here," he continued, "and he'll want to know what we did." I promised David before, and repeated the promise today, if another therapist requests a summary of the work we did, I will furnish it.

When I told him I had to meet with a patient at 4:30 and would have to end the conversation in about five minutes, he became even more insistent I give him the notes, though his tone was not as ugly as it had been when we have talked about this issue before. But he did make what sounded like a veiled threat. I can't recall the full statement, but he said, "I do X [whatever it is] when people do things like that [he meant my not giving him the notes]." When my patient knocked at the door I told David I had to say good-by. "I hope your patient is doing well," he replied in a way that made me wonder if he meant it, and hung up. (See Epilogue.)

PART II

Analysis of David
Helbros's Psychopathology

Chapter 5

੭**੶**

Sociopathy, Borderline Splitting, and Self-Deception

The primarily descriptive account of David's illness in the preceding journal will now be focused more sharply into a three-part thematic analysis:

1. David as Sociopath
2. An Existential–Phenomenological Inquiry into David's Borderline Splitting
3. Borderline Splitting and Self-Deception

This analysis was written during the last months of 1984 and January 1985, as our work together was coming to an end. Some material covered in therapy sessions not written up for the journal is included here.

DAVID AS SOCIOPATH

"I can't make it in the system." "I can't play it straight." "I've always had trouble with authority." These admissions could stand as David's epitaph.

All through this text, David has been saying, sometimes shouting, he is at odds with this country, with its values, and with its laws. The moments I felt he was most in touch with his feelings and most behind his words were those when he talked about how, when he was strong enough ("light on my feet again," as he put it), he would "subvert" this country and everything it stands for. How? Through what he calls "revolutionary thinking" and by breaking the law. "After I get over this illness," he said often, "I'll have to be one mean motherfucker."

David insisted, time and again, he does not like "nice" people, that is, people who work for a living, obey the law, and respect the rights of others. "They're hypocrites," he said bitterly when I asked why he feels this way. "They don't mean it." He told me he began hating his father when he was seven because his father ran his business within the law and didn't realize he could do much better by breaking it. In grammar school, David organized a ring of his classmates to steal books from the school bookstore and sell them to the students at reduced prices. He felt he was performing a real service. "I was ahead of all of them," he told me once with pride, as if he believed stealing is what life is all about. "I'm a criminal," he said another time, as if he is comfortable being one.

David feels "nice" people are fools. He prefers the company of those outside, or on the fringes of, the law, even when they take advantage of him. These are the people he respects. When David won some money at cards from an acquaintance—a petty criminal and drug dealer who refused to pay him—David said, "What I should do is get into a game with the flunkies from Lawrence Farms [an upper-middle-class residential neighborhood in the city]. They pay. That's their code." It was clear from the way David spoke he feels contempt for these people because they have a sense of fair play. He admires the guy who wouldn't pay him because that's the code he subscribes to. Once, after David was robbed at gunpoint (this happened several times), I asked how he felt about being victimized. "Do you blame them?" was his response. "After the way they have been treated?" He was identifying with a criminal and potentially violent act.

David's last major breakdown occurred in the spring of 1979, after his father liquidated the family business David hoped to take over. "My mistake was letting my family know what I had on my mind," David said about his unsuccessful attempt to convince his father to turn the company over to him. "They resented me for it." At first, he told me his father balked at his suggestions to modernize the operation of the business, implying this had been the main point of disagreement between them. "He wouldn't listen to me," David said, again and again, bitterly. But later, he added: "There were all kinds of possibilities for what could have been done with the business. It could have been used as a base for setting up an alternative press or an alternative film studio. It's done all the time. My father just didn't see it. He has no imagination. He's boring. He's a boy. People like that should be killed." There is no question by "alternative" David means radical and subversive. Several times he has said, "I'm trying to subvert this country, twenty-four hours a day." David also considered distributing marijuana through the company and using what he called "sexual favors" to promote business. "Why not?" he asked. "You're crazy," his father told him when David revealed these plans.

Many times, David complained his father used his history of mental illness against him. "My parents could never relate to me when I was healthy," he said, time and again. "Selling those books back to the students at reduced prices was a good thing. Why should the school profit? And burning religious books was healthy, too. [These books were used in a class in the Episcopal school David attended.] I was acting on my feelings. That's good. My parents didn't understand this. They disapproved of everything I did—the way I dressed, how I kept my hair, my friends, the girls I brought home. They couldn't stand anything about me. They could never communicate with me directly. They paid therapists to do this. They tried to buy me off. They could only relate to me when I was sick [presumably, when he was under a therapist's care or in a mental hospital]. Then, they paid attention." Clearly, David believes his plans for expanding his father's business were, as he put it, "healthy"; it is his parents who were sick. That, he feels, is why he had a major breakdown in 1979, after his father liquidated the company. "They never heard me," he said. "They made me sick. I internalized their illness." And what is "their illness"? They felt the business should be run within the law.

As already noted, David considers his father a "fool" because he worked hard and respected the law. "His work was never liberating," David insists. "He was repressed." Does "liberating" mean, to David, breaking the law and subverting capitalism in the process? Does being "repressed" mean staying within the law? I believe so. Not only was David asking his father to affirm him by allowing him to take over the business, he was asking him to affirm his most basic need—to be a criminal! David's mistake, as he sees it? "I let them know what I was thinking. I'll know better next time." David claims his father was jealous of him. "I could feel the resentment," he insisted. "My father was threatened by my brains and by my skill with women. He knew I could outfox and outsteal him at every turn."

It seems all David's actions and plans for the future, including what are obviously fantasy plans, ultimately tend toward the criminal and the subversive. "I should have stolen my father blind while I worked for him," he told me many times. (He once claimed he stole $20,000 from the business between 1976 and 1978. I'm not sure I believe him.) During the year David was in Chicago (1978–1979), he worked in a bookstore for about three months. He told me he stole more than $2,000 during that time. (I do believe this.) Sometime later, when he mentioned having this job, I asked why he didn't work there longer. "I had to leave," he replied, without any apparent regret. And when a friend was trying to help him get a job with a utility company, David told me, "He thinks I'm just a nice guy down on my luck who's looking for some honest work. Just wait. He'll find out."

David speaks often of going to graduate school to get a Ph.D., so he would have the credentials to teach and write. But several times, in what I sensed were moments of total honesty, he said: "I don't want to be part of a university. I want to subvert it. I want to start my own [subversive?] university." At other times, when he talked about his plans to apply to graduate school and his father's offer of financial help to see him through, David said, "Maybe I'll just take the money and run."

David talks convincingly about getting a job and going back to school. But whenever he gets close to doing anything about either, the underlying criminal intent surfaces.

David was suspicious of me, of my values, and of my intentions from the start. He worried if his father paid me I would become his father's "agent." He often accused me of representing "the authorities," and repeatedly said, "Therapy in this country is surveillance." More than once, he accused me of being in league with the CIA.

I got the impression David felt I was trying to undermine him. Occasionally, he would claim he had no business being in therapy because, as with an artist, therapy would interfere with his creativity. I pointed out his illness has not produced anything that seems creative, and he agreed. But he kept bringing this issue up. At some point, I asked myself what being creative means to David. Is it his commitment to, as he says, "critique" this society and "subvert capitalism twenty-four hours a day?" I believe that just might be the way he sees it. From his perspective, then, if I help him become what society considers "healthy," am I not undermining his commitment to subvert that society? Wouldn't he then be co-opted? Am I not interfering with his fundamental project, which is to be a criminal? I represent the society he detests and the values he insists made him sick in the first place. Does he feel I'm trying to integrate him into the social order he has always been at odds with? No wonder he puts up so much resistance to the work we are doing. Not only is he resisting facing up to his issues, difficult as they are: he is resisting the very notion and possibility of becoming what society considers "well."

David said several times he should have killed his father, rather than brood so long over the loss of the family business. Once, after I pointed out he might have gone to jail for doing this, he seemed unconcerned, even pleased with the prospect. "They would have given me a psychologist there, and I would have made friends with people of my own kind," he told me. Was David saying he would feel more at home in jail and be more fulfilled there?

Harris fused with David, fostered his dependence on him, and consequently fed his illness. The result? David become so dependent he couldn't maintain himself, even minimally — sleeping, eating, organizing his day — and had to be hospitalized. Being "fed" led to his being incapacitated. I, on the other hand, took a stand against David's illness and issued a strong therapeutic invitation to autonomy. The result? Words became fists, and he assaulted me (June 28, 1984). Several months later, he began talking

about "bringing out the guns and knives." To David, moving toward autonomy means moving toward violence.

David is a borderline *and* a sociopath. Neither pathology can be separated
from the other. Each is dialectically intertwined with the other. They are
complementary and understandable only in the light of each other.

Perhaps, feeling he couldn't "make it" in what he experienced as "normal
society," David took on and continued to develop what Erik Erikson calls a
"negative identity," one at odds with social standards. If you can't fit in,
stand against; if you can't join them, try to beat them.

As a sociopath and a borderline, David faces the same problems when he
tries to do something illegal he faces trying to do something not proscribed
by the law. Any action he plans, be it stealing or writing a paper for a course,
seems to activate an anxiety that stops him in his tracks. As a sociopath,
David is caught between being a criminal and being a citizen. As a borderline, he cannot be either very well. He doesn't live in either the world of
the criminal or that of the citizen; he is paralyzed between the two. Kernberg
has described how splitting may interfere with adequate superego formation (1975, pp. 35–36).

Besides the problems nonsociopathic borderline patients have because
they split their experience in the "legal" world, David has the additional
problem of splitting between the legal and criminal worlds. Having, as the
saying goes, one leg in each world, he cannot stand or take root in either.
"Split" so between them, his good-faith efforts in therapy and outside it
(such as they are) to integrate opposite polarizations of his experience, heal,
and become autonomous are ultimately undermined because the values
and meanings of these worlds are incompatible. In phenomenological terms,
this "dual citizenship" is the fundamental reason borderline patients with
antisocial personalities have such a poor prognosis in therapy (Masterson,
1983, pp. 287–294; Kernberg, 1975, pp. 115–117). In essence, these patients
are being invited to integrate themselves into a world (society) they despise
and want only to subvert.

AN EXISTENTIAL–PHENOMENOLOGICAL INQUIRY
INTO DAVID'S BORDERLINE SPLITTING

Many (though not all) borderline patients' principal defense, their way of
not dealing with the ambiguity that inheres in all they live, is splitting
(Muller, 1991a). Splitting makes it possible for these patients to keep separate in their consciousness positive and negative feelings about themselves,
about others, and about everything else in their world (Gabbard, 1989).

In the Western, Cartesian, dualistic world we inhabit, dichotomies are
inevitable. Day–night, light–dark, cold–hot, black–white, high–low, good–
bad are polar opposite ways of constituting and interpreting experience.

Western language, too, inclines us to speak of all experience as pairs of opposites, one of which is generally judged better than the other (Pinderhughes, 1982). From recognizing this component in the structure of Western existence it is just one step—how large?—to naming a defense clinical thinkers starting with Freud have called splitting.

Borderline Splitting and the Negation of Ambiguity

To acknowledge oneself, another person, or some other aspect of the world as ambiguous (good *and* bad, desirable *and* undesirable, etc.) is implicitly to acknowledge an inherent unpredictability in human experience. One never knows what to expect. The world is a dangerous place, and others are dangerous, too. Most people make some kind of accommodation to this reality, painful as it is. To escape the anxiety of the ambiguity they cannot tolerate, some borderline patients live each situation as if it were unambiguous (good *or* bad, desirable *or* undesirable, etc.). In essence, by constituting their experience in this black-and-white, all-or-nothing way, defensively avoiding the "middle ground" that is the terrain of unpathological reality (Lewin and Schulz, 1992), they demand to know ahead of time who they are, who others are, and how a particular situation will turn out. Splitting allows them to do this.

The ambiguity in reality leads to uncertainty, and uncertainty leads to anxiety. This anxiety is precisely what some borderline patients attempt to neutralize through the splitting defense. For as long as another person or a situation is constituted exclusively in a black-and-white, all-or-nothing way, one can create a less anxious identity relating to the person or situation, now "simplified" and rendered unambiguous, though not without paying a price: whoever and whatever is pathologically split is necessarily pathologically distorted. And inevitably, what is pathologically distorted is pathologically lived.

David's principal defense is splitting. When he moves toward, or into, situations that are particularly anxious for him, he uses this defense more vigorously. The greater the anxiety, the greater is his need to defend against it.

Oscillations between David's Opposite Polarizations of Various Issues

What follows in the chart on the next page is a compilation of the issues David "splits" over most frequently, as well as the positive and negative polarizations he makes of these issues. It is the *oscillations* between polar opposite constitutions in feeling and thinking that distinguish borderline splitting from other, more static, uses of this defense (Akhtar and Byrne, 1983).

HIMSELF:	+	I was the smartest person in Atlanta. Everyone came to me for advice.
	–	Eventually, I always backed off on everything.
WOMEN:	+	I've never had problems with women. They're there for me now.
	–	My main problem is my pathology with women. Everything else is secondary. Why wasn't I able to trust women?
PARENTS:	+	My parents did everything for me.
	–	My parents never did anything for me.
	+	My father worked hard, and took care of his family all these years.
	–	My father was programmed. He did what his father told him to do. He was dead. He has no imagination. He's a fool.
ME:	+	You're sharper than Harris and Stacey. You understand my illness better. Working with you is the best thing I ever did.
	–	You're too one-sided. There are too many things you don't understand. I can tell by the language you use. Being in therapy with you isn't cost-effective. It's a waste of time.
DR. HARRIS:	+	I really respect him. He hung in there all those years and paid his dues to the profession. He's one of the best therapists in the city.
	–	Harris was incompetent. He didn't know what was going on. He tried to bring me back into the fold. He was "the authorities."
ACADEMIC WORLD:	+	The university is the only place I've ever been happy. That's where I belong—reading, writing, and thinking.
	–	The academic world isn't real. It's just a lot of bullshit.
BUSINESS WORLD:	+	I have the stock market in my blood. I started making money trading when I was fifteen. I had it all down.
	–	There's nothing real about trading stocks. I can't stand the language. I can't stand the people. I had my last breakdown in 1979 because I was playing the market.
WORK:	+	I have to work to regain my self-respect and to be independent of my parents. No one should take money from their parents after the age of eighteen. They should have cut me off then. I would have had to go to work.
	–	My father could have set things up so I would have been taken care of. It's done all the time. He's a millionaire. Why should I have to kill myself?
CAPITALISTIC SOCIETY:	+	It's not that bad. I just make it so.
	–	It all has to be subverted, twenty-four hours a day.

Keeping Opposite Affective States Separate

When David changes his constitution of some issue from one polarization to another, he does so without seeming to have any memory of the recent opposite polarization. He seems to live each polarization of the issue as if the opposite one does not exist for him at that moment. I asked him about this several times, and he told me he remembered what he had just said, but it was clear that the disparity between the two seemingly incompatible positions did not bother him.

Kernberg maintains that borderline patients cannot integrate the cognitive and affective components of their split constitutions of an issue: "The patient is aware of the fact that at this time his perceptions, thoughts, and feelings about himself or other people are opposite to those he has had at other times; but this memory has no emotional relevance, it cannot influence the way he feels now. At a later time, he may revert to his previous ego state and then deny the present one, again with persisting memory, but with a complete incapacity for emotional linkage of these two ego states" (1975, pp. 31–32). While splitting and oscillating back and forth between opposite polarizations of an issue, David can sometimes recall the polarization he is implicitly denying at the moment I point this out, but he does not integrate the affect associated with its content, nor does he live its meaning.

Once when I pointed out to David he had reversed himself on an important point he made just the day before, he replied, "That was yesterday," as if the passing of twenty-four hours justified the change. The situation had remained the same. Only his constitution of it changed — 180 degrees. Some time later, he acknowledged at times the oscillation between opposite polarizations of certain issues occurs within seconds. As far as I can tell, this happens during periods of unusual stress and anxiety.

Splitting Leads to "Slips of the Tongue"

Sometimes when he is splitting, I get the impression David's left hand doesn't know what his right hand is doing. It occurred to me this may be one reason for his frequent "slips of the tongue." As he "splits" more, he "slips" more. Many times, as he says something directly contrary to his usual stance on an issue, I ask myself, "Why is he telling me this? Doesn't he know what he's revealing? Doesn't he realize how what he is saying goes against his usual efforts to cover up?" Is this "slipping" what, in part, David is referring to when he often says he is not "as fast on [his] feet now" as he once was? Has he lost some of his traction because of this? How can he "dance around things," as he puts it, when he "slips" so, and has such poor footing?

The Depolarization of Affect

By alternately living each polarized fragment of the ambiguity of a situation as if it were the whole truth, splitting borderline patients discharge some of the anxiety inherent in the ambiguity. Paradoxically, the polarization induced by the splitting defense actually *de*polarizes the lived situation, literally taking some of the emotional charge off it. By having it one way and then the other, borderline patients can have it both ways without having to follow through on the consequences of having it either way. Splitting results in what Kernberg calls "mutually dissociated or split-off ego states [so that] haughty grandiosity, shyness, and feelings of inferiority may coexist without affecting each other" (1975, p. 265). Kohut describes the consequences of splitting as "the side-by-side existence of disparate personality attitudes in depth" (1971, p. 183).

Splitting and the "Two Davids"

Soon after David and I started working together, I recognized there were "two Davids." One was essentially "in touch" with his situation and could during this time, however briefly, accept ambiguity in himself, others, and the world without splitting. The other was "in flight," and split ambiguity into all-good–all-bad constitutions, pathologically "simplifying" his experience to avoid the complexity he could not handle. Often during an hour session, David would oscillate from being "in touch" to being "in flight" several times. Doing this, he seemed like two different persons. More than once, when I asked why he made such vicious remarks about me during a previous session, he said emphatically, "Don't pay any attention to that," as if these remarks had been made by someone else. During a phone conversation, his father told me at times he also senses David is two different persons.

I tried to forge a therapeutic alliance with the "in touch" David, the "part" of him who wanted to be whole. I challenged the "in flight" David by taking a stand against his defensive splitting while offering him support to momentarily relinquish the defense. My therapeutic tack was to have him spend, through repeated supported challenges (Lewin and Schulz, 1992), as much time as possible during a session "in touch," realizing he could face unsplit reality only for brief periods and would shortly "fly" again.

Inconsistency and Alienation

Because he uses the splitting defense so effectively, David cannot constitute himself, others, or any situation consistently. This is one of the major reasons he cannot commit himself to anyone or to any project. David, a "split self," lives in a "split world" inhabited by "split others." He cannot take root anywhere in this world because he destroys its ground, nullifying whatever continuity and solidity if offers. His world is a kaleidoscope of meanings and values. No issue is ever settled for him. Because of his ever-changing constituting of himself, others, and his world, David doesn't feel real or present in his kaleidoscopic world. He feels an abiding confusion and emptiness. Often, he shows extraordinary insight into every aspect of his illness. For brief periods, it seems he is owning this insight and that it is touching him. But the insight always slips away, as if it were insight into another person, not David.

David reads often and widely. But what he reads slips through his fingers. One day an idea means one thing, the next the diametric opposite. It is a juggling act, pluses and minuses polarized now to one extreme, only to be repolarized later to the other. There is no integration of his opposite consti- tutions. They stay separated in his perception, his feelings, and his will like the lumps in tapioca pudding. He can't go anywhere with his thinking be- cause the fragments of opposite polarity that result from splitting make it impossible to set a course and stay with it. Sometimes when I point this out, he responds by citing Heraclitus that "Being is a flux" or Nietzsche that "There is no Being, just becoming." This is his "in flight" justification. When he is "in touch," he acknowledges this is not what Heraclitus or Nietzsche had in mind and that his thinking is going nowhere. He takes a fragment of the truth and magnifies it to the point where it becomes the whole truth (for him), which is to say it no longer bears any resemblance to the truth. The fragment, so magnified, becomes a grotesque distortion and a pathological lie.

When the "in flight" David talks about philosophy or literature, his prin- cipal interests, he usually sounds off the wall — often like a crazy man grasp- ing at straws, trying to nourish himself on food he has rendered nonnutritive. During one session when he was "in touch," I pointed out how the lack of consistency in his thinking is death to the scholarship he says he aspires to. He agreed. When F. Scott Fitzgerald wrote, "The test of a first-rate intelli- gence is the ability to hold two opposed ideas in the mind at the same time, and still retain the ability to function" (1945, p. 69), he was not thinking of a splitting borderline!

While "in touch" and not splitting, David sees things more or less in con- text, which is to say situated in a consensual fabric of ongoing intentions and meanings, his and others. What he says makes sense and sounds "right." But when he uses the splitting defense and is "in flight," that context dis- appears. His observations and judgments are wrenched out of the consensual fabric and become grossly, sometimes bizarrely, distorted, at times appear- ing to be the fruit of primary process thinking (Searles, 1969; Sternbach et al., 1992).

Splitting Results in David's Living between Various Worlds

I have already shown how David inhabits what seems like eight different "worlds" (see journal entry for July 28, 1984):

(1) Autonomous world ↔ (2) Infantalized world
(3) Idea world ↔ (4) Business world
(5) Legal world ↔ (6) Criminal world
(7) Heterosexual world ↔ (8) Homosexual world

The "in flight" David lives less *in* any of these worlds than somewhere *between them*. While oscillating back and forth, he can't take root anywhere. I would like to look briefly now at how he moves in, through, and between these different worlds.

1, 2. (1) David does make some autonomous moves. In 1982, for example, he went from a hospital to a halfway house and from there to several apartments. He took graduate courses. He read a number of books. (2) But he did not work and earn a living, though he made numerous inquiries about jobs. He not only takes his father's support but expects and demands it.

3, 4. (3) David spends a great deal of time "reading, writing, and thinking," as he puts it. The people he spends most of his time with either have Ph.D.s or are working on them. He talks constantly about going to graduate school. (4) He also speaks by phone often to a close friend from Atlanta who is a very successful stockbroker, keeping up with the latest developments in the market. He even got involved for a time in the market recently, speculating with $100,000 he raised from two men he barely knew. David lives in the "idea world" and the "business world," but only to a point. Eventually, he loses what autonomy (1) he has in both worlds, becoming infantalized (2) and backing off (he balked at going to graduate school and stopped trading stocks after several months).

5, 6. (5) David conforms to the law, for the most part, probably because he recognizes most of what is out there is, strictly speaking, "legal." (6) But if I hear him correctly, he is biding his time until, as he says, he is "light on my feet again." He speaks often (usually obliquely) of doing illegal things later on, particularly stealing and dealing in drugs. As far as I can tell, when David considers working, he is ultimately thinking of doing something criminal or subversive. I have speculated before if David wasn't a borderline, he might have become a "successful" criminal. But the paralyzing anxiety that arises when he considers doing something legal must also come when he considers doing something illegal.

7, 8. (7) After leaving the hospital in June 1982, David had several brief sexual encounters with women and a sexual relationship with a woman who was about ten years younger than he that lasted several months. As he spent less time with (and talked less about) women, he spent more time with (and talked more about) men. (8) He admits having sexual feelings for men since what he calls "a near miss encounter" with a male teacher when he was in prep school. While living in the same house with the biophysicist-musician, David became close to him and often spoke of him in ways suggesting sexual longing. He acknowledges having a problem "separating," as he put it, from his friend after he moved to New York and being depressed after he left. He lived in a neighborhood where many gay men live and socialize. He never gave the impression he disapproved of their presence. David denies having any physical contact with men. He continues talking with disinterest and sometimes with contempt about women and with increasing enthusiasm about the men he spends time with.

Unable to live satisfactorily in any of these worlds, David lives in the cracks, as an alien, an extraterrestrial.

BORDERLINE SPLITTING AND SELF-DECEPTION

Because borderline patients who split constitute their experience to suit a particular defensive need, their world is a unique one. It is different in significant ways from the world of someone who does not use the splitting defense. From the point of view of the "nonsplitter," the "splitter" distorts the truth of what is there (i.e., how the world is seen without the splitting defense). While splitting and using the associated defenses of denial, projective identification, devaluation, and fantasy gratification, borderline patients live a fragment of the truth as if it were the whole truth. They transform the situation as it is there (from the perspective of the "nonsplitter") to meet their needs. They cut the world down to their size, to something that makes them less anxious and therefore less uncomfortable. In other words, while attempting to prevent a poorly differentiated, poorly integrated, chronically unstable self from becoming more acutely threatened in the face of some anxious personal challenge, they deceive themselves.

Self-deception is the lie we tell ourselves (as contrasted to the lie we tell others). It is how we trick ourselves out of facing the truth—the reality—of a situation we experience as too painful to acknowledge and live for what it is. Self-deception is universal. We all deceive ourselves, and often. "Every man," Dostoevsky observed, "has some reminiscences which he would not tell to everyone, but only to his friends. He has others which he would not reveal even to his friends, but only to himself, and that in secret. But finally there are still others which a man is even afraid to tell himself, and every decent man has a considerable number of such things stored away" (1960, p. 35).

Dostoevsky was a good psychologist, like so many of the best novelists, playwrights, and poets. He not only intuited the essence of self-deception but understood how this defense is rooted in anxiety. Ibsen spoke of the "vital lie," the lie we must tell ourselves—and live—to survive. What the French existential philosopher Gabriel Marcel (1965) said about betrayal—

that it seems forced on us by the very shape of our world—is equally true of self-deception.

In his film *Rashomon*, Akira Kurosawa interrogates the phenomenon of self-deception by having the three protagonists of a violent act (a rape followed by a murder) give three not only different but incompatible versions of what happened. Each tells the court what is necessary to preserve his or her sense of what honor is. Who is lying? We never find out. We are left wondering what truth is and under what conditions truth may be known. The following is a brief exchange between the Commoner and the Priest, two peripheral characters in the film whose honor is not at stake in constituting the "truth" of the violent act (Kurosawa, 1969, pp. 88–89).

COMMONER: Well, men are only men. That's why they lie. They can't tell the truth, not even to themselves.

PRIEST: That may be true. But it's because men are so weak. That's why they lie. That's why they must deceive themselves.

We constitute the "truth" of a situation to suit our needs, to preserve our "honor," to make the foundation on which we must stand or be no one at all.

Sartre, in *Being and Nothingness* (1956, pp. 47–70), insists that consciousness is transparent to itself (i.e., that the self—what he calls Being-for-itself—is a unity and knows what it thinks and does). He makes this point an important part of his rebuttal to Freud, who distinguishes between conscious (ego) and unconscious (id) knowing and behavior and proposes a censor (superego) that keeps experience unacceptable to the ego out of consciousness. With a nod to Sartre, it is tempting to speculate that self-deceivers know–do not know those facets of reality they deny at a given moment by simply knowing where *not* to look! Sartre saw self-deception as a particular way of using one's freedom—a choice made to avoid facing an anxious, unpalatable truth. Self-deceivers *trick* themselves, through "an attitude of excuse," into believing what is necessary to keep the ever-needy self on the course of its "project," a Sartrean notion that encompasses and transcends the more familiar notion of identity. When one's project is threatened by some encroaching facet of self–other–world, the "trick of bad faith" may come into play to defensively neutralize the anxiety.

No example in Sartre's *Being and Nothingness* reveals more fully the essence of self-deception than this account of a mother who first believed her daughter's accusation of sexual abuse by her father then, in the daughter's words, "eventually chose not to know about the incest again." The mother told the victim's therapist: "I have no reason not to believe my daughter, but if I believe her I'll have to leave my husband, and I can't live without him" (Cutting, 1993, pp. 52 and 54). The mother denies what would effectively end her marriage—talking herself out of what she formerly "knew."

Of course, as soon as self-deception begins to involve others, as it ultimately almost always does, these others are deceived as well.

Fingarette (1969; Haight, 1980) both challenges and affirms Sartre's theory of self-deception and makes two important contributions to understanding this phenomenon. First, he sees what is avoided or denied in self-deception is not "spelled-out" (i.e., made explicit, or thematized, in either thought, language, or behavior). This is a kind of denial, what he calls a "disavowal," a way of keeping part of the truth of a situation out of conscious awareness. Second, Fingarette recognizes what a person disavows in self-deception is foreign to, and in conflict with, his or her perceived identity. Self-deception is a way of dealing with a conflict of this kind by denying some facet of it — whatever links the person to the conflict. The mother in the example above who denies the convincing evidence her husband molested their daughter says, in effect, this cannot be true because it would destroy my life. Is an unconscious censor at work here, as Freud claims? To Sartre, the deception is a deliberate choice (how, he asks, would an unconscious censor know what to disavow [deny] if the threat were not perceived in some way by the conscious ego?). To Fingarette, the deception is a failure to make sufficiently explicit something important enough to be made explicit — so important in an anxious and threatening way that spelling it out is deliberately avoided.

We all deceive ourselves, but borderline patients who split, because of the very structure of their illness and emergent personality (Engel, 1980; Goodman, 1991), deceive themselves to a greater degree. To say borderline patients act impulsively (i.e., in an unplanned, unmeasured way) is akin to saying their choices are often of the all-or-nothing, black-and-white kind that exclude the "middle ground." Surely, it could be argued to the degree self-deception involves a choice, that choice is less deliberate for borderline patients who split than for those who do not use this defense (in Freudian terms, the result of a greater dominance of conscious processes by the unconscious). Particularly during periods of anxiety and stress, self-deception driven by splitting appears to be activated by a "hair trigger."

David: Self-Deception through Borderline Splitting

The splitting defense seems to serve as a "template" for much of what David thinks, says, and does and to drive his self-deception. When David was "in flight" during our sessions (splitting, denying, projecting, etc.), he did not seem "behind his words," as Hellmuth Kaiser describes the response this bad faith evokes in the therapist (Fierman, 1965). In contrast, during those periods when he was "in touch" (not splitting, etc.), he did seem to mean what he said.

The "in touch" David has keen insight into the defenses of the "in flight" David and sees vividly how these defenses limit him. "I hate this illness. I can beat it," he says often when not defending. "How could I have done this to myself?" He talks as if he has the will and the resolve to turn his illness around. The "in flight" David, on the other hand, has no insight into his situation whatever because as he splits and uses the other defenses that accompany borderline splitting, he is blinded by his pathological constitution of himself, others, and the world. "I've always felt better away from therapists," he says often while "in flight," denying he has any problems. "There is no such thing as mental illness," he would insist. "It's an invention of the authorities."

David revealed his global self-deception often during our sessions but never more strikingly than through five declarations I will recall now. These acknowledgments of his true feelings and motives show the fundamental dishonesty with which he faces the world—the changing masks and poses he uses as fronts for his chameleon existence (Muller, 1987, pp. 103–132).

1. For as long as we worked together, David talked about going back to school to get a Ph.D. in an interdisciplinary program of literature and philosophy. "The university is the only place I've ever felt at home," he said, again and again. "I won't be happy anywhere else." He criticized his father bitterly for telling him, "You can't eat books," when he was considering applying to graduate school while he worked in Atlanta between 1976 and 1978, and he claimed his father's "disapproval" is the reason he didn't apply then.

   About a year after we began our work, David's father agreed to help him financially if he were accepted into a graduate program. David made a list of the schools that interested him most, wrote for catalogs, and talked to various people about what these schools had to offer. At least twice when I brought up the subject of his going to graduate school and reminded him of his father's promise to help support him, he said, *What I should do is talk baby talk to him for a while, then take the money and run.*

2. David misrepresents himself about going to graduate school in another way, too. "I should have done it in 1976," he told me often. "I could have done it then," he insisted. *"I was always good at fooling people."* In other words, at the time he told me this, David no longer felt up to "fooling people" and thus no longer up to going to graduate school.

3. While describing a sexual advance made by one of his teachers when he was in prep school, David said, *"I wish now I hadn't turned him down. It cost me Yale"* (implying, I assume, the teacher could have gotten him into Yale). Neither before nor since, did David give any hint he was interested in Yale. I doubt he ever was. What refusing the teacher did cost him was his chance to do something about his sexual feelings for men. I believe David has repressed these feelings since at least that time and now regrets doing so, particularly since meeting the biophysicist-musician, who seems to have helped him crystallize his latent homosexual feelings. Most of the time, David splits and denies these feelings.

4. While telling me about a woman he knows who talked about the possibility of their getting married, David said, after a long discussion of the pros and cons, *"She didn't have enough money to take care of me."* He sounded as if this is his ultimate criterion for marriage.

5. David made many attempts to find a job, half-hearted attempts for the most part. Once, he talked with an acquaintance who worked for a utility company about the possibility of getting a job there. *"He thinks I'm just a nice guy down on my luck who's looking for some honest work,"* David told me. *"Just wait. He'll find out."* It was clear from David's tone what he wanted from the company was a chance to "steal it blind," as he said he wished he had done when he worked for his father's company, and which he said he did when he worked at a bookstore in Chicago (1978–1979). He told me he stole more than $2,000 from that bookstore.

Each of these five revelations shows a profound difference between the face David presents to the world on an important issue and his true feelings which, through splitting, he has kept even from himself (in a certain sense) for much of his life. He split off and denied his sexual feelings for men and his criminal intentions as he lived mostly in, and moved through, the heterosexual and "legal" worlds. In each case, the self-deception was revealed through a proposed deception of another person. The lie David lives for himself necessarily becomes a broader lie when he deals with others. The revelations on all five issues came at moments of extreme stress for him, as he struggled to find himself in each issue. It was as if, under great pressure, he could no longer maintain the lie. Momentarily, the mask slipped off and the truth slipped out *de profundis*.

PART III

Three Global Analytical Views

I have tried to understand David's psychopathology here in three ways:

1. From an Existential–Phenomenological Perspective
2. As an Instance of Karen Horney's "Resigned Person"
3. As an Instance of Borderline Personality Disorder

Each of the three perspectives offers a different kind of insight. Ultimately, the interpretations are compatible and complementary.

Chapter 6

ॐ

An Existential–Phenomenological Perspective

David has told me the following story several times. During the first year he worked for his father in Atlanta (1976), he took two courses in philosophy at a university there. He was also playing the stock market. He had been following a particular stock closely for some time. One day, after finishing an afternoon class, he learned the stock had suddenly dropped. "I lost $8,000 during that class," he said.

The comment itself did not strike me as unusual, but something in his tone the last time he told me the story did. He had been talking about whether he would go into business or go to graduate school with the idea of eventually getting a teaching job. Listening to him tell how he had lost all that money during a philosophy class, I got the impression that to him this meant he had no reason to commit himself to either business or graduate school. He had no obligation to go any further. He couldn't win either way.

This story was my first clue that David is caught between two worlds— his mother's and his father's—which he cannot reconcile, integrate, or live. His mother comes from a family of physicians, Greek Orthodox priests, and scholars. In college, she studied literature, philosophy, and the piano, seriously. His father, on the other hand, comes from a family of businessmen. He started college but did not graduate because he had to earn a living. According to David, he has little regard for any academic study that does not have a practical payoff. "You can't eat those books you read," he advised his son.

Two worlds. To David, the world of his mother represents what is high, ascetic, sacred, appreciative of art and study, feminine. The world of his father, in contrast, stands for what is base, worldly, profane, concerned only with making money, masculine. David has a foot in each world, and lives fragments from each world: he has a large library and likes to read and discuss ideas; he idolizes certain writers and professors; many of the people he spends time with are Ph.D.s; he talks about going to graduate school. But he has also made money on the stock market, admires the power of people high up in the corporate world, worked as an adolescent in his father's business, routinely talks on the phone to a stockbroker friend in Atlanta about the market, and reads *The Wall Street Journal*.

But David cannot make enough of a commitment to either world to take hold in it, stake a claim, and do something meaningful and productive there. Instead, he makes timid forays, first in one world then in the other, always hedging, always retreating in disappointment, disillusion, and defeat after a short time. Unable to live fully in either world and unable to integrate the parts of both worlds that appeal to him, he lives paralyzed between them. Committing himself to the academic life would mean moving toward and identifying with his mother; but that would be tantamount to becoming reconciled to her coldness and to her disapproval of him. Committing himself to the business world would mean moving toward and identifying with his father; but that would be tantamount to selling out to what he sees as a "lower" order and to a bourgeois capitalistic society he despises. Finding both worlds ultimately uninhabitable, he lives in a no-man's land.

David has said several times he feels his mother married his father for money. "She liked the bucks," he told me. After her marriage, according to David, she lost most of her interest in literature and art. She turned her energies to raising money for the symphony and for various charities and to keeping up with the Atlanta social scene. David disapproves of all this. He sees it as a sellout.

David is perpetually angry, depressed, and anxious. It is time to inquire about what these feelings mean.

Anger

Implicit in David's anger at his parents is the claim things should have been otherwise: he had a *right* to be given more authority in the business and to take it over when his father retired; his mother had the *obligation* to approve of what he did and accept him as he was. When his father sold the business, other paths (choices) were open to David—other jobs, graduate school, travel. To embark on one of these, however, he would have had to deal with the disappointment he felt following his father's rejection. He would have had to acknowledge what happened as a loss and do the work of mourning it. He would have had to take up the pain of loss and strike out on another path in spite of it. He would have had to see his father's side of the situation and, to some extent, forgive him for what he saw as an injustice. But instead, David responded to the situation something like this: If I can't have things my way, I won't have them at all. It's too difficult to go on considering what happened to me, what my father did to me. Because I have been so wronged, it is no longer necessary for me to put one foot in front of another, struggle for what I want, take risks, accept setbacks, and in general act as if what happens to me will be a consequence of what action I take.

David's anger at his parents is a choice, though he does not recognize it as such, and it serves a purpose. It is a "solution" to his disappointment and a way out of the conflict that disappointment created. It is an escape. David has magically transformed his world so there is no longer any need for him to go on. He has convinced himself — really, tricked himself into believing — this is so. Anger absolves him of the necessity to continue. And he luxuriates in that anger.

To take another job or go to graduate school after his father liquidated the business would have required David to be patient until his efforts came to fruition. It would have taken time, perhaps years, for something to come of his gambit. But David saw no need for patience. He wanted something — a part of his father's business — and he wanted it *then*. Not willing to put in the time and effort required to achieve an alternate "healthy" goal through instrumental action, he chose an immediate pathological one instead. Anger gave him the gratification he needed. And he received his reward instantly. No waiting required. No risk, either. Satisfaction guaranteed.

Depression

The world of a person who is depressed is different from that of someone who is not depressed. Jean-Paul Sartre gives a differential description of these two worlds, as well as an intentional explanation of what it means to go from a "normal" world to a depressed one. He calls this process a "magical transformation" (Sartre, 1948; Muller, 1991b, pp. 39–40).

People may become depressed in response to some negative experience or to a situation they constitute as unsatisfactory. They may suffer a loss or a disappointment, a betrayal, or a failure.

How did David become depressed? His world was once a highly differentiated one: he went here and there, saw this person and that person, did this and that, all in accord with the value he placed on these interactions, even though he may not have recognized it explicitly. He was willing to be patient, to tolerate setbacks, to overcome obstacles, to take risks. He acted as if what he did would influence what happened to him. In short, he acted instrumentally.

But then the family business, which his father promised would be his one day, was sold out from under him. David was bitterly disappointed. He felt betrayed by his father. A road had come to an end for him. He was obligated, therefore, to find a new road. But this is precisely what he did not wish to do. Other jobs were offered to him, but he refused them. With one possibility closed off, he denied the need to pursue new possibilities. This, he felt, would be too much to ask. How could the world make this demand of him, considering what he had been through? Lacking the will to go on in spite of the disappointment, he acted as if the world no longer required anything of him, or him of it.

In short, David has "magically transformed" his world from an instrumental, highly differentiated one, where certain persons and things were valued and pursued, to a world that is undifferentiated and homogenized, where no one or nothing is valued. His world became, as Sartre describes it, "a totally undifferentiated structure . . . an affectively neutral reality" (1948, p. 65). David is depressed! His depression is a way of making it unnecessary for him to overcome the disappointment of losing the family business and go on to something else. In effect, he is depressed because he *chooses* to be depressed by refusing to take the next step and overcome his disappointment with a new victory. He has stopped acting instrumentally and now acts in a "magical" way, as if the normal requirements—the requirements for people who live in the "normal," instrumental world—no longer apply to him.

Being depressed (de-pressed), David lives life heavily, as a burden. The weight of the world he spurns pushes him down. His body is stiff. He has trouble walking. The loneliness of his isolation is crushing. He can spurn the world, but he cannot get rid of it any more than he can get rid of himself. While rejecting new possibilities, he regrets the loss of these possibilities. Somehow, though he is reluctant to acknowledge this, he knows he is cheating himself. But he does not have the will to choose out of the depression that cheats him.

How does one transform the instrumental world into a magical one? By a trick of "bad faith," Sartre feels. We lie to ourselves. We tell ourselves we cannot go beyond our disappointment, that it is *too difficult* to do so—which, of course, relieves us of the obligation of having to put one foot in front of the other and try again. People who are depressed have lied to themselves about what they are capable of doing in the face of a negative experience or situation they constitute as unsatisfactory. Their depression is an inauthentic choice of the magical world over the instrumental world vis-à-vis that experience. To Sartre, to deceive oneself is to be inauthentic.

What it means to magically transform one's world through depression (and anger) is not an easy notion to grasp. There are other ways to "transform" the mundane, baseline world we inhabit most of the time, and perhaps the magical transformation Sartre proposes as the basis for depression would be easier to understand if it were contrasted with some of these other transformations.

After a long period of physical exercise, the world seems a brighter, more vital, more highly delineated and differentiated place. I, too, feel brighter, have more energy, and feel more up to doing what I need to do. I constitute myself as being more capable of acting instrumentally. This is an "up" transformation. If, on the other hand, I drink several vodkas and tonics, I change my world in a different way. The edges of the instrumental world are no longer as sharp as before; they have been rounded off somewhat. The burden of what I will have to face tomorrow does not seem so heavy. The pain of a recent disappointment does not seem so acute. For a few hours, something that has been bothering me recedes into the background, and I may think of other things. This is a "down" transformation. To some degree, my world has been dedifferentiated.

Both the physical "up" and the alcoholic "down" are transformations that come about through chemical substances — adrenalin and neuropeptides for the physical "up" transformation, ethanol for the alcoholic "down" transformation. And each is reversible over the course of several hours. The magical transformation Sartre believes leads to depression, on the other hand, originates in how I constitute myself and my world, and alters the very essence of that world by denying its instrumentality, and thus its reality, almost certainly altering brain neurochemistry in the process. (This discussion of Sartre's notion of the "magical transformation" in depression was taken from a longer work [Muller, 1991b, pp. 39–40]).

Anxiety

David is also anxious. In refusing to take a new road after the disillusioning experience with his father's business and face the uncertainties and consequent anxiety he would encounter by doing this — in other words, *existential anxiety* — he set himself up for the *pathological anxiety* that comes with self-deception. There is no way he can take a stand in a world he has magically transformed to rid himself of the need to take a stand. Any effort he makes to do this necessarily comes into conflict with a world of his creation that does not require this effort.

Unlike existential anxiety, pathological anxiety undermines the very sense of self. While existential anxiety can be the basis for creative action, pathological anxiety necessarily short-circuits creative action. Not only must David deal with the anxious (existential) feelings that accompany thoughts such as "I'm not up to it" and "I can't do it," but with the anxious feelings that originate in his magically transformed (pathological) belief that "There is no reason for me to do it."

The magical transformations of anger and depression make it impossible for David to confront — and overcome — the anxiety that inheres in any choice. Thus, when he considers his possibilities in business, the stock market, or academia, he becomes pathologically anxious because of the way he constitutes his world. Being anxious is a way of being in a situation. And when one is in a situation anxiously, either existentially or pathologically, the sense of who one is is radically called into question. Identity becomes problematic. This is the existential–phenomenological meaning of anxiety (Fischer, 1988).

Chapter 7

ε**

An Instance of Karen Horney's "Resigned Person"

Karen Horney (1885–1952) identified and described three major neurotic personality types, which she saw as originating in three neurotic solutions, chosen early in life, to the problem of basic anxiety. The data of David Helbros's case are consistent with one of these — the "resignation" solution.

David's psychopathology will be reanalyzed in the light of Horney's theory. First, however, it is necessary to look into the basis for Horney's typology and summarize her description of the "resigned person."

Basis for Horney's Typology

Horney discarded Freud's notions of instinct and drive and came to understand neurosis as a failure of interpersonal relations. She saw neurosis as "a disturbance in one's relation to self and to others." Her theory was presented in its fullest development in her seminal work, *Neurosis and Human Growth* (1950).

Implicit in Horney's theory of neurotic transformation are the notions of freedom and choice. Though her language is strongly psychoanalytic — she often uses the quantitative terms of natural science — she is phenomenological to the degree of punctiliously describing what she sees as three neu-

Some of the discussion in this section appeared first in R. J. Muller, Karen Horney's "Resigned Person" Heralds DSM-III-R's Borderline Personality Disorder, *Comprehensive Psychiatry* 34 (1993): 264–272.

rotic personality types, always staying close to the phenomenon of the pathology, not distancing herself from it by imposing constructs between what she observed and what she wrote. Horney is interested in the meaning of a particular neurotic choice, the purpose it serves, and how it functions as a defense in the solution to a specific problem in interpersonal relations. She gives detailed empirical descriptions of pathological self-other–world relations and, in the process, overflows her psychoanalytic perspective.

Horney sees neurosis as originating in a particular way of dealing with anxiety, which she defines as "the feeling of being isolated and helpless in a world conceived as potentially hostile." The feelings of isolation and hopelessness come from being in a situation that is lived ambiguously; in the face of an ambiguous situation, I am no longer certain who I am, who the other is, or where I stand vis-à-vis him or her. Who I am is called into question, and I find this ambiguity uncomfortable because I want to know who I am (and who the other is). I am not at ease with the ambiguity that has been introduced. The world is no longer familiar now, but alien and hostile. I become anxious.

Horney recognized that in the face of an anxious situation, a person may move — respond — in one of three ways: *toward, against,* or *away from.* Emotionally healthy people can move in one, two, or all three ways depending on the meaning of the situation to them. They are (relatively) flexible and spontaneous. They can see the ambiguity in the situation, take it up, and respond accordingly.

For example, a friend whose opinion I respect may disagree with me on a major issue. If I am emotionally healthy, I will be able to hold on to my position, or alter it if my friend is finally convincing, and still maintain a sense of who I am and of who he or she is. The implicit response of emotionally healthy people to such a situation would be something like, "Can we agree to disagree?" They can live with the ambiguity in the disagreement itself and with the ambiguity the disagreement introduces into the friendship. "Perhaps my friend is seeing something that I am missing" is a thought they could entertain without undermining their sense of who they are. Responding this way, the healthy person moves to a degree, toward, against, and away from the disagreeing friend appropriately and realistically.

But for those who have not, to give a nod to Erik Erikson (1950), "solved" the problem of basic anxiety early in life, that kind of open, flexible, and spontaneous response would not be possible. In the hope of avoiding the ambiguity in the situation, and ultimately the ambiguity of *who they are* and *who the other is* in the face of the situation, these people may be able to move in one way only, either toward, or against, or away from, excluding the other possibilities. In doing this, they preserve their notion of who they are (and who the other is, as well) at the expense of neurotically transforming and distorting that who. They narrow the possibilities of their response, take a part for the whole, and live that part defensively rather than spontaneously.

Continuing with the example given above, let us look at how someone who had responded to an anxious situation early in life by adopting each of the three neurotic solutions to an anxious experience (what Horney calls basic anxiety) and then continued to live out this solution might respond later in life to a disagreement with a close friend.

1. The solution of moving exclusively "toward" is a self-effacing solution. Those who have made this response to basic anxiety early in life will seek accommodation at any price. They will surrender their point of view because they are afraid of losing the friendship, support, or love of the other if they stand their ground. They seek the approval of others in everything they do. They will go to any length to avoid taking a stand in a conflicted situation with someone who is important to them. "Of course, you're entirely correct," the self-effacing person would say to his or her disagreeing friend.

2. The solution of moving exclusively "against" is an expansive solution. Its purpose (meaning) is to be always in control and to master the other. For those who have made this neurotic transformation early in life, to admit the other might be correct and they incorrect would be to suffer defeat at the hand of the other. Being "right," they retain control; being "wrong," they lose control which, for them, is everything. For someone who has opted for the expansive solution, there can be no mutuality with another person. "You're crazy," he or she would say to a disagreeing friend, not yielding an inch.

3. The solution of moving exclusively "away from" is a solution of resignation — literally, a resignation from the situation and from any person involved in it. It's purpose (meaning) is to be free from anything or anyone that might call for taking a stand. To those who make this fundamental choice, there is nothing worth putting themselves on the line for. To move "toward" involves a risk of one kind, to move "against," a risk of another — better to just stay out of the whole thing. These people feel if they can just stay uninvolved, they will be safe and out of harm's way. "What difference does it make?" a "resigned person" would say to his or her disagreeing friend. "Let's forget the whole thing."

Description of the "Resigned Person"

To read Horney's account of the "resigned person" is to see David in every paragraph. In the hope of doing justice to her psychological insight and skill as an observer, I have excerpted, verbatim, parts of the description of the resignation phenomenon she gives in *Neurosis and Human Growth* (1950, pp. 259–290), fashioning these summaries, somewhat arbitrarily, around eight cardinal points.

1. How can we account for this appeal of [resignation]? . . . There were often cramping influences against which the child could not rebel openly, either because they were too strong or too intangible. . . . He may have received affection, but in a way that more repelled than warmed him. . . . There was an environment which made explicit and implicit demands for him to fit in this way or that way and threatened to engulf him without sufficient regard for his individuality, not to speak of encouraging his personal growth. (p. 275)

2. [The resigned person is] an *onlooker at himself and his life.* . . . [He may] develop a picture of himself replete with a wealth of candid observation. But . . . all this knowledge [changes nothing] . . . for none of his findings has been an experience for him. Being an onlooker at himself means just that: not actively participating in living and unconsciously refusing to do so. In analysis he tries to maintain the same attitude. He may be immensely interested, yet that interest may stay for quite a while at the level of a fascinating entertainment—and nothing changes.

When the analyst perceives his "avoidance" tactics and tells him, "Look here, this is *your* life that is at stake," the patient does not quite know what he is talking about. For him it is not his life but a life which he observes, and in which he has no active part. (pp. 260–261)

[His expectations from therapy] are limited and again negative. Analysis he feels should rid him of disturbing symptoms. . . . Whatever he hopes for should come easily, without pain or strain. The analyst should do the work. . . . He is willing to wait patiently for the analyst to present the clue that will solve everything. . . . He may not mind observing things in himself. What he always minds is the effort of changing. (pp. 262–263)

[The resigned person] may have had a long experience with the analyst's patience and understanding and yet, under duress, may feel that the analyst would drop him at a moment's notice in case of open opposition. (p. 278)

3. [The resigned person avoids any serious striving for achievement and is averse to putting out any sustained effort.] He minimizes or flatly denies his assets, and settles for less. (p. 261)

He may compose beautiful music, paint pictures, write books—in his imagination. This is an alternative means of doing away with both aspiration and effort. He may actually have good and original ideas on some subject, but the writing of a paper would require initiative and the arduous work of thinking the ideas through and organizing them. So the paper remains unwritten. He may have a vague desire to write a novel or a play, but waits for the inspiration to come. Then the plot would be clear and everything would flow from his pen.

What does he actually want to do with his life? The question has never occurred to him and is easily discarded, as if it were none of his concern. (p. 262)

[He believes] that it is *better* not to wish or to expect anything. Sometimes this goes with a conscious pessimistic outlook on life, a sense of its being futile anyhow and of nothing being sufficiently desirable to make an effort for it. (p. 263)

4. [He] may . . . have plenty of transient sexual relations, backing out of them sooner or later. They should not, as it were, degenerate into love. (p. 264)

5. In or around adolescence he often does things which show remarkable energies and gifts. He may be resourceful, surmount economic handicaps, and make a place for himself. He may be ambitious in school, first in his class, excel in debating or some progressive political movement. At least there often is a period in which he is comparatively alive and interested in many things, in which he rebels against the tradition in which he has grown up and thinks of accomplishing something in the future.

Subsequently there is often a period of distress: of anxiety, of depression, of despair about some failure or about some unfortunate life situation in which he has been involved through his very rebellious streak. After that the curve of his life seems to flatten out. People say that he got "adjusted" and settled down. (p. 269)

6. If they have no financial means [resigned persons] may take occasional jobs or else sink down into a parasitic existence. Or, if moderate means are available, they rather restrict their needs to the utmost in order to feel free to do as they please. The things they do, however, often have the character of hobbies. Or they may succumb to a more or less complete inertia. (p. 282)

The inertia in thinking can be well observed in analysis and often is a great hindrance to work. Simple mental operations become difficult. Whatever is discussed during one hour may then be forgotten — not because of any specific "resistance" but because the patient lets the content lie in his brain like a foreign body.

The [inertia] chokes off the very aliveness it was meant to preserve. Hence when his emotional life becomes paralyzed he suffers under the resulting deadness of his feelings more than other patients, and this may be the one thing which he does want to change. (p. 283)

7. The resigned person is a subdued rebel. . . . [Whether his rebelliousness remains passive or becomes active] depends on the relative strength of expansive and self-effacing trends and on the degree of inner aliveness a person has managed to salvage. The stronger his expansive tendencies and the more alive he is, the more easily he will become discontented with the restrictions of his life [and the more active his rebellion will become].

The environmental situation — home, work — may become so unsatisfactory that the person finally stops putting up with it any longer and in some form or another rebels openly. He may leave his home or his job and become militantly aggressive toward everybody with whom he associates as well as toward conventions and institutions. His attitude is one of "I don't give a damn what you expect of me or think of me." (pp. 283–284)

8. Another characteristic of the resigned person is his *hypersensitivity to influence, pressure, coercion* or *ties* of any kind. This is a relevant factor too in his detachment. Even before he enters into a personal relationship or a group activity the fear of a lasting tie may be aroused. And the question as to how he can extricate himself may be present from the very beginning. Before marriage, this fear may grow into a panic. (p. 266)

The sensitivity to coercion constitutes a real difficulty in analysis — the more difficult the more the patient is not only negative but negativistic. He may harbor an everlasting suspicion that the analyst wants to influence and mold him into a preconceived pattern. This suspicion is all the less accessible the more the patient's inertia prevents him from testing out any suggestion offered, as he is repeatedly asked to do. On the grounds of the analyst's exerting undue influence, he may refute any question, statement, or interpretation that implicitly or explicitly attacks some neurotic position of his. What renders progress in this respect still more difficult is the fact that he will not express his suspicion for a long time, because he dislikes friction. (p. 267)

David: A "Resigned Person"

By matching the data of David's case with each of the eight cardinal points from Horney's descriptive typology, I will show how these data are consistent with what she calls the resignation solution to the problem of basic anxiety. (It has been shown that these eight points from Horney's description of the "resigned person" match DSM-III-R's criteria for border-line personality disorder [Muller, 1993].)

1. **How can we account for the appeal of resignation?** Horney feels the resigned person was not encouraged sufficiently as a child to become his or her own person, and whatever encouragement may have been given had unpleasant consequences. It is as if these children could receive affection only on their parents' terms, only if they did what the parents wanted. The initial autonomous moves "toward" and "against" their parents bring these children pain.(basic anxiety), so they "resign" from any possible future conflict by not moving "toward" or "against" again, but "away from."

David's basic complaint against his mother is that she would never accept him as he was. At some point we can imagine him feeling he could never please her, at least not on terms acceptable to him, and so he stopped trying. Several years ago, when David showed his mother a paper he had written on Camus, her only comment was that there were several typographical errors. "How could you hand in something like that?" she asked. From what he has told me, I doubt David could please his father either.

The notion of David being caught between "two worlds"—his mother's and his father's—explored in the preceding section also has relevance here. To move "toward" his mother, to try to please her by becoming an academic professional, writer, or artist, would be to give in to the demands for her approval and to sanction her world, which he had come to despise. To move "toward" his father and go into business or the stock market seriously would be to acquiesce to the father's world, which he also despised. Moving "toward" and "against" his mother and father by identifying with what they stood for may have become too painful for David. To spare himself future conflict and disappointment, he may have moved "away from" both parents, disengaging himself from the conflict. But through splitting, he reengaged in an even greater pathological conflict driven by an oscillating identification–nonidentification with them that ultimately neutralized any movement one way or the other.

2. **The resigned person is an onlooker at himself and his life. He complies with the "rules" of therapy, but to no therapeutic effect. He is angry at the therapist, but holds back his ultimate criticism for fear of being deserted by him.** David is a master at distancing himself from his feelings by intellectualizing and rationalizing. He talks about his problems eloquently and incisively and with all kinds of insight. But none of this insight touches his life. It is as if he were talking about someone else. Right up to the last day he worked with Harris, he expected Harris to come up with something that would "solve" his problem. At bottom, David believes the solution is out of his hands and that it must come from the outside. Something or someone else must change. He wants to be free of his pain, but *he* does not want to change. When David was in the hospital for six months in 1980, he

told me, he followed the regimen precisely. He took part in the group therapy sessions, participated in the planned activities, and got a good deal of exercise running, playing tennis, boxing, and swimming. "I did everything they asked me to do at the hospital," he said. "I played all their little games." Games, exactly. Because it was a game, most of what he did at the hospital did not touch him, and he did not heal.

Not only would David not cut himself loose from Harris, in spite of his reservations about his effectiveness as a therapist; he felt Harris might *drop him.* "He would have probably been glad to get rid of me," David said.

3. **The resigned person avoids any serious striving for achievement and is averse to putting out any sustained effort.** Being paralyzed between two worlds — the "higher" world of academia and art he associates with his mother and the "lower" world of business and the stock market he associates with his father — David is not required to achieve anything in either. He is relieved of the obligation of doing something productive, testing himself out and putting himself on the line. He will go to graduate school or write something — someday.

David undercuts the long-range goals he considers by telling himself the end result just isn't worth it. To him, the academic world isn't the "real" world. But neither is the business world. (I have come to the conclusion that the real world for David, the only world in which he can function at present, is the pathologically transformed world of his illness.) "Academicians never take risks in the real world," he has said often. "Anyone can make money in business, it's no challenge," he has said just as often.

4. **The resigned person may have numerous sexual relations, backing out of them sooner or later. They should not, as it were, degenerate into love.** David's sexual history fits this brief description perfectly. He says he has had intercourse with about five hundred women since becoming sexually active at thirteen (this number is probably exaggerated, but by any standard David has had numerous sexual partners). He claims he has "enjoyed" sex with only three. He mentioned his ex-wife and Sally.

I have little doubt David was frightened by how much Sally meant to him ("Sally didn't realize how much I needed to get away from her"). Yet, when she became involved with someone else soon after he left this city, he was deeply hurt and resentful. It appears David was not willing to take responsibility for what he felt for Sally. He invited her to visit him in Atlanta and even asked her to live with him there. But he was not willing to make any commitment to her and continued to have sexual relations with a number of other women.

5. **In and around adolescence he often does things which show remarkable energies and gifts.** David claims, with a stake from his father, he made $100,000 in the stock market before he was twenty. He advised his friends on how to invest, and they too made money. David was also a successful

gambler during his late adolescence. He made enough at cards to pay part of his college tuition. His academic performance was uneven. He would do well for a semester or two, then not so well. In high school, he played football and ran track. He worked in his father's business during that time and, as he put it, learned it from the inside out. He was, by his standards, successful with women.

At twenty-one, a serious relationship with a woman ended, sending him into a major depression. He sought psychiatric help, and was later hospitalized. (This therapeutic relationship ended when David and his psychiatrist, a woman about ten years older than he, had intercourse in her office.) In college, David was active in the antiwar movement, participated in rallies and marches, and avoided the draft. He also became heavily involved with drugs for two years during that time.

Clearly, adolescence was a hopeful, though not untroubled period for David. He must have thought of himself as having a future, quite possibly in his father's business. He had developed many talents and acquired some skills. Looking back, it seems he accomplished more during adolescence than during any later period. In a sense, everything afterward was downhill.

6. **If he has no financial means, the resigned person may sink down into a parasitic existence. If moderate means are available, he may restrict his needs to the utmost in order to feel free to do as he pleases. Or he may succumb to a more or less complete inertia. This inertia bears within it the danger of deterioration.** During the three years before we began therapy, David had what Horney calls "moderate means." He had a series of part-time jobs as cab driver, switchboard operator, and hotel desk clerk. He restricted his activities and expenditures, probably more than his financial situation demanded. During this time David began his demand for financial "reparations" from his father in the form of support, a demand he continued through our fifteen months of work together and after. At times, I can imagine David becoming totally dependent on others or living frugally on the interest of the considerable inheritance he will receive. He recalls with pride how Henry Miller sponged off others in Paris during the 1920s and 1930s while writing *Tropic of Cancer*.

7. **The resigned person is a subdued rebel.** David has been a rebel all his life. In the seventh grade, he organized a book stealing ring. In the eighth grade, he burned religious books. In college, he took part in antiwar demonstrations. David is deeply at odds with the values of this country. He feels capitalism is evil because it exploits workers. He despises his parents' upper-middle-class way of life. He has little regard for social conventions and prefers the company of people from the lower classes. He admires the revolutionary spirit and idolizes revolutionary leaders like Lenin, Castro, Fanon, and Guevara. He acknowledges, however, that he has done little with his revolutionary consciousness except talk from the safety of the sidelines.

David's anger, depression, and anxiety may result in part from a subdued rebellion (i.e., one not actualized and lived out productively). He is paralyzed. In effect, he is a rebel without a lived cause.

8. **The resigned person is hypersensitive to influence, pressure, coercion, or ties of any kind.** Clearly, David is hyperreactive to everyone and everything in his world. He vigorously fights off what he sees as his parents' efforts to make him "normal," "nine-to-five," as he often says. His resistance to my challenging his pathology underlies most of the friction in our sessions. And David feels constantly pressured, too, by how society—"this capitalistic country"—wants him to conform to its rules and standards.

In her description of the behavior of the "resigned person," Horney recognizes that while "resigned" overall, the expansive and self-effacing trends characteristic of the other solutions to the problem of basic anxiety—the solution "against," which involves mastering the situation (the expansive solution) and the solution "toward," which involves identification and merging with the conflicted situation (i.e., the self-effacing solution)—are not entirely eradicated and can coexist in an alternating way as the "resigned person" attempts solutions to intra- and interpsychic conflicts. During an expansive trend,

[in] his feelings about himself he may tend to be his proud self. The attributes, though, of which he is proud—in contrast to the expansive type [who chooses the expansive solution to the problem of basic anxiety]—are in the service of resignation. He is proud of his detachment, his "stoicism," his self-sufficiency, his independence, his dislike of coercion, his being above competition. (Horney, 1950, p. 271)

On the other hand,

if self-effacing trends are in the foreground, resigned people tend to have a low estimate of themselves. They may be timid and feel that they do not amount to much. They may also show certain attitudes which we would hardly recognize as self-effacing, if it were not for our knowledge of the full-fledged self-effacing solution. They are frequently keenly sensitive to the needs of other people, and may actually spend a good deal of their lives in helping others or serving a cause. They often are defenseless toward impositions and attacks and would rather put the blame on themselves than accuse others. They may be overanxious never to hurt others' feelings. They also tend to be compliant. This latter tendency, however, is not determined by a need for affection, as it is in the self-effacing type, but by the need to avoid friction. (Horney, 1950, pp. 271–272)

It seems reasonable that a "resigned person" who experiences alternating expansive and self-effacing trends would exhibit behavior similar to that of a borderline patient who splits. This oscillation of polar opposite constitutions of self–other–world is consistent with the instability of self-image, interpersonal relationships, and mood characteristic of both the "resigned person" and the borderline personality. Horney's observation that only some of her "resigned patients" display alternating expansive and self-effacing trends parallels the clinical observation that only some patients who make DSM-III-R criteria for borderline personality disorder show evidence of using the splitting defense (Muller, 1991a).

As a "resigned person," David showed alternating expansive and self-effacing trends strongly evident during the time we worked together and very likely witnessed by those who knew him outside the therapeutic hour as well.

Chapter 8

ε&

An Instance of Borderline Personality Disorder

This third perspective on David's illness derives from a classification of psychopathology known as borderline personality disorder. Perhaps the term *borderline* is unfortunate because it reminds us of borderline schizophrenia and borderline psychosis. In fact, borderline patients rarely become schizophrenic; and if they do develop psychotic symptoms, these symptoms usually do not last long. One way of understanding the term *borderline* is as signifying an illness with a degree of life disturbance between that experienced by patients with neurotic disorders and those with psychotic disorders.

For the theoretical background on borderline personality disorder necessary to examine David's case, I have drawn mainly from James F. Masterson's description and analysis of this pathology given in *Psychotherapy of the Borderline Adult* (1976) and *The Narcissistic and Borderline Disorders* (1981). Masterson, along with Gunderson (1984), Kernberg (1975, 1982) and Kohut (1971), is one of the principal architects of the current concept of borderline pathology. Although there are significant differences in these authors' formulations of borderline phenomena, I have chosen to emphasize Masterson's presentation because his dynamic theory—particularly the emphasis on oscillating self and object part-units generated by splitting—offers such a satisfying model for understanding David's pathological life-story.

While not explicitly spelled out here, it should be clear from reading the journal and this multiperspectival analysis that David easily meets DSM-III-R criteria for borderline personality disorder (APA, 1987).

Masterson's Formulation of Borderline Personality Disorder

Unlike the quasi-phenomenological language Karen Horney uses to describe the resigned person, Masterson's language is primarily mechanistic and derives from a branch of psychoanalysis known as object relations (Guntrip, 1959). (*Object*, meaning another person, may be as unfortunate a term as *borderline*.) Masterson speaks of an ego split into two parts, of split object relations units, and of object inconstancy. The criticism can be made that this language is not descriptive, that there is no such thing as a "split" ego, or that interpersonal relations can be "split" into "units" such as the "rewarding object relations part-unit" and the "withdrawing object relations part-unit." But reading Masterson's books one cannot fail to recognize that while the language itself may not be descriptive, the phenomena revealed are often seen in clinical practice.

Margaret Mahler (Mahler, Pine, and Bergman, 1975), who closely studied the relationship between infants and their mothers, sees the borderline syndrome as one that originates in the failure of the infant to accomplish the task of separation-individuation. During this period, which occurs during eighteen to thirty-six months, the infant is epigenetically challenged to emerge from symbiosis (mutual dependence) with the mother, strike out on its own, and start the process of becoming its own person. The infant, who still needs the mother, returns to her periodically for reassurance and support.

In normal development, when the mother is sufficiently secure to not be threatened by a lessening dependence of her child, she encourages this process of separation and rewards the child for moves toward autonomy. If, however, the mother is not prepared emotionally to allow her child to become independent because she herself needs to be depended on, she may implicitly or explicitly discourage the child's efforts to separate from her. Sensing this, the child will become anxious and conflicted in the face of further attempts to separate and will experience what Masterson calls "feelings of abandonment," which include depression, rage, panic, guilt, passivity, helplessness, and feelings of emptiness. If the infant is not rewarded (or worse, is actually punished) for its efforts to become independent, it will not feel secure enough to make further moves toward autonomy. This conflict may result in an arrest of psychological growth—a developmental snag—so the capacity of the borderline person to relate to others and to function in the world is seriously diminished. The condition may remain largely asymptomatic during childhood, adolescence, or even early adulthood and become manifest only when the incipient borderline is faced with a serious life crisis.

It should be apparent that Masterson's hypothesis of developmental arrest leading to borderline personality disorder based on Mahler's notions of failed separation-individuation, is strikingly similar to Karen Horney's description of the "resigned person," where the child moves "away from" the parents because its efforts to move both "toward" and "against" them are not sufficiently supported or are unsuccessful for some other reason (Muller, 1993). In both psychodynamic formulations, the infant or child cannot tolerate the ambiguity and concomitant anxiety that come with separating from the unsupporting parents in the move toward autonomy. At this point the borderline splitting defense comes into play.

Borderline Splitting

The purpose of the splitting defense is to keep separate in the infant's consciousness the conflicting affective responses arising from the mother's ambiguity toward its newly declared autonomy. The infant comes to associate pleasure with its reward for remaining dependent on the ("all good") mother and pain with its punishment for attempting to separate from her (the "all bad" mother). By alternately constituting the mother as all-good and all-bad, the infant attempts to preserve its identity by avoiding the ambiguity of experiencing the unsplit reality of a mother who rewards *and* punishes.

A distinction needs to be made between two common uses of the term "splitting" (Muller, 1991a). The *primitive splitting* described above defines a hypothetical defensive process carried out by an infant during separation-individuation. It is postulated that this primitive defense leads later in life to *borderline splitting*, a descriptive term that specifies how some borderline patients constitute their experience of self and others in fragments of alternating polarity (e.g., idealization-devaluation). Primitive splitting is considered a normal defense (i.e., one not leading to serious, chronic psychopathology) *until* separation-individuation (Klein, 1975), when further developmental growth allows higher level defenses to come into play. Presumably, it is the use of this defense *during* and *after* separation-individuation that leads to developmental arrest.

Many, but not all, patients diagnosed as borderline use the splitting defense *(borderline splitting)*. It is a matter of conjecture by Masterson and others whether they do so because during a failed attempt at separation-individuation they used the *primitive splitting* defense beyond what Melanie Klein considered the "normal" time. It should be pointed out that Masterson (1976, 1981) and Kernberg (1984), who consider splitting to be the core defense in borderline pathology, as well as the cause of ego weakness and distorted object relations, define borderline personality disorder somewhat differently than DSM-III-R (1987). While DSM criteria for this disorder are consistent with the use of the splitting defense, many patients fulfill these criteria without splitting. This author (Muller, 1991a) has argued that the borderline personality disorder diagnosis be subtyped according to whether a patient strongly uses the splitting defense. Since borderline splitting is ultimately lived out as *split behavior,* this subtyping could be implemented in harmony with DSM's behavioral stance toward diagnosis. Making this distinction would help reduce the often-criticized heterogeneity of the borderline diagnosis and encourage a more pointed psychotherapeutic challenge of the patient's pathologically split self–other–world constitutions.

In addition to healing split self and split object part-units, psychotherapy for these patients may imply the "healing"—or annealing—of "split" interhemispheric structures as well (Kandel, 1979). If, as this author proposes (Muller, 1992a, *vide infra*), borderline splitting does have a neural substrate, it follows that the splitting borderline patients described by Masterson and Kernberg have a different illness than those caught in the wide net of DSM-III-R's borderline personality disorder diagnosis who do *not* split.

The Split Ego

In the split ego, one "part" functions in response to being rewarded for remaining dependent on the mother, while the "remainder" of the ego tries to deal autonomously with self, other, and world by withdrawing from the mother and is punished for this. The split ego leads to an unintegrated self-image (i.e., a good self–bad self dichotomy).

The Split Object Relations Unit

For the splitting borderline patient, the object relations unit (another person) is split through the internalization of the infant's interactions with the split maternal object (rewarding mother–punishing mother). Consequently, in addition to the mother, others are seen as either all good or all bad as well. Again, the existentially painful ambiguity that is the reality of any involvement with another person—the other is almost always good *and* bad—is denied and defended against through splitting. For as long as the infant (through primitive splitting) and the adolescent or adult (through borderline splitting) can constitute another person or situation exclusively one way or the other—all good *or* all bad—he or she can maintain an identity relating to the less "anxious" split good or bad constitution, although at a cost. Necessarily, this defensive maneuvering occurs at the expense of pathologically distorting the other person or situation, as well as the splitting or split self.

Splitting prevents the borderline patient from achieving object constancy, which is the ability to see objects as whole and constant over time. The result is that the other, who may be seen as all good at one point may be quickly reconstituted as all bad when the relationship is frustrated in some way. The other will be judged at any particular moment according to the changing emotional and cognitive needs of the borderline patient, regardless of the merits of the situation. The split ego and the split object relations unit render this patient incapable of what Matthew Arnold called "seeing life steadily and seeing it whole."

A further consequence of splitting borderline patients' object inconstancy is that they cannot successfully mourn the loss of anyone or anything significant to them. Having altered their constitution of the lost person or negative experience so many times according to the defensive needs of the moment (i.e., changed the meaning), these patients cannot face the loss in its full reality and ambiguity, the starting point for successful mourning (Muller, 1992b). The abandonment depression characterized by Masterson (1976, pp. 228–250) that borderline patients experience so often and so profoundly following loss or disappointment is undoubtedly exacerbated by splitting.

Relation between the Split Object Relations Unit and the Split Ego

For the infant whose autonomous moves toward separation-individuation (eighteen to thirty-six months) are thwarted by the mother (because her own pathology requires that the infant remain dependent on her), the conflict between the developmental call to be autonomous and the mother's discouragement of independence and reward of continued dependence can so overwhelm the infant that, to preserve ego–self–identity, it deintegrates in consciousness its constitution of self and mother into two parts. The *withdrawing object relations part-unit* (WORU) is triggered when the infant attempts to separate from the mother and be autonomous; the *rewarding object relations part-unit* (RORU) comes into play when the infant clings to the mother, maintaining its dependence on her. The infant experiences the mother's unavailability as punishment (the bad mother) and feels guilty when it acts autonomously through the WORU structure. It feels rewarded by her and loved (the good mother) when it clings to her through the RORU structure.

In the table on the next page, Masterson summarizes the relation between WORU and RORU part-object and part-self representations, and the affect that links them.

The WORU and the RORU are each made up of a part-object representation, a part-self representation, and an affect that "links" the two. The infant is rejected by the mother, made to feel angry and frustrated and as though it is bad for acting through the WORU. Conversely, the infant is rewarded by her, made to feel wanted and as though it is good for acting through the RORU.

Masterson's identification of the WORU and the RORU part-units is particularly useful in understanding the dynamics of the splitting borderline patient's behavior. For the borderline patient who splits, the WORU and the RORU are inextricably and dialectically linked. To make any autonomous move, according to Masterson, is to rekindle the feelings of abandonment that occurred when the infant made its first autonomous moves and was discouraged by the mother from doing so. Using a mecha-

Relation between the Part-Object Representation, the Part-Self Representation, and the Accompanying Affect for the WORU and the RORU in Borderline Splitting

	Withdrawing or Aggressive Object Relations Part-Unit (WORU)	Rewarding or Libidinal Object Relations Part-Unit (RORU)
Part-Object Representation	A maternal part-object which is attacking, critical, hostile, angry, withdrawing supplies and approval in the face of assertiveness or other efforts toward separation-individuation.	A maternal part-object which offers approval, support and supplies for regressive and clinging behavior.
Affect	Chronic anger, frustration, feeling thwarted, which cover profound underlying abandonment depression (rage, depression, fear, guilt, passivity and helplessness, emptiness and void).	Feeling good, being fed, gratification of the wish for reunion.
Part-Self Representation	A part-self representation of being inadequate, bad, helpless, guilty, ugly, empty, etc.	A part-self representation of being the good, passive compliant child.

Source: Masterson, 1976, p. 58.

nistic, natural science term, Masterson claims the borderline patient's WORU automatically "activates" the RORU, which may then be projected onto or acted out against the WORU, to defend against the feelings of abandonment and fulfill the wish for reunion with the mother.

The rewarding part-unit (RORU) becomes the borderline's principal defense against the withdrawing part-unit (WORU). In terms of reality, however, both part-units are pathological; it is as if the patient has but two alternatives, viz., either to feel bad and abandoned (the withdrawing part-unit), or feel good (the rewarding part-unit) at the cost of denial of reality and the acting out of self-destructive behavior. (Masterson, 1976, p. 63)

In other words, as soon as the splitting borderline patient attempts an autonomous move of any kind, he or she becomes anxious and conflicted and backs away from the move so as to neutralize the anxiety and conflict. Acknowledging this dynamic associated with borderline splitting does not require postulating primitive splitting as a necessary antecedent. Masterson's description of the splitting defense can be accepted without accepting his developmental explanation for it.

Broadening the Psychoanalytic View on
Borderline Personality Disorder

The theory of borderline splitting proposed by Mahler, Masterson, Kernberg, Kohut, and others is based on a fixation–regression model of psychopathology: something goes wrong at one of the crucial stages of development, and the opportunity to complete the developmental task of that stage is missed or only partly accomplished. A developmental snag occurs, making it more difficult to resolve favorably the issues of the stages that follow, condemning one to repeat throughout life pathological patterns anchored in an epigenetic failure. For borderline personality disorder, the failed developmental task is separation-individuation, and the time period epigenesis purportedly allows for resolving the issues of this stage is eighteen to thirty-six months.

The fixation–regression model of psychopathology has been challenged as reductive, particularly as to the temporal point of origin of pathology and the hard-and-fast link to a specific developmental phase and its associated task. Stern (1985) and others have proposed what they call a continuous construction model of psychopathology that leaves open the question of origin of pathology and focuses on the content (meaning) of the psychic trauma experienced. According to the continuous construction model, borderline personality disorder would not necessarily have its origin at eighteen to thirty-six months and would not specifically require the infant's mother to thwart the task of separation-individuation during this time.

In principle, the *primitive splitting* defense proposed by Masterson, Kernberg, and others as the basis for borderline pathology could be used to skirt *any* psychic trauma, including the trauma of sexual or physical abuse so often reported by patients with the borderline diagnosis. Trauma leading to splitting could occur much later than the period assigned to separation-individuation in the fixation–regression model. While the infant may be more vulnerable to psychic stressors at eighteen to thirty-six months, vulnerability could continue through childhood and beyond.

A Possible Neural Substrate for Borderline Splitting

Elsewhere, I have proposed that borderline splitting and borderline pathology may have a neural substrate (Muller, 1992a; see Appendix). It is possible that for an infant who, in response to emotional trauma, splits its constitution of its mother during separation-individuation or even considerably later, while interhemispheric communication leading to integration is not yet complete (Yakovlev and Lecours, 1967, pp. 3–70), the split "good mother"–"bad mother" engram may be lateralized in the brain in a more exaggerated way than it is for an infant who does not use this defense beyond what Melanie Klein (1975) considers the "normal" time. Once myelination between the hemispheres reaches a certain stage, two split, unintegrated—and alternating—mental systems may become hardwired to create a neural "template" that would facilitate the splitting of all further experience and behavior through these two systems. It is also possible that the brains of some infants (or older children) may be more susceptible to the effects of early trauma and so be predisposed to using the splitting defense or more sensitive to its consequences.

A genetic component to a possible diathesis for borderline splitting cannot be ruled out, nor can the possibility that a splitting "template" may be hardwired at or before birth, so borderline splitting can occur later in life even without prior undue trauma. As already noted, the trauma leading to splitting may be other than failed separation-individuation, and may include sexual or physical abuse in infancy or beyond.

David: A Splitting Borderline Patient

David's case is reexamined now as a possible instance of borderline personality disorder. Another quotation from Masterson serves as a starting point.

During young adulthood (20's and 30's) the behavioral, rebellious type of acting out seen in adolescence decreases and the principal presenting problems that take its place are difficulties with work and with close relationships. As the borderline moves into his late 20's or early 30's, either his difficulty with intimacy prevents him from a continuous close relationship and thereby confronts him with the problem of loneliness, or he establishes a continuous relationship—married or not—and runs into trouble as the involvement invokes his fear of engulfment and/or abandonment and activates his clinging and/or distancing defenses. (1976, p. 73)

As an adolescent, David stole books from the school bookstore and burned religious books from the school library. Now his main difficulties are with work and his relationships with women. He has not made any real commitment to a career. He has taken a number of jobs for short periods that require little risk or responsibility, and are not in line with his intelligence and education. One could imagine David's conflict over committing himself to a career originating in the anxiety he experienced when he moved away from his mother during infancy in an attempt at separation-individuation. Any movement toward autonomy made through the WORU (withdrawing object relations part-unit) threatens him with the prospect of a recurrence of the initial primitive abandonment anxiety and the depression that accompanied it. This anxiety then "activates" (Masterson's term) the RORU (rewarding object relations part-unit), and David calls off his autonomous move, reenacting the initial primitive return to the mother that was rewarded by her.

Whenever David makes a plan to do anything that requires putting himself on the line by committing himself to something or someone, he instinctively pulls back. This has been the pattern in all his efforts to make a start in both an academic and a business career, and in his relations with women as well.

The following are examples of David's moves toward autonomy that were quickly undermined by his need to not be autonomous, but to stay passive and dependent instead.

1. There is a pattern to David's academic performance in high school and college. He did well for a semester or two, and then did poorly for some period. This cycle was repeated many times.

2. David, a good athlete, played basketball in high school. His father came to some of the games and noticed his son was reluctant to make a shot even when he was in a good position to do so. Instead, David passed the ball to another player, who then made the shot. His father was sufficiently concerned to discuss this with the coach.

3. I asked David why he was putting so little effort into a paper for a course he was taking, though the paper was the only criterion for the final grade and in spite of the fact he had little else to do at the time. He said he just didn't see the point in going all out on the project.

4. David claims when he reads serious philosophical books by Sartre and Camus, for example, and gets an idea or has an insight, he becomes terrified.

5. David told me that once, after losing a chess game, his opponent said he could not understand how someone who was so far ahead at the start of the game could then make so many bad moves and lose. David implied this was not an isolated incident.

The pattern here fits borderline patients' need to back away from whatever autonomous moves they begin. Does David set himself up to lose because winning is intolerable to him? He talks on and on about what he will do *someday*: he will go to graduate school, open an investment consulting business, write a book, make a film, start a publishing house, take part in the coming revolution, start his own mental hospital, and so on. Masterson points out how it is characteristic of adult borderline patients to substitute fantasy gratification for the achievements they fear. More than once, when David was in an expansive mood and looking back on how badly things had gone for him, he said, throwing his hands in the air, "I should have made a movie out of it." That he does not know how to make a movie did not concern him.

David has told me of several instances where he was not able to move autonomously out of what he considered a bad situation. At some point during the time he was working for his father in the family business between 1976 and 1978, he realized his father was not going to make good on his promise to give him more authority in the business. He agonized about confronting his father and finally did, but then he did not get out of this situation, which was intolerable to him, until more than a year later. Meanwhile, there were other possibilities in business and chances for working with people he knew who were involved in the stock market. "I just couldn't leave," he said once in a way that made me think he didn't know why he couldn't leave.

There is an apparent similarity between David's inability to leave his father's business and his reluctance to break with Harris who, he acknowledged many times, wasn't doing him any good. Masterson could have had Harris and David in mind when he wrote about how a therapist can fail a borderline patient and why the patient will continue "therapy" that is doing him no good. Harris did not take a stand against David's illness and was passive with respect to it. He fused with David's psychopathology and fed it.

The therapist who adopts a consistently passive stance appropriate for the neurotic patient will meet with failure with the borderline patient since the two developmental necessities — a real object and a real ego — will be lacking. The therapist's passivity will so correspond to the patient's projection of his withdrawing maternal part-image that the patient will not be able to distinguish between his WORU projection and the reality of the therapist's behavior. Consequently he will enter a transference psychosis. This will activate the RORU unit which will produce resistance and the therapy will stop. Moreover, the therapist's failure to confront the destructiveness of the mechanisms of the patient's pathological ego — avoidance, denial, projection, acting out the wish for reunion — will leave the patient at the mercy of these mechanisms. The therapy may stop in a dramatic, catastrophic fashion with the patient abruptly not returning or refusing to return; however, more often *there is a prolonged stalemate, since the borderline patient is a master at compliance with the therapist's unconscious wishes. The patient's lack of involvement remains hidden beneath his defenses while he presents the therapist with an illusion of therapy.* (Masterson, 1976, p. 108; emphasis added)

The message is clear: The patient's feelings of infantile deprivation are so fundamental, so deep, and the feelings of abandonment so painful that he is willing in therapy, as he was as a child, to sacrifice *anything* to fulfill the fantasy of reunion while at the same time avoiding the pain of abandonment. (Masterson, 1976, p. 109)

From what David has told me, it seems Harris treated his illness as an Oedipal (neurotic) phenomenon, rather than a pre-Oedipal (borderline) one. Masterson maintains that some therapists, particularly orthodox Freudians, dogmatically insist that the Oedipal conflict is the *only* primary source of emotional conflict, and ignore the pre-Oedipal separation-individuation failure postulated to lead to developmental arrest in borderline patients (Masterson, 1981, p. 228).[1]

The conflicts borderline patients have with intimacy are similar in structure to the conflicts they have in committing themselves to work or to any other action requiring autonomy. According to Masterson, as soon as some degree of autonomy is established through the RORU (rewarding object relations part-unit), the WORU (withdrawing object relations part-unit) is "activated," and the borderline patient pulls back. For these patients, attempts at close emotional involvement alternate between fusion with the love object (being "too close") and total separateness (being "too far"). Neither is satisfactory. Each is lived out through a split ego toward a split love object. The seemingly gratuitous oscillations between being "too close" and "too far" that occur with borderline splitting reflect the borderline patient's inability to find a comfortable emotional distance with another person (Melges and Swartz, 1989). True intimacy for the borderline patient—at least for any extended period of time—is therefore impossible.

Let's look again at David's relationship with Sally, whom David claims was one of the three women in his life he really cared for. When David went back to Atlanta in September 1976 to work for his father, that relationship was, by his own admission, in good shape. But after going with David for nearly two years, Sally was asking, perhaps more implicitly than explicitly, for some kind of commitment from him. She did not expect marriage at this point, but she did want some assurance their relationship would continue in spite of the geographical separation. David invited her to visit him in Atlanta and promised to help her find a job if she decided to move there. He even suggested they live together. But Sally probably sensed something lacking in David's commitment to her. He had, after all, slept with other women during their last year together and continued to do so in Atlanta. Were these "side affairs" initiated, at least in part, to deal with the anxiety of engulfment he most likely felt because of his growing involvement with Sally (RORU)? Were they a way of pulling back through the WORU?

When David came back to see Sally in November and learned she had become seriously involved with someone else, he was devastated. He was now "too far" from someone he still cared for very much. He could not handle this situation any more than he could handle the situation before he left in September, when he was "too close." By January 1977, when David came back to see Sally a second time, their relationship had been smashed beyond repair.

In love, as in work, David sets himself up to lose. There is no question he cared for Sally. But it seems he could not handle the feelings that came with this close emotional involvement. For much of his life, David has compulsively engaged in brief affairs and one-night stands. Was this one way of discharging his fear of intimacy with women, as well as holding off his latent sexual feelings for men?

During the fifteen months we worked together, David, by his own choice, was not significantly involved with any woman, though there were several one-night stands. Sexual isolation is a frequent consequence of the schizoid alienation from self and others that occurs with borderline patients who have "split egos" and "split object relations units." David did not feel himself as real, and he was unable to experience others, particularly women, as real, either. He did not feel the coincidence of his self with his body, as an emotionally healthy person does. He was *dis*embodied, which is to say he was not centered in his body. David's near-celibacy during the time we worked together could be looked at as a hysterical impotence, a conversion and extension of his general paralysis.

Schizoid persons, who do not feel their bodies as real, may alternate between sexual overstimulation and sexual inhibition. For many years, David lived his sexuality compulsively, chalking up a high body count. But when his defenses collapsed, overstimulation gave way to inhibition, which was more "appropriate" to his disembodied self. Harry Guntrip gives this account of the schizoid's sexuality:

The tragedy is that although the schizoid so desperately needs human relationship, he cannot enter into it because his fears do not allow him either to trust or to love, and he feels so weak that he expects the mental proximity of another person to overwhelm him. He may oscillate between being in and out of personal relations. When he is afraid of his inner loneliness, he may rush into a precipitate overintense friendship or infatuation, or try to substitute sexual activity for the personal relationship he cannot achieve, and end up disillusioned because he is still basically withdrawn. When his fear of commitment to close relationship is dominant, he will become shy, detached, asocial, or sexually anesthetic, frigid, impotent, and inhibited as a substitute for genuine independence and for the capacity for self-reliance of the nonanxious person. (1971, p. 169)

There is a structural and dynamic similarity between Guntrip's description of schizoid sexuality as either overstimulated or inhibited and Masterson's account of the "too close" and "too far" extremes to which borderline patients go in their attempts at love. If schizoid persons do not feel themselves as real and embodied, it seems likely they will not be able to feel this way about potential sexual partners either. Until 1979, when David's defenses were still in place and he was still relatively functional, he acted out his schizoid (and borderline) sexuality by overstimulation. When the defenses no longer served him well, he all but abandoned sexual activity. Guntrip sees the switch from overstimulation to inhibition in the schizoid person as a signal the illness is becoming more serious.

Sexual inhibition is more deeply psychopathological than overstimulation, because it is more totally dominated by schizoid withdrawal and despair. Neither are desirable, but at least in sexual overstimulation, the starved ego is putting up a fight for life, however dangerous the results, while in sexual inhibition something vital has gone dead, given up the struggle; fears have mastered and repressed needs. Both are conversion hysteria symptoms masking a schizoid problem. Either a starved infantile ego or else a frightened and withdrawn one finds expression through the body. In inhibitions, a lost function is a clue to a lost part of the self. (1971, pp. 169–170)

People may lie to themselves and to others, but their bodies do not lie. Through its impotence, David's body lived his psychic death.

David's Illness: A Series of Abandonment Depressions

David's serious emotional problems did not begin until he was about twenty-one, though he did a good deal of sociopathic acting out before then. His psychiatric history could be looked at as a series of abandonment depressions (Masterson, 1976, pp. 228–250) that followed serious loses. This kind of depression is seen often in borderline patients, who are not able to effectively mourn the loss of anyone or anything important to them. The abandonment depression is thought to originate in the rejection of the infant by the mother for its efforts to move autonomously away from her. This initial loss of her affection and support, according to Masterson's theory, is relived by borderline patients later in life whenever they experience a serious loss. The inability to mourn, work through, and transcend a loss is due to the borderline patient's ambivalence (which originates in a split self part-unit and split object part-unit, whether this splitting is due to antecedent primitive splitting) toward whomever or whatever has been lost. One reason borderline patients cannot deal with and work through a loss effectively is that they are not sure, emotionally or cognitively, what it is they have lost and what it meant to them (Muller, 1992b).

David has had three major breakdowns, each precipitated by a loss, each followed by an abandonment depression:

1. He was hospitalized for the first time when he was twenty-one (1971), following the breakup of a serious relationship with a woman. He was depressed, had trouble functioning, and became involved with drugs for about two years during this time.

2. The next breakdown occurred after the separation and eventual divorce from his wife several years later. He was hospitalized for two years, he was psychotic during part of that time, and he was treated with Thorazine. After his release from the hospital, he began psychoanalysis with Harris. The analysis was terminated in 1976 when David returned to Atlanta.

3. When David left Atlanta in 1978 and went to Chicago, he was angry and depressed at what he saw as his father's betrayal for not turning the family business over to him. A role in the business had been one of David's fantasy possibilities for a career. He could not mourn and work through the loss after his father sold the business, and he had another breakdown in Chicago during the spring of 1979. (How does a splitting borderline patient successfully mourn a fantasy that was lived as reality?) He moved back to this city in the fall of 1979 and continued therapy with Harris. He was angry, anxious, and depressed. He was hospitalized again for six months in 1980 and continued therapy with Harris after he was discharged. In spite of intense psychotherapy and drug treatment, David did not improve; he was hospitalized again in March 1982 for about three months. During these last hospitalizations and the periods between, David's depression continued, as did his rage at his father for not turning the business over to him.

Depression for borderline patients who strongly use the splitting defense in all likelihood is a more complex phenomenon than depression without this defense (Muller, 1992b). Splitting keeps separate in consciousness all-good–all-bad constitutions of a lost object or negative experience that need to be integrated if successful mourning and working through can occur. If borderline splitting does have a neural substrate (Muller, 1992a), the "template" that facilitates the splitting of so much of the borderline patient's experience may also "hold apart" split constitutions of loss and negative experience *neurally*, making depression in these patients more difficult to challenge therapeutically and pharmacologically. Post (1992) has proposed that early psychosocial trauma is transduced through the protooncogene c-fos to alter the gene expression of neurotransmitters, neuropeptides, and receptors — in effect imprinting the memory of these stressors on neural tissue, creating vulnerability to affective illness later in life. It is tempting to speculate that Masterson's abandonment depression may have its roots in this neural developmental arrest.

The Borderline Patient's Talionic Impulse

One of the enduring characteristics of David's illness has been his anger — at his parents, at me, at the world. Masterson, who has seen this global rage in every borderline patient he has worked with, calls it the "talionic impulse":

The borderline child experiences the parents' exploitation of his dependency and helplessness as the grossest form of cruelty and torture. This leads to an abandonment depression, an essential part of which is rage. Unable to express his hurt and rage because of his need for and fear of his parents, he attempts to master it by internalizing it, using the mechanism of identification with the aggressor. He creates an internalized drama of a medieval spectacle, where the patient is both attacker and victim. He discharges the rage by attacking himself, fantasying revenge on the parents and fulfillment of his talionic impulses by destroying their possession. This is at the same time a defense against the underlying talionic, homicidal urges toward the exploiting object. There is also a compensatory accompanying fantasy that, if he dramatizes his sorrowful state sufficiently, the parents will provide the wished-for response. This results in a failure to master the talionic impulse, which is destructively acted out on the self. Aggression is thus not free for release in self-assertive, adaptive behavior. (1981, pp. 187–188)

During most of the time I worked with David, he seemed at least as interested in luxuriating in his rage against his parents and punishing them as in working through his illness.

The borderline wants primarily revenge, to get back — not to get better. The second critical crossroad comes in treatment when the patient must make a choice between getting back or getting better. [The first comes when the illness is felt as ego alien. For David, this occurred (in part, anyway) shortly before we started working together. The third critical point is working through the anxiety that comes with separating from the therapist.] He cannot have both. As long as his aggression is channeled into revenge, it is not possible to build a psychic structure. He must give up the idea of revenge, that is, he must master the talionic impulse, and free his aggression to be used to support his self-image, rather than to attack it. By overcoming and mastering his talionic urge for revenge, he lays the groundwork for the beginning of an objective sense of morality—he puts aside the immediate but destructive and fantasy pleasure of revenge for the more long-term but more realistic objective and enduring satisfaction of aiding and abetting his own growth. He tolerates current discomfort in pursuit of future objectives. (Masterson, 1981, p. 188)

The Borderline Patient's Narcissistic Defense

Masterson has observed that borderline patients sometimes develop a narcissistic defense against their borderline problem (1981, p. 32). The infant who experiences rejection from its mother for acting autonomously may turn to its father for "rescue." This seems to have been the case with David. Implicit in his response to the liquidation of the family business is a demand his father "activate" him by providing him the means to earn his living. When the business was liquidated, David made little serious effort to start another career. Instead, he went into a narcissistic rage that lasted several years. Another manifestation of David's narcissistic relation to his father is his claim he did not go to graduate school and pursue an academic career because his father told him, "You can't eat books." He took this as a put-down of his plans and often cites his father's words as the reason he did not continue his education.

Projective Identification

Psychodynamically, David's taking up his father's words, "You can't eat books," in this way can be understood as projective identification, a term used differently by various authors (Grotstein, 1981; Goldstein, 1991). After splitting off his need *not* to do something, David projected the all-bad constitution of the fantasized project onto his father, then identified with the projection, justifying his failure to act. As part of this process, David's father was made to feel as if *he* were responsible for his son's paralysis. Many times I too became the object of David's projective identification, the reason for his doing, or not doing, something—as did his mother, his teachers, and his close friends. Clearly, self and object boundaries are blurred in this dynamic, which is facilitated by David's intense splitting.

NOTE

1. Working with borderline patients whose major defense is splitting, I often feel the infantile states they lapse into during psychotherapy are a strong intuitive argument—one "proved on our pulses" (Lewin and Schulz, 1992, p. 15)—that splitting is

rooted either in a developmental arrest due to trauma experienced during infancy or in regression due to trauma experienced later during childhood or adolescence that "undoes" a (perhaps faulty) developmental achievement at that stage. That emotional, sexual, or physical trauma could eventually induce the defense of borderline splitting having such a devastating effect on personality structure and function is consistent with the hypothesis that borderline splitting is a behavioral manifestation of a "split" neural substrate (Muller, 1992a; see Appendix).

Epilogue

After not hearing from David Helbros for six years (the last journal entry was September 6, 1985), I called him in New York in August 1991. He had held several jobs, including one at the New York Public Library, taken some graduate courses in philosophy and literature, learned French, written a long book review for a journal of social criticism, and begun working part time as a tutor in philosophy at two universities in New York. He was seeing a number of people, including a woman he had known for over a year, getting around to different parts of New York City, and taking an interest in the neighborhood where he has an apartment. He was enthusiastic about his work with his students.

I sent David a copy of the manuscript of this text. He felt what I wrote was for the most part a fair account of the work we did together, though he took issue with some of the interpretations. He had no objection to this book being published.

David's father died of leukemia in September 1990. Since then, David has been close to his mother, calls her often, and visits her occasionally in Atlanta.

This brief summary of David's life in the summer of 1991 shows an improvement in his quality of life and level of function over that of the winter of 1985 when we stopped therapy. He did go to New York; he did take graduate courses there; he did find some work; he did make new friends; he was not hospitalized again; he was not taking any medication. And he did reconcile with his mother after his father died, a turn of events that seemed unlikely during the time we worked together.

On the other hand, it was clear from talking to David that he is still very angry about and conflicted over many of the same issues. Although he learned French and took graduate courses, he did not enroll in a graduate degree program (he told me he could have gotten into one in New York). When I asked why, he said he was afraid of the pressures and struggles associated with that kind of commitment. David is working with another therapist now.

Reading the journal of our therapy sessions, considering the therapeutic impasse of the final weeks and the sudden termination, the fifteen months' course could be seen as a treatment failure. But even at the time we finished, I felt David was at a plateau from which he could later go on to integrate more of what he still needed to split off and defend against.

Outcome studies that follow borderline patients through the decades of their lives (Stone, 1990) show that for many, with time, the most fulminant expressions of the illness subside and quality of life improves. I would like to think I helped David reach a stage where further treatment and his own hard work will allow him to achieve more.

Appendix

৶

Is There a Neural Basis for
Borderline Splitting?

Is There a Neural Basis for Borderline Splitting?

René J. Muller

It is proposed here that borderline splitting and border-line pathology may have a neural basis. For the infant who splits its emotional and cognitive constitution of its mother during separation-individuation, the "good mother"–"bad mother" engram may be lateralized in the brain in a different way than for an infant who does not use this defense. The infant may be developmentally vulnerable to the effects of splitting during separation-individuation (18 to 36 months) because interhemispheric communication necessary for mental unity is not possible at this time, since neurons connecting left and right hemispheres are not totally myelinated and because the infant has not yet fully acquired language, a prerequisite for an integrated psychological reality. Two separate, unintegrated—and alternating—mental systems may come into being. Later, as myelination is completed, the infant's split emotional and cognitive constitutions of mother and of self may create a neural "template" for splitting all further experience and behavior through the two separate, alternating mental systems. The possibility that emotional trauma occurring later than separation-individuation, and involving other issues, may be the occasion for splitting is considered, as well as the possibility that a congenital abnormality in brain structure or function may be a primary factor in borderline pathology. Ways to test the hypothesis that borderline splitting has a neural basis are suggested.
Copyright © 1992 by W.B. Saunders Company

By dividing everything you think you can pass between.
—*John le Carré, A Perfect Spy*

SPLITTING is the main defense many persons with borderline personality disorder (BPD) use to skirt the anxiety inherent in life's ambiguous situations. Attempting to neutralize the painful emotional content of even the most ordinary daily experience, they alternately split their concepts of themselves, others, and the world into all-good/all-bad fragments. By construing and living an ambiguous experience first with one polarity, then with the other, the borderline avoids having to cope with the uncertainty and anxiety of the full experience, but at the cost of denying reality, and thus life itself. Like all psychodynamic defenses, splitting fails to give borderlines the security they seek, and leads to some of the most interesting and therapeutically challenging pathology this side of psychosis.

The phenomenology of BPD given in DSM-III-R[1] and the role of the splitting defense thought to underlie it have come to be well understood only during the last two decades. In contrast to schizophrenia, bipolar affective disorder, depression, and anxiety, no drug has been found to counteract the core illness, although drugs are used with some success to treat incidents of anxiety, depression, and psychosis secondary to it.[2,3]

In the psychoanalytic literature, borderline splitting is seen strictly as a psychodynamic defense. The psychiatric literature is largely silent on a possible biological basis for BPD, although borderlines have been studied with electroencephalography (EEG),[4] and efforts have been made to link BPD and organic brain dysfunction.[5] I will suggest here that a neural concomitant of borderline splitting may indeed exist. But first the psychoanalytic perspective on BPD will be reviewed, particularly the explanation for the origin of the splitting defense.

BORDERLINE SPLITTING: THE PSYCHOANALYTIC VIEW

BPD has been tied to a deficit in development sometime between 18 to 36 months, when the infant fails at the task of separating from its mother, due to her lack of support for its moves toward autonomy.[6-8] The infant in such a situation can respond in two ways: it can comply with the mother's need for it to remain infantile and be rewarded, or it can move autonomously and be rejected by her. To the infant, neither course is satisfactory. Rather than deal with the conflict and anxiety inhering in this dilemma, the infant may defend itself by alternately splitting its emotional and cognitive constitution of the mother (i.e., what it makes her out to be, emotionally and cognitively) into all-good (rewarding mother) and all-bad (punishing mother) fragments; thus sidestepping the conflict. Using this defense, the infant tries to rid itself of the

From the Department of Psychiatry, University of Maryland School of Medicine, Baltimore, MD.

Address reprint requests to René J. Muller, Ph.D., 3900 N Charles St (1103), Baltimore, MD 21218.

anxiety that would come in dealing with the ambiguous (rewarding and punishing) mother constituted in her totality.

As the infant splits its constitution of the mother, it also splits its own self-constitution and that of others into good-self/bad-self fragments. Consequently, the infant has no steady, integrated view of the mother, itself or anyone, or anything, else. These split fragments of self and others are internalized by the infant and become structural components of its ego. The internalized, unintegrated fragments remain separate in the borderline's consciousness, and conflicted there. Later in life, according to psychoanalytic theory, this conflict is manifested by borderline pathology, whose principal features include a shaky sense of identity, inability to be alone, inability to maintain stable relationships, unusual sensitivity to real or imagined rejection, periods of depression and hopelessness, and impulsive, self-destructive acts.

DSM-III-R defines BPD so broadly that it is possible for some patients who do not use the splitting defense to meet criteria. Yet, in the psychoanalytic formulation of BPD just summarized, splitting is thought to be the principal pathogenic factor, and to underly the structure of borderline behavior. Perhaps the confusion surrounding this point will eventually be resolved by defining two categories of BPD, one, the narrower, being reserved for patients whose pathological behavior takes the form of splitting.[8a] (Lesser degrees of the splitting defense are seen with patients who do not meet criteria for BPD. Being more toward the neurotic end of the psychopathology spectrum, these patients are not as drastically affected by splitting as borderlines.)

In the brief summary of the psychoanalytic interpretation of BPD given above, "splitting" has been used to describe two distinct phenomena. *Borderline splitting* is a descriptive term that specifies how borderlines constitute their experience of self and others in fragments of alternating polarity (e.g., idealization-devaluation). *Primitive splitting* defines a hypothetical defensive process carried out by an infant during separation-individuation, which may or may not be responsible for later borderline splitting and borderline pathology.

It is not known if some structural diathesis in the brains of persons who become borderline makes them unusually susceptible to the consequences of the type of anxiety thought to trigger the original, primitive splitting defense (infants who do not become borderline may also face this same kind of anxious situation) or if congenital brain pathology is mainly, or even entirely, responsible for the psychopathology known as BPD. The theory that primitive splitting during separation-individuation leads ineluctably to borderline splitting later in life is compelling, but other factors may be involved, and may be even more important.

BORDERLINE SPLITTING: A NEURAL BASIS?

At times, therapists who work with borderlines feel they are dealing with two different persons. How could "one" person be 100% in favor of something (or someone) yesterday, and 100% against it today, when no objective change occurs in between? This cycling between positive and negative constitutions may occur over shorter periods, and when a borderline is very anxious, a cycle may be completed in seconds. Alternately splitting an ambiguous life situation into all-good/all-bad fragments, the borderline often appears to have two personalities. Unlike the true multiple personality,[9,10] who has two or more complete (though not necessarily equal) consciousnesses with totally different personalities, borderlines have one consciousness and one personality that alternately splits ambiguous life experiences into all-good/all-bad constitutions of these experiences. Borderlines' personalities are not multiple, but their constitutions of their experiences are.

Considering how borderlines split their experience so palpably and so universally, is it too large a stretch to suppose that something in their brains may be split as well? (The converse would require that the brain remain whole as the mind splits all it encounters.) During separation-individuation (18 to 36 months), as the infant constitutes its mother as alternately all-good and all-bad, could this split impression of "mother" be laid down in the brain differently than with an infant who does not use the splitting defense?

Why would the primitive splitting defense used at the time of separation-individuation have such a profound effect? Why should the brain be so sensitive to split constitutions of the infant's experience that the resultant engrams (hypothetical alterations of living neural tissue posited as an explanation for memory) make such a pathological mark on brain function? Perhaps because, at this point, the neural connections between left and right brain hemispheres are not fully myelinated, prohibiting the interhemispheric communication necessary for integrated brain function. "During this period," Gazzaniga and LeDoux maintain, "it is as if the child has a split brain"[11] (p. 82). If the infant splits the emotional and cognitive constitution of its mother into oppositely polarized fragments, this sensory experience may be encoded in the brain in a way that makes it impossible to lay down an integrated engram of "mother."

During separation-individuation, the infant's sense of what the world is—what reality is—comes primarily from its relationship with its mother. If she is not what Fairbairn calls "a good enough mother"[12] (p. 97), the infant has nowhere else to turn for the encouragement and affirmation it needs for normal development. And having only rudimentary language at this stage, the infant has no opportunity to reason its way out of the freedom-restraint dilemma (that takes the form of a double bind) it faces with the mother. What Gazzaniga and LeDoux say about how the emotional tone of preverbal experience influences later life seems particularly applicable to the infant who uses the splitting defense:

"... there is the critical period during development before language is a functional mechanism. During this period, important conditioning that bears fruit for a variety of adult motivational states is surely ongoing. Responses are extensively examined by the young child when considering the smile or the frown of those around him, and these play a huge role in controlling behavior. The behavioral tone of the emerging adult is largely set in these preverbal years, and adult impulses—which is to say, response patterns—can largely be determined by the early associations"[11] (p. 158).

Language, it seems, uniquely allows man to verbalize his fragmented experience and create a personal conscious reality from engrams encoded in each brain hemisphere.[13] It is only through the integrating power of language that a person can rise above his or her own limited experience and come anywhere close to Matthew Arnold's elusive ideal of seeing life steadily

and seeing it whole. No wonder, then, that the preverbal infant who is discouraged by its mother from making moves toward autonomy during separation-individuation should be vulnerable to splitting its constitution of her both mentally and neurally. At this point in the infant's development, neither mind nor brain may be capable of handling that kind of experience nonpathologically.

As the infant grows beyond separation-individuation and the neural connections between hemispheres become complete, engrams of its emotional and cognitive constitutions of "mother" and of self from primitive splitting may be programmed in an unintegrated configuration. It is conceivable that what can be thought of as two separate, unintegrated mental systems may come into being, one coded for a predominantly positive constitution of self, other and world, the other for a predominantly negative one. The fully myelinated interhemispheric circuits could then form a neural "template" for two separate mental systems that would be maintained throughout life. All experience, language and behavior would then be split between two alternating systems of polar opposite constitution. With both brain and mind split, such a person would be destined to live life with borderline pathology. (An infant of comparable age who does not use the splitting defense, on the other hand, will in time have integrated engrams of "mother" and of self programmed between the hemispheres.)

The theory of borderline splitting proposed by Mahler, Masterson, Kernberg, and others is based on a fixation-regression model of psychopathology. Something goes wrong at one of the crucial stages of development and the opportunity to complete the developmental task of that stage is missed, or only partly accomplished. A developmental snag occurs, making it more difficult to favorably resolve the issues of the stages that follow, condemning one to repeat throughout life pathological behaviors anchored in an epigenetic failure. For BPD, the failed developmental task is separation-individuation, and the time period epigenesis purportedly allows for resolving the issues of this stage is 18 to 36 months.

The fixation-regression model of psychopathology has been challenged as reductive, particularly as to the temporal point of origin of pathology and the hard-and-fast link to a specific developmental phase and its associated task. Stern and others have proposed what they call a continuous construction model of psychopathology that leaves open the question of origin of pathology and focuses on the *context* (meaning) of the psychic trauma experienced.[14,15] According to the continuous construction model, BPD would not necessarily have its origin at 18 to 36 months and would not specifically require the infant's mother to thwart the task of separation-individuation during this time. In principle, the splitting defense underlying borderline pathology could be used to skirt *any* psychic trauma, including sexual abuse, in infancy and beyond, which is part of the history of so many patients with the borderline diagnosis, and this could occur much later than the period assigned to separation-individuation in the fixation-regression model. While the infant may be more vulnerable to psychic stressors at 18 to 36 months, vulnerability could continue through childhood and beyond. As to the possible susceptibility of the brain to the consequences of splitting while myelination is incomplete and interhemispheric communication is compromised, it has been shown that myelination of some fibers through the corpus callosum may be delayed as long as adolescence.[16,17] Finally, a genetic component to a possible diathesis cannot be ruled out.

EXPERIMENTAL EVIDENCE FOR HEMISPHERIC LATERALIZATION

It is generally agreed that, overall, the right brain hemisphere is more involved with emotion, the left hemisphere with cognition and language. There is also evidence that the right hemisphere is more involved with negative emotion than the left. It could be imagined, then, that in lateralization accompanying primitive splitting during separation-individuation, splitting could lead either to an imbalance in distribution between the hemispheres of the infant's emotional and cognitive constitution of the mother, or to an imbalance in the hemispheric distribution of "good mother" and "bad mother" emotional engrams. When brain and mind are working in sync, emotion and cognition can each be thought of as "informing" the other, so

as to allow an integrated, balanced, and consistent constitutive view of ambiguous life experience. But if brain structure and function are such that emotion (right hemisphere) and cognition (left hemisphere) do not "inform" the other, integration, balance, and constancy may not be possible. It is just these characteristics that the borderline lacks.

We have, as yet, no neural foundation for consciousness. But we do know that there is no such thing as a "mother cell" in the brain. An infant's constitution and memory of its mother are distributed in many cells throughout both hemispheres. In each hemisphere, different cells encode and remember different facets of "mother" (rewarding mother, punishing mother; tranquil mother, angry mother, etc.). The integrated brain working normally encodes a relatively balanced and realistic impression of what the mind encounters in its environment. Through memory, the "glue" of psychic life, the brain can then make available a balanced and realistic gestalt on which a person may interpret future experience and base future behavior.

The discussion, so far, has been limited to theory. I will now summarize some of the experimental evidence for hemispheric lateralization of emotion and show how aberrant asymmetrical distribution of engrams between hemispheres could underlie borderline splitting, whether this is due to a neurally programmed reactivation of the original primitive splitting defense, or to a structural diathesis of the brain that is itself responsible for the aberrant asymmetry.

Depression and the Right Hemisphere

Evidence is accumulating that in sad mood and depression the right hemisphere is more involved than the left, which is to say depression "resides" here disproportionately.[18] Depressed subjects show greater EEG activity of the right hemisphere, particularly in temporal and frontal areas compared to nondepressed controls.[19,20] Neuropsychological tests show decreased cognitive function of the right hemisphere in depressed patients.[21] Patients successfully treated for depression by electroconvulsive therapy (ECT) performed better on neuropsychological examinations sensitive to right hemisphere dysfunction than before treatment.[22] And while stroke patients with left-hemisphere lesions become depressed and sometimes have catastrophic reactions (consistent with the idea that positive emotions reside mainly in the left hemisphere and have their neural substrate compromised by the lesion), patients with right-hemisphere lesions do not.[23] Right-hemisphere stroke patients often seem indifferent to their condition, and there are reports of an increase in emotional tone for some of these patients.

When the left brain hemisphere is inactivated by unilateral, intracarotid injections of central nervous system depressants (e.g., sodium amytal or amobarbital), the subject becomes depressed, but when the same injection is given on the right side (that presumably underlies most negative emotion) the opposite response occurs. Terzian gives the following account of his experience with this procedure, describing first the inactivation of the left hemisphere:

> "The patient especially when spoken to, despairs and expresses a sense of guilt, of nothingness, of indignity, and worries about his own future or that of his relatives. . . . The injection of the same dose [of sodium amytal] in the contralateral [right] carotid artery of the same subject or in subjects not having received the same injection, produces on the contrary a complete opposite reaction, [a] euphoric reaction that in some cases may reach the intensity of maniacal reactions"[24] (p. 235).

This procedure was introduced by Wada, and bears his name; it was first used by him to determine the side of cerebral speech dominance before neurosurgery, particularly for people who are left-handed or ambidextrous.[25]

Lateralized Film Viewing

Hoping to find further experimental support for the notion that left and right hemispheres encode and process emotional experience differently, Dimond et al.[26] asked normal subjects to view motion pictures through contact lenses specially designed to lateralize the film to one hemisphere or the other. Three films were shown to each subject: a Tom and Jerry cartoon, a film showing a surgical operation, and a travel film of Lucerne. The films were shown without sound. After viewing a film, subjects were asked to score forms rating the film in four categories—humorous, unpleasant, horrific, and pleas-

ant—on a scale of 1 to 9. All films were first viewed with normal, bilateral vision and then through the specially designed contact lenses, with left and right hemisphere alone. Subjects wore the lenses in both eyes, so vision was binocular (but not bilateral) for all trials.

When the three films were seen through the lateralizing contact lenses, there were significant differences between left and right hemispheres in subjects' ratings for the category of unpleasant, the right hemisphere making a more negative rating. Significant differences between left and right hemispheres were also observed in subjects' ratings for horrific with the Tom and Jerry cartoon and the medical film, but not with the travel film (where, presumably, horrific scenes were minimal); again, the right hemisphere rated more negatively than the left.

In contrast, much smaller differences between left and right hemispheres were noted when subjects with lateralized vision rated the humorous and pleasant categories in these films. Ratings in all categories for the three films made with bilateral vision were similar to those made with the left hemisphere alone, except in the unpleasant rating for the medical film. And ratings made with the right hemisphere alone were significantly higher than those made with bilateral vision for the categories unpleasant and horrific (except for the travel film), but not for the categories humorous and pleasant.

Dimond et al. concluded that each hemisphere of the human brain has an essentially different "emotional vision" of the world, and each makes a unique contribution to the bilateral whole. The left hemisphere sees the world pretty much as do left and right hemispheres working together, and it is likely that in everyday experience the left hemisphere predominates over the right by, in effect, forcing its vision on the whole. The right hemisphere appears to encode negative (unpleasant and horrific) experience more strongly. These negative engrams are probably held in check to some degree by the left hemisphere in bilateral experience most of the time, insuring a degree of integration and balance.

If left hemisphere–right hemisphere differences in emotional response to negative experience are significant in a brain where interhemispheric communication is normal, as is the case for Dimond's adult subjects, even larger differences in emotional response between the hemispheres would be expected in brains where the communication is less, as would be the case for the infant who uses the splitting defense during separation-individuation (18 to 36 months), when neurons connecting the hemispheres are not fully myelinated. It seems plausible, then, that the "bad mother" engram resulting from primitive splitting during a time when interhemispheric communication is not at full capacity would be laid down even more asymmetrically than with an infant who does not use this defense. Splitting may, in effect, lead to a unique kind of experiential lateralization. Furthermore, considering that the greatest differences in emotional response between left and right hemispheres in the four categories of response Dimond et al. measured—humorous, unpleasant, horrific, and pleasant—are with the negative emotions unpleasant and horrific, it seems plausible that it is the "bad mother," rather than the "good mother" engram that is split and laid down most asymmetrically.

Using the same technique to lateralize visual input to left and right hemispheres, Dimond and Farrington[27] measured the response in normal subjects of heart rate to each of the three films used in the above study. Subjects showed a greater emotional response (as measured by heart rate) with the left hemisphere than with the right while viewing the Tom and Jerry cartoon, a result consistent with the notion that the left hemisphere is more involved in processing positive emotions. The right hemisphere, on the other hand, had a higher response to the film showing a surgical operation, which is consistent with the idea that the right hemisphere is partial to processing negative emotions. Since ratings measuring differences in heart rate were made as the films were being watched, these differences represent a more direct emotional response to the visual stimulus than in Dimond's earlier experiments[26] where the films were rated in each of the four categories after the films were viewed. Clearly, there is some cognitive component in the judgments of emotional experience made here.

Dimond's characterization of the difference in emotional vision between left and right hemispheres may provide a clue to understanding a particularly dramatic aspect of borderline pathology. While borderlines do split their constitutions of self, other, and world into all-good/all-bad fragments, they also have extended periods, usually when they are calm and emotionally unchallenged, when they show a relatively balanced and integrated constitution of the same experiences they have split before, and will split again at a later time. Could an anxious experience trigger a dyscontrol mechanism of the right hemisphere that perturbs the emotional-cognitive balance needed for an integrated view of ambiguous life experience? (Overexcitation caused by epileptic seizures originating in the right hemisphere provokes strong negative emotions; this does not occur with seizures occuring in the left hemisphere.) Could a "pathological" neural circuitry created by primitive splitting during separation-individuation make the right hemisphere unusually labile to the stress of negative emotion, so that the relative balance between positive and negative constitutions which the borderline achieves for brief periods is tipped in favor of the negative constitution of life events so typical in borderline splitting?

If the left brain vision does predominate in ordinary experience when left and right hemispheres operate together, as Dimond's data suggest, then what Dimond calls the "extra dimension" of the ordinarily suppressed right brain may be triggered into play and assert its predominantly negative emotional vision as the borderline is confronted with the anxiety of ambiguous experience he cannot live ambiguously, i.e., normally, nonpathologically. If this is so, an incident of borderline splitting later in life may reenact the original perturbation, now ingrained neurally, of left brain–right brain balance and integration brought on by primitive splitting made in response to the first ambiguous situation with the mother that the infant experienced pathologically.

It is well known that borderlines cannot tolerate for any length of time the ambiguities implicit in intimacy. An intimate situation (whether this involves love, friendship, work, or anything else) is often initially constituted by the borderline as all-good (idealized), only later to be resplit into the opposite all-bad constitution (devalued) when the emotions associated with intimacy become threatening, and thus negative. Where ambiguous emotions are involved, the borderline is either too close, or too far away, alternately experiencing engulfment or abandonment. And because borderlines cannot integrate and live the opposite polarities that inhere in ordinary ambiguity—they oscillate between the opposite polarities of the ambiguity—they have great difficulty with any relationships or projects they attempt.[28,29]

Lateralized Lesions and Memory Recall

Most studies of the effects of organic brain disease on memory emphasize the quantitative aspects of memory, i.e., the number of items recalled in a given memory task. Relatively little has been done to investigate the qualitative aspects of memory, i.e., the capacity to recall the emotional contents of material presented and the symbolic distortions made. Wechsler filled this void with an important study comparing the ability of subjects with left hemisphere, right hemisphere, and bilateral lesions to recall the content of an emotionally charged text and a neutral narrative text.[30] Subjects were read aloud two brief stories, one emotional, the other emotionally neutral. They were scored on their recall, given verbally, of specific items in both stories. Subjects without brain lesions were used as controls.

The data were analyzed for both quantitative and qualitative differences between the groups studied, but only the qualitative differences are of interest here. Thirty percent of the brain-damaged group (left, right, and bilateral lesions) made errors in recalling specific items for the neutral story, compared with 21% for the controls. With the emotional story, on the other hand, 76% of the brain-damaged group made these errors, compared with only 30% of the controls. Clearly, these results show that brain damage effects recall of emotionally charged material more than recall of emotionally neutral material.

More significant for our purpose here is the difference in the number of subjects with right and left cerebral lesions who made errors in the recall of items from both stories. For the story with emotional content, 79% of the right-hemisphere lesioned subjects made errors, compared with 30% for the controls; only 53% of the left-hemisphere lesioned subjects, in contrast, made errors. For the emotionally neutral story, 21% of the right-hemisphere lesioned subjects made errors (21% for controls); left-hemisphere lesioned subjects had an 18% error rate.

Wechsler's results show that right-hemisphere lesions significantly impede recall of memories in the emotionally charged story, but not in the neutral story. Left-hemisphere lesions have a lesser, though significant, effect on recall of the emotionally charged story and no significant effect on recall of the neutral story. These data strongly support the view that the right hemisphere has more to do with processes that underlie emotion and provide additional evidence that engrams associated with emotion are laid down asymmetrically in each brain hemisphere.

Right-Hemisphere Anesthesia and Memory Recall

Building on Wechsler's results, Ross and Homan[31] measured the recall of memorable life events in normal subjects who had the right (nondominant) hemisphere anesthetized with amobarbital. Prior to the right-sided Wada test, subjects were asked to recall an emotionally charged life event. Subjects' verbal descriptions of the event were tape-recorded. Within 24 hours, amobarbital was injected into the right carotid artery and the subject was asked to repeat his recollection of the event with the right hemisphere anesthetized. The speech of all seven subjects showed affective flattening during the Wada test, but none became aphasic. Five of the seven patients showed striking changes in the amount of affect attending their version of the event compared with the original version of the story before right-hemisphere anesthesia, when both hemispheres were involved. After the anesthesia had worn off, subjects were asked to recall the event a third time. Their stories again had the affective coloring of the original version.

Before the Wada test, one subject described a car wreck, following a seizure, where the car left the road and hit a tree. He was thrown from the car, but not seriously injured. Asked to recall how he felt immediately after regaining consciousness, he replied "I was scared, scared to death, I could have run off the road and killed myself or someone else . . . I was really scared."

During the Wada test, the subject was again questioned about how he felt when he woke up from the accident. His answer was "Silly . . . silly." Asked specifically if he was afraid or frightened, he said "Oh . . . maybe a little bit." As the amobarbital was wearing off, he was asked directly a second time if he felt frightened, and he replied ". . . it was a bad accident but . . . it was nothing that was physically damaging to anyone." When he had fully recovered from the anesthesia, he was requested to repeat the story once more, and his version of the incident now was very much like the original version (pre-Wada test), including an emphatic admission of how frightened he was when he woke up after the accident.

These results of Ross and Homan are consistent with the generally held view that the right hemisphere predominantly modulates the affective components of language and behavior, while the verbal-cognitive aspects of language and behavior are predominantly modulated by the left hemisphere. The data are also in line with Wechsler s work, cited earlier, on the recall of an emotionally charged story by subjects with right and left hemisphere lesions. Overall, for our consideration of a possible neural concomitant of borderline splitting, the most significant conclusion of Ross and Homan's study is that in persons with intact brains, various facets of experience, as well as the memory of that experience, are laid down asymmetrically in each brain hemisphere. In addition, their results are consistent with the idea that the right hemisphere encodes engrams of negative experience more strongly than the left.

EMOTIONAL TONE, LATERALIZATION, AND SPLITTING

The borderline's pattern of idealizing-devaluing can be regarded as a pathological mode of approach-avoidance. This pattern is particularly evident in intimate relationships, where any mutuality for the borderline is fleeting (accepting the ambiguity of another person is essential to mutual encounter) and the only long-term alternatives in relating to another person are engulfment or abandonment (the borderline is either too close to another person or situation, or too far removed, consequences of an intolerance of ambiguity).

If, as so much evidence indicates, the left hemisphere has a greater positive emotional tone and a larger capacity for encoding positive emotion, while the right hemisphere has the opposite valencies,[32-34] the borderline's constituting power that alternately lays down all-good engrams of an experience in the left hemisphere and all-bad ones in the right does not permit a realistic (i.e., ambiguous) rendering of the situation to be encoded in *either* hemisphere. Consequently, both hemispheres may be lacking in the balance of positive and negative engrams necessary for the kind of intrahemispheric and interhemispheric integration that underlies nonpathological reality. It is tempting to speculate that the lack of intrahemispheric balance of positive and negative engrams of the borderline's experience may inhibit interhemispheric balance and integration.

Borderlines often act as if they are experiencing and relating to the world with two nonsynchronized half-brains. It is as if each hemisphere "decides" on an opposite interpretation and course of action while responding to a particular experience. This may be why, at times, borderlines can appear to be two different persons—one positive (approach), the other negative (avoidance)—while involved in a situation, switching back and forth in response to external stimuli and internal dynamics. What one hemisphere "knows" about the borderline's world does not appear to be available to what the other hemisphere "knows." The two brain hemispheres do not seem to communicate and integrate their oppositely polarized knowledge, only give opposite versions of it alternately.

Borderlines use language in a way consistent with the supposition of two separate, unintegrated mental systems. What is most striking about the language of borderlines is that often, while talking about themselves, they speak as if they were talking about someone else. The words they use to describe themselves and their situation do not seem to apply to them.

Even with negative emotion brought on by mild anxiety and stress, the right hemisphere seems to be more activated, i.e., attuned and responsive to this pole of emotion, than the left.[35] It is not difficult to imagine how an infant between 18 and 36 months (or, possibly someone much older, particularly if interhemispheric myelination is delayed), caught in the double bind of being developmentally able to act autonomously now on one hand, and being punished for doing so by its mother on the other, would use the splitting defense in an attempt to negate the psychic trauma of the double bind. While constituting the mother in a purely negative way as she punishes the infant for making an autonomous move, that negative constitution of her and all that comprises the experience could be encoded exclusively (or nearly so) in the right hemisphere. Similarly, during the infant's all-good constitution of the mother, while she rewards it for going against its developmental instinct and staying symbiotically related to her, this split positive constitution could be encoded exclusively (or nearly so) in the left hemisphere. It is conceivable that a double bind of any kind—where two opposing emotional or cognitive demands are made simultaneously—involving *any* issue, may prompt the infant, child or adolescent to use the splitting defense.

Over a period of months or years, this way of splitting experience—in essence, of lateralizing it—could lead to an accretion of split positive and negative engrams, unbalanced and unchecked by opposite emotional engrams in the *same* hemisphere, as would occur during normal development, when the splitting defense is not used. And then, as myelination between left and right hemispheres becomes complete, however many years this may take, the selectivity of the left hemisphere for split positive emotions, and that of the right for split negative emotions could become hard-wired, inclining all subsequent experience to be split and lateralized in this way as well. By hard-wiring here we mean that the fully myelinated interhemispheric brain circuitry perpetuates the near-exclusive receptivity of the left hemisphere for the positive emotional engrams associated with an emotionally charged experience, as well as the near-exclusive receptivity of the right hemisphere for the negative engrams.

For someone whose psyche and brain have been touched by the splitting defense, the behavioral manifestations of splitting may not appear in infancy or childhood, but only in adolescence or early adulthood, after significant emotional and cognitive demands have been felt.

As mentioned earlier, the possibility that borderline splitting and borderline pathology are due primarily to a congenital malformation of brain structure or function cannot be ignored. The notion that faulty connections between brain hemispheres may be part of the underlying pathophysiology of schizophrenia has been seriously considered,[36,37] and it is possible that similar malformations of interhemispheric circuitry may have a significant causative effect on the behavior we describe as borderline splitting.

Some brains may be wired from birth in such a way that the right hemisphere inordinately encodes the negative engrams of an emotionally charged experience, and the left hemisphere the positive engrams. This would amount to a diathetic set-up for prospective borderlines, making their brains unusually susceptible to encoding the split engrams that could result from facing even ordinary double bind situations. If such a neural predisposition to splitting does exist, the onus of pathogenic responsibility is lifted from the mother (or mother substitute), since any of the common double bind situations people of any age routinely find themselves in could lead to emotional engrams being pathologically split between the hemispheres. For such cases, the brain, rather than the mind (in this artificial and often misleading distinction) or the environment, can be thought of as taking the lead in the genesis of what eventually would be manifested as borderline splitting.

As a neural basis for borderline splitting is sought, an open mind should be trained on all possible ways the brain could come to underlie this phenomenon.

TESTING THE UNIFIED HYPOTHESIS OF BORDERLINE SPLITTING EXPERIMENTALLY

Hypotheses are made to be tested. Dimond's procedure[26] for studying the "emotional vision" of left and right hemispheres could be used to test the unified hypothesis of borderline splitting proposed here. Subjects should meet DSM-III-R criteria for BPD and, in addition, be actively using the splitting defense.[8a] (As noted earlier, patients can meet these broad criteria even if their pathological behavior does not take the form of splitting, or seem to derive from the splitting defense.) Because borderlines are less able to integrate the opposite "emotional visions" of each brain hemisphere, one would predict a difference in their response, compared to controls, to the films used by Dimond: the right hemisphere should "see" more negatively, the left more positively. It is also likely that when emotionally charged scenes are shown to both hemispheres simultaneously, borderlines would have a greater (and sharper) response than controls. Moreover, the polarity of the borderlines' response would be expected to oscillate back and forth from positive to negative over time more often and more sharply than controls as external stressors impinge on and modify the borderlines' first reported reaction to the films.

If these differences in response between borderlines and controls could be established, a more elaborate experiment might be considered. Scenes could be shown to borderlines and to controls from feature-length films, some emotionally neutral, others highly emotionally charged that might be expected to elicit a splitting response (scenes between husbands and wives, lovers, parents and children, friends; also those depicting commitment to careers and political involvement). Subjects could view these film clips first bilaterally, then with each hemisphere alone through lateralizing contact lenses, just as in the Dimond experiment. Questions probing subjects' emotional and cognitive reactions to each film clip could be asked and tape recorded for analysis. As with the Dimond films, comparisons could then be made between the responses of borderlines and controls, with both brain hemispheres operating simultaneously and with each hemisphere operating alone.

The procedure used by Ross and Homan[31] to measure the retrieval of emotionally charged memories in persons with anesthetized right hemispheres (Wada test) could also be adapted to test the unified hypothesis of borderline splitting. As noted earlier, Ross and Homan observed a flattening of negative affect in emotional memory with the right hemisphere anesthetized, compared with the same memory recalled with both hemispheres functioning, before and after the Wada test. If the right brain has its own "emotional vision" that supplies an "extra dimension" suppressed in ordinary bilateral experience, as Dimond maintains, a borderline may be expected to recall an emotionally charged memory under right hemisphere anesthesia differently than with both brain hemispheres operating, and differently than a non-borderline subject challenged with the same tasks. Many factors could come into play in these experiments, making predictions of outcome difficult, though it might be safe to predict that under right hemisphere anesthesia, borderlines would split less negatively.

Perhaps the most direct and definitive way to determine if anything is structurally and functionally different about the brains of persons who use the borderline splitting defense would be to apply a technique developed by Petersen et al.[38] to measure with positron emission tomography (PET) changes in regional cerebral blood flow (rCBF) as single words are perceived and pronounced. Subjects are flashed words, and then asked to pronounce and verbally associate tasks to these words. Changes in rCBF paralleling the brain's activity have been measured quantitatively in both brain hemispheres. Using a method of tomographic separation, it is possible to determine in normal subjects what areas of the brain are involved—and to what degree—in visually perceiving, processing and verbally associating a task to single words. Other tests were done to measure changes in rCBF as spoken words were presented to subjects.

If persons using the borderline splitting defense do have a neural "template" that prompts them to split emotional and cognitive constitutions of their experience as is proposed here, single words having emotional content may be processed in their brains differently than in normal persons, and the underlying pathological structure and function may give rise to different patterns of rCBF as measured by PET. First, actively splitting borderlines and controls could be scanned without sensory challenge to check for differences in rCBF that might represent intrinsic differences in left hemisphere–right hemisphere brain structure. Borderline subjects could then be given single words representing persons, issues, events, etc. known to evoke from them split responses. A series of tomograms for borderlines and controls challenged with the same words could be examined and compared for gross interpretable differences.

Using PET, Reiman et al.[39] found that patients with panic disorder who were vulnerable to lactate-induced panic attacks showed abnormally low ratios of left-to-right parahippocampal blood flow, blood volume, and oxygen metabolism in the resting, nonpanic state. Possible reasons for these regional PET abnormalities include a relative or absolute increase of neuronal activity in the right parahippocampal region, anatomical asymmetry, and a relative or absolute increase in blood-brain barrier permeability in the right hippocampal region. Reiman proposes that the parahippocampal abnormality amounts to an anatomical predisposition to panic attacks and that these attacks are triggered through this abnormal structure and/or function. These results offer encouragement that PET may reveal a neural correlate for borderline splitting.

The results of one or more of the experimental methods suggested above may provide data necessary to begin evaluating the unified hypothesis of borderline splitting. In each, an attempt is made to create a situation to elicit and measure the behavioral consequences of borderline splitting. This is an important and difficult experimental challenge. In essence, one is looking for a behavioral response consistent with splitting that can be correlated with some abnormal neural structure or function.

It must be acknowledged that even if experimental evidence for an aberrant neural "template" consistent with borderline splitting were found, this would not establish a causal link between neural pathological structure and function and the primitive splitting hypothesized to occur during separation-individuation. As noted earlier, primitive splitting is one explanation for the pathology ascribed to borderline splitting in BPD, but a congenital brain defect could not be excluded as being responsible, in whole or in part, for any aberrant neural structure that may underlie this pathological condition.

IMPLICATIONS FOR BPD TREATMENT

Borderlines are known to respond well to intensive psychoanalytically oriented psychotherapy.[6-8] If, as suggested here, borderline splitting has a neural concomitant, successful therapeutic intervention may be accompanied by the laying down of new, integrated engrams that would take precedence over existing split engrams. In other words, as therapy promotes healing of a borderline's split emotional and cognitive constitutions of self and others, new neural circuits between brain hemispheres may form, which could then provide a more integrated neural "template" for subsequent experience and behavior.

Neuropsychologists distinguish between what they call "special purpose" neural mechanisms that are hard-wired into the nervous system and "general purpose" ones that are programmed by a person's learning experiences[13] (p. 275). It seems most likely that it is the "general purpose" neural mechanisms that are newly programmed as psychological integration occurs during successful psychotherapy. One can imagine an annealing of the two, separate, alternating mental systems that may come into being with primitive splitting, or result from some structural diathesis. If, as it has been suggested, psychological integration and neural integration occur concomitantly during psychotherapy,[40] it seems reasonable to ask whether some drug could facilitate the creation of new neural pathways, or the reactivation of compromised ones, between brain hemispheres, and "catalyze" the therapeutic process.

One can also imagine a drug that would desensitize the "trigger" of the process that leads borderlines to split constitutions of their experience into polar opposite fragments (e.g., idealization-devaluation), or dampen the amplitude of the back-and-forth oscillations between these lived polarities. That none of the drugs used so far has worked against core borderline pathology may be because no drug tried has addressed the neural pathology underlying it. Most of the drugs tested have been selected from those effective against other mental illnesses[3] with biological pathologies vastly different from that suggested here for BPD, and would, in any case, not be expected to promote formation of new neural interhemispheric circuitry, activation of dormant interhemispheric circuitry, or desensitization of the mechanism that triggers borderline splitting.

CONCLUSION

Whether there is a neural basis for borderline splitting is part of a larger issue, what is universally known as the mind-brain problem. Some theoreticians and clinicians study psychopathology from the perspective of consciousness, others from the perspective of neural function, and some—relatively few, it seems—try to understand these phenomena from both perspectives. Edmund Husserl, the founder and father of the phenomenological method in the human sciences (an approach that seeks to rescue all psychological investigation from the reductions of natural science), wrote around 1935:

"If . . . a really exact explanation and consequently a similarly extensive scientific practical application is to become possible for the phenomena belonging to the humanistic sciences, then must the practitioners of the humanistic sciences consider not only the spirit as spirit but also must go back to its bodily foundations, and by employing the exact sciences of physics and chemistry, carry through their explanations. The attempt to do this, however, has been unsuccessful (and in the foreseeable future there is no remedy to be had) due to the complexity of the exact psychophysical research needed . . ."[41] (p. 152).

When Husserl wrote this, more than 50 years ago, the "foreseeable future" was nowhere in sight. It seems now that we may be catching up with the future. To some, anyway, it is becoming clear that the mind-brain dichotomy does not exist in lived human experience, but only in our inadequate attempts to understand it.[42] By using the techniques of modern science and overcoming the limits of Cartesian dualism, it may be possible to show that the psychopathology and neuropathology of borderline splitting are two sides of the same coin.

REFERENCES

1. American Psychiatric Association. Diagnostic and Statistical Manual of Mental Disorders. 3rd ed. rev. Washington, DC: APA, 1987.

2. Gunderson JG. Pharmacotherapy for patients with borderline personality disorder. Arch Gen Psychiatry 1986; 43:698-700.

3. Cowdry RW, Gardner DL. Pharmacotherapy of borderline personality disorder. Arch Gen Psychiatry 1988;45:111-119.

4. Cowdry RW, Pickar D, Davies R. Symptoms and EEG findings in the borderline syndrome. Int J Psychiatry Med 1985-1986;15(3):201-211.

5. Andrulonis PA, Gluek BC, Stroebel CF, Vogel NG, Shapiro AL, Aldridge DM. Organic brain dysfunction and the borderline syndrome. In: Stone MH (ed): Psychiatric Clinics of North America. vol 4. Philadelphia, PA: Saunders, 1981:47-66

6. Masterson JF. Psychotherapy of the Borderline Adult: A Developmental Approach. New York, NY: Brunner/ Mazel, 1976.

7. Masterson JF. The Narcissistic and Borderline Disorders. New York, NY: Brunner/Mazel, 1981.

8. Kernberg OF. Borderline Conditions and Pathological Narcissism. New York, NY: Aronson, 1975.

8a. Muller RJ. Distinguishing borderline patients with splitting (letter). Am J Psychiatry 1991;148:1404-1405.

9. Putnam FW. Diagnosis and Treatment of Multiple Personality Disorder. New York, NY: Guilford, 1989.

10. Muller RJ. The Marginal Self: An Existential Inquiry into Narcissism. Atlantic Highlands, NJ: Humanities Press International, 1987:103-132.

11. Gazzaniga MS, LeDoux JE. The Integrated Mind. New York, NY: Plenum, 1978.

12. Guntrip H. Psychoanalytic Theory, Therapy, and the Self. New York, NY: Basic Books, 1973.

13. Buck R. The psychology of emotion. In: LeDoux JE, Hirst W (eds): Mind and Brain: Dialogues in Cognitive Neuroscience. New York, NY: Cambridge University Press, 1986:275-300.

14. Stern DN. The Interpersonal World of the Infant: A View From Psychoanalysis and Developmental Psychology. New York, NY: Basic Books, 1985.

15. Zeanah CH, Anders TF, Seifer R, Stern DN. Implications of research on infant development for psychodynamic theory and practice. J Am Acad Child Adolesc Psychiatry 1989;5:657-668.

16. Randall PL. Schizophrenia, abnormal connection and brain evolution. Med Hypotheses 1983;10:247-280.

17. Yakovlev PI, Lecours A-R. The myelogenetic cycles of regional maturation of the brain. In: Minkowski A (ed): Regional Development of the Brain in Early Life. Philadelphia, PA: Davis, 1967:3-70.

18. Otto MW, Yeo RA, Dougher MJ. Right hemisphere involvement in depression: toward a neuropsychological theory of negative affective experiences. Biol Psychiatry 1987;22:1201-1215.

19. Perris C, Monakhov K, Von Knorring L, Botskarev V, Nikiforov A. Systemic structural analysis of the electroencephalogram of depressed patients: general principles and preliminary results of an international collaborative study. Neuropsychobiology 1978;4:207-228.

20. Schaffer CE, Davidson RJ, Saron C. Frontal and parietal electroencephalogram asymmetry in depressed and nondepressed subjects. Biol Psychiatry 1983;18:753-762.

21. Goldstein SG, Filskov SB, Weaver LA, Ives JO. Neuropsychological effects of electroconvulsive therapy. J Clin Psychol 1977;33:798-806.

22. Kronfol Z, Hamsher K. de S, Digire K, Waziri R. Depression and hemispheric functions: changes associated with unilateral ECT. Br J Psychiatry 1978;132:560-567.

23. Robinson RG, Kubos KL, Starr LB, Rao K, Price TR. Mood disorders in stroke patients: importance of location of lesion. Brain 1984;107:81-93.

24. Terzian H: Behavioral and EEG effects of intracarotid sodium amytal injection. Acta Neurochir 1964:12:230-239.

25. Wada J. A new method for the determination of the side of cerebral speech dominance: a preliminary report on the intracarotid injection of sodium amytal in man. Med Biol 1949;14:221.

26. Dimond SJ, Farrington L, Johnson P. Differing emotional response from right to left hemispheres. Nature 1976;261:690-692.

27. Dimond SJ, Farrington I. Emotional response to films shown to the right or left hemisphere of the brain measured by heart rate. Acta Psychol 1977;41:255-260.

28. Melges FT, Swartz MS. Oscillations of attachment in borderline personality disorder. Am J Psychiatry 1989;146:1115-1120.

29. Gabbard GO. Splitting in hospital treatment. Am J Psychiatry 1989;146:444-451.

30. Wechsler AF. The effect of organic brain disease on recall of emotionally charged versus neutral narrative texts. Neurology 1973;23:130-135.

31. Ross ED, Homan RW. Evidence for differential hemispheric storage of affective and factual memories for an emotionally laden life event in patients undergoing right-sided Wada test. Neurology 1986;36(suppl 1):168.

32. Galin D. Implications for psychiatry of left and right cerebral specialization: a neurophysiological context for unconscious processes. Arch Gen Psychiatry 1974;31:572-583.

33. Ahern GL, Schwartz GE. Differential lateralization for positive versus negative emotion. Neuropsychologica 1979;17:693-698.

34. Ahern GL, Schwartz GE. Differential lateralization for positive and negative emotion in the human brain: EEG spectral analysis. Neuropsychologica 1985;23:745-755.

35. Tucker DM, Roth RS, Arneson BA, Buckingham B. Right hemisphere activation during stress. Neuropsychologica 1977;15:697-700.

36. Nasrallah HA. The unintegrated right cerebral hemispheric consciousness as alien intruder: a possible mechanism for Schneiderian delusions in schizophrenia. Compr Psychiatry 1985;26:273-282.

37. Birchwood MJ, Hallett SE, Preston MC. Schizophrenia: An Integrated Approach to Research and Treatment. Washington Square, NY: New York University Press, 1989: 325-352.

38. Petersen SE, Fox PT, Posner MI, Mintun M, Raichle ME. Positron emission tomographic studies of the cortical anatomy of single-word processing. Nature 1988;331:585-589.

39. Reiman EM, Raichle ME, Robins E, Butler FK, Herscovitch P, Fox P, et al. The application of positron emission tomography to the study of panic disorder. Am J Psychiatry 1986;143:469-477.

40. Kandel ER. Psychotherapy and the single synapse. N Engl J Med 1979;301:1026-1037.

41. Husserl E. Phenomenology and the Crisis in Philosophy. Lauer Q (trans). New York, NY: Harper & Row, 1965.

42. Goldman A: Organic unity theory: the mind-body problem revisited. Am J Psychiatry 1991;148:553-563.

References

Akhtar, S., and Byrne, J. P. (1983) The Concept of Splitting and Its Clinical Relevance. *Am J Psychiatry* 140: 1013–1016.

American Psychiatric Association (1987) *Diagnostic and Statistical Manual of Mental Disorders.* 3rd ed. rev. Washington, D.C.: APA.

Cutting, L. K. (1993) Give and Take. *The New York Times Magazine,* October 31.

Dostoevsky, F. (1960) *Notes from Underground and The Grand Inquisitor,* trans. R. E. Matlaw. New York: E. P. Dutton.

Engel, G. L. (1980) The Clinical Application of the Biopsychosocial Model. *Am J Psychiatry* 137: 535–544.

Erikson, E. (1950) *Childhood and Society.* New York: W. W. Norton & Co.

Fierman, L. B., ed. (1965) *Effective Psychotherapy: The Contribution of Hellmuth Kaiser.* New York: The Free Press.

Fingarette, H. (1969) *Self-Deception.* London: Routledge & Keegan Paul.

Fischer, W. F. (1988) *Theories of Anxiety.* 2nd ed. Lanham, Md.: University Press of America.

Fitzgerald, F. S. (1945) *The Crack-Up.* New York: New Directions.

Gabbard, G. O. (1989) Splitting in Hospital Treatment. *Am J Psychiatry* 148: 444–451.

Gendlin, E. T. (1978) *Focusing.* New York: Everest House.

Goldstein, W. N. (1991) Clarification of Projective Identification. *Am J Psychiatry* 148: 153–161.

Goodman, A. (1991) Organic Unity Theory: The Mind–Body Problem Revisited. *Am J Psychiatry* 148: 553–563.

Grotstein, J. S. (1981) *Splitting and Projective Identification.* Northvale, N.J.: Jason Aronson.

Gunderson, J. G. (1984) *Borderline Personality Disorder.* Washington, D.C.: American Psychiatric Press.

Guntrip, H. (1959) Object Relations Theory: The Fairbairn–Guntrip Approach. In S. Arieti, ed., *American Handbook of Psychiatry*, vol. 1. New York: Basic Books.

Guntrip, H. (1971, 1973) *Psychoanalytic Theory, Therapy, and the Self*. New York: Basic Books.

Haight, M. R. (1980) A *Study of Self-Deception*. Sussex, England: The Harvester Press Limited.

Horney, K. (1950) *Neurosis and Human Growth: The Struggle toward Self-Realization*. New York: W. W. Norton & Co.

Kandel, E. R. (1979) Psychotherapy and the Single Synapse. *N Engl J Med* 301: 1026–1037.

Kernberg, O. F. (1975) *Borderline Conditions and Pathological Narcissism*. New York: Jason Aronson.

Kernberg, O. F. (1982) The Psychotherapeutic Treatment of Borderline Personalities. In Lester Grinspoon, ed., *Psychiatry 1982: The American Psychiatric Association Annual Review*. Washington, D.C.: American Psychiatric Press.

Kernberg, O. F. (1984) *Severe Personality Disorders: Psychotherapeutic Strategies*. New Haven: Yale University Press.

Klein, M. (1975) Notes on Some Schizoid Mechanisms (1946). In *Envy and Gratitude and Other Works, 1946–1963*. New York: Delacorte.

Kohut, H. (1971) *The Analysis of the Self*. New York: International Universities Press.

Kurosawa, A. (1969) *Rashomon*. New York: Grove Press.

Lewin, R. A., and Schulz, C. (1992) *Losing and Fusing: Borderline Transitional Object and Self Relations*. Northvale, N.J.: Jason Aronson.

Mahler, M. S., Pine, F., and Bergman, A. (1975) *The Psychological Birth of the Human Infant*. New York: Basic Books.

Marcel, G. (1965) *Being and Having*, trans. K. Farrer. New York: Harper Torchbooks.

Masterson, J. F. (1976) *Psychotherapy of the Borderline Adult: A Developmental Approach*. New York: Brunner/Mazel.

Masterson, J. F. (1981) *The Narcissistic and Borderline Disorders*. New York: Brunner/Mazel.

Masterson, J. F. (1983) *Countertransference and Therapeutic Technique: Teaching Seminars on Psychotherapy of the Borderline Adult*. New York: Brunner/Mazel.

Melges, F. T., and Swartz, M. S. (1989) Oscillations of Attunement in Borderline Personality Disorder. *Am J Psychiatry* 146: 1115–1120.

Muller, R. J. (1987) *The Marginal Self: An Existential Inquiry into Narcissism*. Atlantic Highlands, N.J.: Humanities Press International.

Muller, R. J. (1991a) Distinguishing Borderline Patients with Splitting (letter). *Am J Psychiatry* 148: 1404–1405.

Muller, R. J. (1991b) Sartre Viewed Becoming Pathologically Depressed as a "Magical Transformation." *The Psychiatric Times*, December 1991.

Muller, R. J. (1992a) Is There a Neural Basis for Borderline Splitting? *Compr Psychiatry* 33: 92–104.

Muller, R. J. (1992b) Depression in Borderline Patients Who Split (letter). *Am J Psychiatry* 149: 580–581.

Muller, R. J. (1993) Karen Horney's "Resigned Person" Heralds DSM-III-R's Borderline Personality Disorder. *Compr Psychiatry* 34: 264–272.

Pinderhughes, C. A. (1982) Paired Differential Bonding in Biological, Psychological, and Social Systems. *Am J Social Psychiatry* 2: 5–14.

Post, R. M. (1992) Transduction of Psychosocial Stress into the Neurobiology of Recurrent Affective Disorder. *Am J Psychiatry* 149: 999–1010.

Sartre, J-P. (1948) *The Emotions: Outline of a Theory*, trans. B. Frechtman. New York: The Wisdom Library.

Sartre, J-P. (1956) *Being and Nothingness: An Essay on Phenomenological Ontology*, trans. H. E. Barnes. New York: Philosophical Library.

Searles, H. F. (1969) A Case of Borderline Thought Disorder. *Int J Psycho-Anal* 50: 655–664.

Stern, D. N. (1985) *The Interpersonal World of the Infant: A View from Psychoanalysis and Developmental Psychology*. New York: Basic Books.

Sternbach, S. E., Judd, P. H., Sabo, A. N., McGlashan, T., and Gunderson, J. G. (1992) Cognitive and Perceptual Distortions in Borderline Personality Disorder and Schizotypal Personality Disorder in a Vignette Sample. *Compr Psychiatry* 33: 186–189.

Stone, M. H. (1990) *The Fate of Borderline Patients: Successful Outcome and Psychiatric Practice*. New York: Guilford Press.

Yakovlev, P. I., and Lecours, A-R. (1967) The Myelogenetic Cycles of Regional Maturation of the Brain. In A. Minkowski, ed., *Regional Development of the Brain in Early Life*. Philadelphia: F. A. Davis.

Index

Covers Part II and Part III only.

ABOUT THE AUTHOR

RENÉ J. MULLER, Ph.D., is a psychotherapist in private practice in Baltimore. His research interests include characterizing the effect of the splitting defense on cognition, affect, and behavior in borderline personality disorder, and identifying a possible neural substrate for this defense. He is author of *The Marginal Self* (1987) and many articles in psychiatric journals.

ISBN 0-275-94975-3

HARDCOVER BAR CODE